TRIM & TERRIFIC

AMERICAN
FAVORITES

Also by Holly Berkowitz Clegg

A Trim & Terrific Louisiana Kitchen
From a Louisiana Kitchen

HOLLY BERKOWITZ CLEGG is the author of two best-selling
cookbooks. She is a frequent guest on NBC's "Weekend Today"
show, and the cooking and housewares spokesperson for Mercantile
Department Stores. Holly has had recipes and feature articles in
Cooking Light magazine, *Shape* magazine, and other national magazines
and newspapers. Holly studied at the Cordon Bleu, and lives
in Baton Rouge, Louisiana, with her husband and three children.

TRIM & TERRIFIC
AMERICAN
FAVORITES

OVER 250 FAST AND EASY LOW-FAT RECIPES

HOLLY BERKOWITZ CLEGG

CLARKSON POTTER/PUBLISHERS
NEW YORK

To my dear husband, Mike, who has encouraged and pushed me to be what I am; to my three precious children, Todd, Courtney, and Haley, who are #1 on my list; to Mae Mae, who has been my Baton Rouge mother; and, most important, my parents, Jerry and Ruth, who have listened to each and every stage of my career with enthusiasm.

Published by Clarkson N. Potter, Inc., 201 East 50th Street, New York, New York 10022. Member of the Crown Publishing Group.

Random House, Inc. New York, Toronto, London, Sydney, Auckland

http://www.randomhouse.com/

CLARKSON N. POTTER, POTTER, and colophon are trademarks of Clarkson N. Potter, Inc.

Printed in the United States of America

Design by Susan DeStaebler
Illustrations by Marlies Merk Najaka

Library of Congress Cataloging-in-Publication Data
is available upon request.

ISBN 0-517-70256-8
10   9   8   7   6   5   4   3

ACKNOWLEDGMENTS

It is hard for me to believe that my dreams have become a reality! Without my wonderful support group, I would never be where I am today. For this reason, it is my pleasure to take this time to thank these special people in my life . . .

To my husband, Mike (my #1 attorney), for sharing my life, my family, and my career with me. You make it all worthwhile and make my life as special as it is. See, my cooking did pay off! ♥ To Todd for always unloading my cookbooks, for tasting the recipes even with onions, and doing whatever I ask with a smile. ♥ To Courtney, my love, for being the best executive secretary a Mother could ever have. ♥ To Haley, my baby, for understanding the meaning of "cookbook business" and for all the hugs. ♥ To my parents, Jerry and Ruth, who I am fortunate enough to be their child. They have given me the love and tools in life to be able to achieve my goals. I will continue to share every aspect of my life with you because you are my life. ♥ To Mae Mae and Charles, my Baton Rouge parents, for all your help, love, and support. ♥ To my sister, Ilene, who is my sounding board for advice, trivia, and my best friend! ♥ To my sister-in-law Pam, who dresses me, and is always there to cook, listen, or have fun. ♥ To Aunt Rose and John John . . . you are always on call and here to help in a flash! Thanks. ♥ To Chuck (Uncle Finky), who has helped me with my children, the most important job of all! ♥ To Francine for listening, getting excited, listening, getting more excited, and still listening to more. A special friend who has shared it all with me. ♥ To Gail, my dear friend, I thank you and your family for being my most devoted tasters. I could always look forward to sharing my afternoon with you after a long day of cooking. ♥ To my special tennis team, who has shown me how much fun girlfriends can have. ♥ Louise, my partner (don't forget me), Mary, our chief, Lynell, Regina, Brenda, Carol B., Dorraine, Carole S., Monica, Andrea, Gail, Francine . . . to Janet for always knowing what I think and being there . . . Melanine, for your creative input, Marty, Louann, and the many others. ♥ To Lynda for doing a super typing job . . . Freddie, my cookbook mentor . . . Andy Pargh, your good advice and guidance . . . Toni, a great sounding board . . . Karen Osofsky, for the Keebler ten million coupon opportunity . . . Shirley, for the many hours of testing recipes . . . Hans and Donna Sternberg, for giving me my start in my cookbook career in 1982. ♥ To the NBC Weekend *Today* Show, Robin, and the Executive Producers for giving me my first opportunity to appear on network television and for having me on regularly. I am so grateful! ♥ To Mike Schneider for giving me the confidence in network television and making it fun. ♥ To *Cooking Light Magazine* and Jill Melton for the wonderful articles, all the covers, and for trusting me with some great opportunities. I am so excited to be a part of this magazine. ♥ To *Shape Magazine* and Nancy Gottesman for their great articles and continual support. Thanks for including me in *Shape Cooks,* your new magazine. ♥ To all those many people out there who are cooking from *A Trim & Terrific Louisiana Kitchen,* I thank you. I am so excited to share more recipes, and keep spreading the word! ♥ To Pennington Biomedical Research Center and Dr. Cathy Champagne for doing a great job with the nutritional analyses. Thanks for always taking the extra steps whenever needed. ♥ To Mercantile Corporation: I am so excited to be your national spokesperson and look forward to a long relationship and being an important part of all the Mercantile stores. Get ready! ♥ To Gene Winick, my agent, for the time and effort spent in taking care of me.

To Clarkson Potter . . . You are a dream that has come true! Thank you for giving me this wonderful opportunity and I look forward to being a Clarkson Potter girl for many years. You have taken my books to another level. Thanks also to the many production editors, art department, and others who have spent time on this project to make it the success it is.

To my editor Katie Workman, I thank you for making this day possible. With your expertise, enthusiasm, and ideas you have helped to create my book and make it the best it can be. I treasure you as my boss, and, most important, as my friend. My gratitude goes beyond words.

CONTENTS

INTRODUCTION

I guess you think I am here to tell you that you have to eat all the tasteless, boring, diet food. Let me get one thing straight: I hate diets and anything that tastes like cardboard. However, with today's knowledge that there is a direct correlation between our diet and our health, I believe we have to make changes in our lives. With this in mind, I became inspired to write this book, *Trim & Terrific American Favorites*. I want to prove that you can have "good" food that is "good" for you.

This cookbook contains easy, everyday recipes for all your favorite dishes. I have included convenience products, such as canned soup and frozen vegetables, to make the preparation times even faster. Also, luckily for us, the low-fat products today are of better quality than they were in recent years. Use your judgment; and decide which products you like best. I am not as fond of nonfat mayonnaise, therefore, I will combine low-fat mayonnaise with nonfat sour cream to get the right taste. I prefer the reduced fat cheeses over the nonfat as they do melt and have flavor. However, the nonfat cream cheese usually works fine. As you go back to old favorite recipes, keep these products in mind and make adjustments where appropriate.

I do believe in moderation, and, therefore, I am able to use real ingredients. You will not find substitutes in my cookbook such as Egg Beaters or Butter Buds. Instead, to lower the fat content of dishes, I use a combination of eggs and egg whites, smaller amounts of olive or canola oils, and nonstick cooking spray. You will find all of the ingredients at your regular grocery store or supermarket, if you don't happen to have them already in your home. I want my book to be a way of life, not a book you only use every so often.

The recipes are probably for dishes you had for dinner last night, except these are low-fat. But if you don't tell your family, they won't be able to tell the difference! And remember, moderation is the keyword. If you cook out of my cookbook on a daily basis, then it is fine to have the hamburger or your favorite dessert when you are dining out. I do it all the time!

I also feel very fortunate to have worked with the Pennington Biomedical Research Center who have one of the most sophisticated data base systems, therefore, you have the most correct analyses. All the recipes in the book have 30 percent or less of their calories from fat. I feel these are moderate guidelines, and if you use 30 percent as a daily *average,* you will find you have a lot more freedom than you think you do. In other words, if you eat a piece of fruit with almost no fat, you can have a cookie with 50 percent fat, and it will balance out. I have also used no-salt-added tomato products to keep the sodium to a minimum, but you can substitute any tomato product if sodium is not a concern for you. You will notice I have included salt and pepper to taste in the recipes so you can season the recipes to your liking. The ♥ on most recipes indicates that the cholesterol content is less than or equal to 60 mg per serving, which means the recipe is low in cholesterol. Also, I am very pleased to include a complete list of diabetic exchanges for those who need them at the end of the book.

Time is another very important element. I am a mother of three, which means I am always running carpool, helping out with homework, or watching a Little League game. You can understand why I don't believe you have to spend a lot of time in the kitchen to make a great meal. Most of my recipes can be made in less than thirty minutes. Whether you are working late or picking up kids or both, you still can get a delicious, healthy meal on the table with ease.

There is an extra bonus to eating this way: I have actually received numerous letters from people who have lost weight cooking from my recipes. It has been very rewarding to me to know that I have helped people to make a positive change in their lives, and enjoy themselves at the same time. These recipes prove that there is more to eating right than broiled chicken or a plain baked potato.

In the end, I always strive to keep life as simple as possible. Never go back to the grocery store—if at all possible, just leave that ingredient out! Changing your diet doesn't require many major changes in the way you live your life, but you will find yourself enjoying life more fully. Begin with small changes, and soon you'll find yourself "Trim & Terrific."

MENUS

All-Occasion Brunch
- Breakfast Casserole (page 30)
  Hot Fruit Casserole (page 31)
  Good Morning Grits (page 26)
  Morning Muffins (page 22)

Luscious Lunches
- Cold Peach Soup (page 34)
  Curried Chicken Salad (page 51)
  Morning Muffins (page 22)
  Tiramisù (page 197)

- Shrimp and Artichoke Soup
  (page 32)
  Rigatoni with Roasted Tomato
  Sauce (page 121)
  Tiramisù (page 197)

- Cream of Spinach Soup (page 30)
  Shrimp Basil (page 102)
  Broiled Tomatoes (page 62)
  Coffee Cheesecake (page 191)

Family Pleasers
- Smothered Round Steak (page 90)
  Garlic Mashed Potatoes (page 65)
  Cheesy Spicy Squash (page 56)
  Pistachio Layered Dessert
  (page 196)

- Chicken Scaloppine (page 74)
  Broccoli Casserole (page 58)
  Barley Casserole (page 70)
  Banana Cream Pie (page 187)

- Pan-Fried Fish (page 106)
  Green Bean Casserole (page 59)
  Cherry Gelatin Mold (page 50)
  Chocolate Brownies (page 175)

- Chicken Scampi (page 74)
  Fiesta Potato Casserole (page 64)
  Squash and Zucchini Medley
  (page 56)
  Coffee Angel Food Cake (page 165)

Sunday Dinners
- Pork Tenderloin with Mustard
  Sauce (page 96)
  Tipsy Mushrooms (page 54)
  Potatoes au Gratin (page 66)
  Baby Lima Beans (page 63)
  Caramel Delight Crunch (page 198)

- Quick Cheesy Potato Soup (page 28)
  Spicy Meat Loaf (page 92)
  Cauliflower with Creamy
  Mustard Sauce (page 57)
  Blueberry Cobbler (page 184)

Souper Suppers
- Caesar Salad (page 40)
  Black Bean Soup (page 132) or Chili
  (for meat eaters) (page 134)
  Spinach Bread (page 21)
  Blueberry Cobbler Cake (page 166)

- Spinach Salad (page 39)
  Italian Soup (page 33)
  Beer Bread Muffins (page 16)
  Apple Crumble Pie (page 186)

Children's Favorites
- Oven-Fried Chicken Tenders
  (page 84)
  Macaroni and Cheese (page 70)
  Cranberry-Glazed Baby Carrots
  (page 54)
  Chocolate Brownies (page 175)

- Oven-Fried Chicken Breasts Supreme
  (page 85)
  Parmesan Potato Sticks (page 68)
  Green Bean Casserole (page 59)
  Chocolate Chip Cookies (page 174)

- Oven-Fried Chicken Tenders
  (page 84)
  Garlic Mashed Potatoes (page 65)
  Broccoli with Dijon Sauce (page 58)
  Peanut Butter Brownies (page 178)

Vegetarian Time

• Caesar Salad (page 40)
  Eggplant Parmesan (page 143)
  Italian Linguine Casserole
     (page 150)
  Cherry Crisp (page 183)

• Corn Soup (page 28)
  Excellent Eggplant Pasta (page 112)
  Spinach Stroganoff (page 53)
  Triple Chocolate Cake (page 171)

• Quick Vegetarian Chili (page 154)
  Garden Enchiladas (page 156)
  Sautéed Cherry Tomatoes
     with Basil (page 63)
  Chocolate Espresso Pie (page 189)

• Fruity Tossed Green Salad with
     Strawberry Dressing (page 38)
  Eggplant and Zucchini Lasagne
     (page 149)
  Caramel Delight Crunch (page 198)

• Wild Rice and Feta Salad (page 41)
  Broccoli Vermicelli Salad (page 48)
  Waldorf Carrot Salad (page 42)
  Bran Muffins (page 23)
  Triple Chocolate Cake (page 171)

Southwestern Buffet

• Tortilla Shrimp Bites (page 8)
  Tamales (page 131)
  Tex-Mex Dip (page 130)
  Southwestern Round Steak
     (page 136)
  Black Bean Soup (page 132)
  Baked Mexican Spinach Dip
     (page 129)
  Corn and Zucchini Salsa (page 130)

Cocktail Buffet Party

• Stuffed Mushrooms (page 10)
  Sweet-and-Sour Shrimp and
     Peppers (page 9)
  Italian Squares (page 12)
  Glazed Chicken Strips (page 79)
  Artichoke Dip (page 4)

Pork Tenderloin with Mustard
  Sauce (sliced) (page 96)
Chocolate Mint Brownies (page
  176)
Lemon Squares (page 180)

Football Fever Buffet

• Hamburger Dip (page 4)
  Italian Squares (page 12)
  Shrimp Cocktail Spread (page 5)
  Spinach Balls with Jezebel Sauce
     (page 7)
  Tex-Mex Dip (page 130)
  Peanut Butter Brownies (page 178)
  Coffee Toffee Brownies (page 177)

Summer Salad Trio

• Shrimp, Spinach, and Pasta Salad with
     Poppy Seed Dressing (page 48)
  Tuna and White Bean Salad (page 45)
  Cherry Gelatin Mold (page 50)
  Lemon Bread (page 19)
  Pistachio Layered Dessert (page
     196)

When Asked to Bring:

• *a Casserole*
  Shrimp Casserole (page 104)
  Chicken Pot Pie (page 81)
  Shrimp Jambalaya (page 102)
  Chicken Vermicelli (page 120)

• *a Dessert*
  Chewy Caramel Brownies (page
     179)
  Pineapple Sheet Cake (page 162)
  Coconut Cake (page 164)

• *an Appetizer*
  Italian Squares (page 12)
  Shrimp Cocktail Spread (page 5)
  Tex-Mex Dip (page 130)

• *a Salad*
  Seven-Layer Salad (page 42)
  Italian Pasta Salad (page 47)

APPETIZERS

HOT SPINACH DIP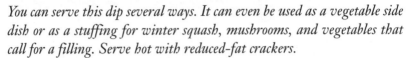

You can serve this dip several ways. It can even be used as a vegetable side dish or as a stuffing for winter squash, mushrooms, and vegetables that call for a filling. Serve hot with reduced-fat crackers.

2 tablespoons tub-style light margarine
1 onion, finely chopped
2 tablespoons finely chopped jalapeño peppers
2 tablespoons minced garlic
3 (10-ounce) packages frozen chopped spinach, thawed and squeezed dry

$\frac{1}{8}$ teaspoon cayenne pepper
$\frac{1}{4}$ teaspoon white pepper
Dash of nutmeg
1 cup evaporated skimmed milk
$\frac{1}{2}$ cup nonfat sour cream, or more if necessary

Melt the margarine in a large skillet coated with nonstick cooking spray. Add the onions, jalapeños, and garlic, sautéing until soft, about 4 minutes. Place the spinach in a food processor and process until pureed. Add the spinach to the skillet with the cayenne, white pepper, and nutmeg. Mix well. Gradually add the evaporated milk, stirring. Remove from the heat and stir in the sour cream. If too thin, add more sour cream.

Makes 12 servings (about 2½ cups)
Nutritional information per serving

Calories	45	Cal. from Fat (%)	19	Sodium (mg)	126
Fat (g)	1.2	Saturated Fat (g)	0.2	Cholesterol (mg)	1

BLACK-EYED PEA DIP ♥

This dip is perfect for New Year's Day, since black-eyed peas are eaten for luck in the South, traditionally on the first day of a new year. Serve this dip with low-fat chips. I also use this as a vegetable side dish.

1 onion, chopped
$\frac{1}{3}$ cup chopped green bell pepper
1 tablespoon chopped jalapeño peppers
2 (15-ounce) cans black-eyed peas, drained

3 tablespoons all-purpose flour
1 (10-ounce) can diced tomatoes and green chilies
4 ounces reduced-fat Monterey Jack cheese, shredded

In a pot coated with nonstick cooking spray, sauté the onion, green pepper, and jalapeños over medium-low heat until tender, about 5 minutes. Add the black-eyed peas and stir in the flour. Gradually add the tomatoes and cheese, stirring until melted and hot throughout.

Makes 10 servings (about 5 cups)

Nutritional information per ½ cup serving

Calories	114	Cal. from Fat (%)	19.7	Sodium (mg)	470
Fat (g)	2.5	Saturated Fat (g)	1.3	Cholesterol (mg)	8

HOT CREAMY VEGGIE DIP

This recipe doubles easily and can be made ahead—a delicious, no-think dip. You can always use canned mushrooms if you like. Serve with reduced-fat crackers.

1 (10-ounce) package frozen chopped broccoli
1 (10-ounce) package frozen chopped spinach
1 onion, chopped
½ pound fresh mushrooms, sliced
1 (10¾-ounce) can 97% fat-free cream of mushroom soup

3 ounces light pasteurized processed cheese spread
1 (8-ounce) package fat-free cream cheese
1 tablespoon Worcestershire sauce
½ teaspoon hot pepper sauce
1 (8-ounce) can sliced water chestnuts, drained

Cook the broccoli and spinach according to package directions, omitting any salt. Drain well and set aside. In a pot coated with nonstick cooking spray, sauté the onion and mushrooms over medium heat until tender. Add the cream of mushroom soup, cheese spread, cream cheese, Worcestershire sauce, and hot pepper sauce. When the cheese is melted and the mixture is well combined, stir in the cooked broccoli, spinach, and water chestnuts.

Makes 6 to 8 servings (about 4½ cups)

Nutritional information per tablespoon serving

Calories	9	Cal. from Fat (%)	20	Sodium (mg)	41
Fat (g)	0.2	Saturated Fat (g)	0.1	Cholesterol (mg)	1

ARTICHOKE DIP ♥

Here's another one of those wonderful dips that you thought you might have to give up to eat healthy—not so! Serve with fresh veggies or reduced-fat crackers.

½ cup nonfat sour cream
½ cup fat-free mayonnaise
1 (.65-ounce) package cheesy
   Italian dressing mix

1 (14-ounce) can artichoke
   hearts, drained and finely
   chopped

Mix the sour cream, mayonnaise, Italian dressing mix, and artichoke hearts together in a bowl.

Makes 4 to 6 servings (about 1½ cups)

Nutritional information per tablespoon serving

Calories	16	Cal. from Fat (%)	0.9	Sodium (mg)	173
Fat (g)	0	Saturated Fat (g)	0	Cholesterol (mg)	0

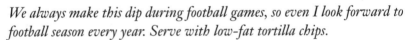

HAMBURGER DIP ♥

We always make this dip during football games, so even I look forward to football season every year. Serve with low-fat tortilla chips.

1 pound ground sirloin
1 onion, chopped
1 pound mushrooms, sliced
1 (10-ounce) can diced
   tomatoes and green chilies

4 ounces light pasteurized
   processed cheese spread
1 (8-ounce) package fat-free
   cream cheese

Coat a heavy pot with nonstick cooking spray and cook the sirloin, onion, and mushrooms over medium heat for 6 to 7 minutes, until the meat is well browned. Drain off any liquid. Add the tomatoes, cheese spread, and cream cheese. Stir over medium heat until the cheese is melted.

Makes 6 to 8 servings (5 cups)

Nutritional information per tablespoon serving

Calories	17	Cal. from Fat (%)	28.1	Sodium (mg)	47
Fat (g)	0.5	Saturated Fat (g)	0.3	Cholesterol (mg)	3

DIP FOR FRESH FRUIT ♥

I don't count fruit as a dessert unless I get to dip it in something tasty. This is a great dip to use in the summer when fresh fruit is plentiful. And nothing could be faster! This will keep in the refrigerator for 1 week.

2 (8-ounce) cartons low-fat lemon yogurt
¼ cup blanched almonds, chopped and toasted

1 teaspoon grated orange rind
2 tablespoons orange liqueur or orange juice

Combine the lemon yogurt, almonds, orange rind, and orange liqueur and mix well. Refrigerate at least 1 hour to blend the flavors.

Makes 2 cups

Nutritional information per tablespoon serving

Calories	19	Cal. from Fat (%) 27.2		Sodium (mg)	8
Fat (g)	0.6	Saturated Fat (g)	0.1	Cholesterol (mg)	1

SHRIMP COCKTAIL SPREAD

Shrimp cocktail is always a popular dish, and this dip combines all the cocktail parts into one zesty spread. Make this ahead and pull it out for company. When crabmeat is in season, substitute it for the shrimp or use a combination of the two. If there is any left, it will keep several days in the refrigerator. Serve with reduced-fat crackers.

2 (8-ounce) packages fat-free cream cheese, softened
1 tablespoon Worcestershire sauce
½ teaspoon minced garlic
½ teaspoon hot sauce
1 (12-ounce) bottle cocktail sauce

½ cup sliced green onions (scallions)
2 cups cooked peeled small shrimp
2 tablespoons minced parsley

In a bowl, blend the cream cheese, Worcestershire sauce, garlic, and hot sauce. Spread on the bottom of a 9-inch serving plate. Cover the cream cheese mixture with the cocktail sauce and sprinkle with the green onions, shrimp, and parsley.

Makes 8 (4 tablespoons) servings

Nutritional information per ½ tablespoon serving

Calories	131	Cal. from Fat (%) 3.4		Sodium (mg)	872
Fat (g)	0.5	Saturated Fat (g)	0.1	Cholesterol (mg)	68

SMOKED SALMON SPREAD ON TOAST ♥

This spread is wonderful to have on hand for guests! You can keep it in the refrigerator and make appetizers as needed. The recipe multiplies easily. You can find smoked salmon in a package or at the deli counter, and some supermarkets sell smoked salmon pieces, which would be perfect for this recipe.

6 ounces smoked salmon, chopped
⅓ cup fat-free mayonnaise
2 tablespoons minced onion
2 tablespoons chopped parsley
2 teaspoons lemon juice

Dash of pepper
Dash of cayenne pepper
⅓ cup shredded reduced-fat cheddar cheese
10 to 12 slices of thin white bread or ½-inch slices of French bread

Mix together the salmon, mayonnaise, onion, parsley, lemon juice, pepper, and cayenne. Stir in the cheese. Spread the mixture on each slice of bread and place the slices on a baking sheet. Broil 6 inches from the heat 3 to 4 minutes, or until the cheese melts and the tops are crisp.

Makes 10 to 12 salmon toasts

Nutritional information per serving

Calories	97	Cal. from Fat (%)	19.5	Sodium (mg)	318
Fat (g)	2.1	Saturated Fat (g)	0.7	Cholesterol (mg)	6

SPINACH BALLS WITH JEZEBEL SAUCE ♥

You can freeze the spinach balls on a baking sheet before cooking. When frozen, transfer to zip-top bags and store in the freezer. Take them directly from the freezer to bake in the oven. I've made these spinach balls for years and they are always popular in the Jezebel Sauce, as it has a real "bite."

2 (10-ounce) packages frozen chopped spinach
2 cups herb bread stuffing mix
1 cup finely chopped onions
½ cup grated Romano cheese

1½ teaspoons garlic powder
1 teaspoon dried thyme
⅛ teaspoon pepper
2 large eggs
4 large egg whites
Jezebel Sauce (recipe follows)

Preheat the oven to 350°F. Combine the spinach, stuffing mix, onions, cheese, garlic powder, thyme, pepper, eggs, and egg whites; mix well. Form into small balls about ¾-inch round and bake on a baking sheet coated with nonstick cooking spray for 20 minutes. Serve with the Jezebel Sauce.

Makes 4 dozen

Jezebel Sauce

½ cup apricot preserves
1 (10-ounce) jar apple jelly
2 tablespoons dry mustard

2 tablespoons prepared horseradish
1 teaspoon pepper

Mix the apricot preserves, apply jelly, dry mustard, horseradish, and pepper together. Jezebel Sauce is also great served over fat-free cream cheese on crackers.

Makes 2 cups

**Nutritional information per serving
(1 ball with 1 to 1½ tablespoons sauce)**

| Calories | 57 | Cal. from Fat (%) | 12.4 | Sodium (mg) | 106 |
| Fat (g) | 0.8 | Saturated Fat (g) | 0.3 | Cholesterol (mg) | 10 |

CAPONATA

This recipe makes quite a bit of this flavorful Italian eggplant and vegetable dish, but you can always cut the recipe in half. The caponata will keep, covered, for a few days in the refrigerator. Serve at room temperature with reduced-fat crackers.

2 medium eggplants
2 onions, chopped
1½ cups thickly sliced celery
2 green bell peppers, seeded and cut in 1-inch chunks
2 garlic cloves, minced
2 (14½-ounce) cans Italian stewed tomatoes with their juice

⅓ cup red wine vinegar
2 tablespoons sugar
2 tablespoons dried basil
3 tablespoons tomato paste
½ cup chopped parsley
1 teaspoon pepper
¼ cup sliced stuffed green olives

Cut the unpeeled eggplant into 1-inch cubes. Heat a large pot coated with nonstick cooking spray over medium-low heat and add the eggplant and onions, sautéing until lightly golden, about 6 minutes. Add the celery, green peppers, garlic, tomatoes, vinegar, sugar, basil, tomato paste, parsley, pepper, and green olives to the pot and stir gently but thoroughly. Simmer, covered, for 30 minutes, stirring occasionally. Remove the lid and simmer about 10 minutes more, or until thick.

Makes 3 quarts

Nutritional information per ¼-cup serving

Calories	20	Cal. from Fat (%)	13.5	Sodium (mg)	71
Fat (g)	0.3	Saturated Fat (g)	0	Cholesterol (mg)	0

TORTILLA SHRIMP BITES ♥

These appetizers, which can be made ahead, freeze well. They will make you the star of the party.

1 (8-ounce) package fat-free cream cheese, softened
2 tablespoons light mayonnaise
½ cup chopped green onions (scallions)
1 (4-ounce) can chopped green chilies, drained

½ teaspoon chili powder
½ teaspoon garlic powder
Salt and pepper to taste
½ cup coarsely chopped cooked peeled shrimp
10 (6-inch) flour tortillas
Salsa

In a bowl, blend the cream cheese and mayonnaise. Add the green onions, chilies, chili powder, garlic powder, salt and pepper, and shrimp, mixing well. Place about $\frac{1}{8}$ cup of the filling on one end of a tortilla and roll up, jelly-roll style. Place the rolled tortillas, seam side down, on a tray or baking sheet. Refrigerate until ready to serve, up to several days. Cut each tortilla into 5 pieces. Serve with toothpicks and salsa.

Makes 50 bites

Nutritional information per 1-bite serving

Calories	31	Cal. from Fat (%)	20.3	Sodium (mg)	90
Fat (g)	0.7	Saturated Fat (g)	0.1	Cholesterol (mg)	4

SWEET-AND-SOUR SHRIMP AND PEPPERS

This colorful shrimp dish can be served on top of Bibb lettuce on a platter or mounded individually on plates. If you have trouble finding all the different colored peppers, use what is available. This delicious combination can even be tossed with freshly cooked pasta for a starter or main course.

$\frac{1}{4}$ cup light brown sugar
2 teaspoons dry mustard
$\frac{1}{2}$ teaspoon ground ginger
$\frac{1}{2}$ cup balsamic vinegar
$\frac{1}{4}$ cup water
1 tablespoon Worcestershire sauce
1 tablespoon olive oil

2 pounds medium uncooked shrimp, peeled
$\frac{1}{2}$ cup very thinly sliced red bell pepper
$\frac{1}{2}$ cup very thinly sliced yellow bell pepper
$\frac{1}{2}$ cup very thinly sliced green bell pepper

Combine the brown sugar, mustard, ginger, vinegar, water, Worcestershire sauce, and olive oil in a medium saucepan; bring to a boil, stirring constantly until the brown sugar dissolves. Reduce the heat and simmer, uncovered, 5 minutes. Add the shrimp and cook 3 to 5 minutes, or until the shrimp turn pink. Transfer the shrimp mixture to a bowl, add the peppers, and toss well. Cover and marinate in the refrigerator for 3 hours. Drain the shrimp mixture, discarding the liquid, and serve.

Makes 10 servings

Nutritional information per serving

Calories	97	Cal. from Fat (%)	17.6	Sodium (mg)	173
Fat (g)	1.9	Saturated Fat (g)	0.3	Cholesterol (mg)	129

STUFFED MUSHROOMS ♥

These make a great appetizer or you can put several on a plate as a first course. For a fancier stuffing, add a cup of crabmeat or chopped cooked shrimp to the stuffing mixture.

1 cup chopped celery
1 cup chopped green bell
　pepper
1 cup chopped onion
2 cups Italian bread crumbs,
　or a little more
¼ cup chopped parsley
1 cup grated reduced-fat
　sharp Cheddar cheese

½ cup white wine
1 teaspoon dried thyme
1 teaspoon dried oregano
Salt and pepper to taste
60 medium fresh
　mushrooms

Preheat the oven to 350°F. In a large skillet coated with nonstick cooking spray, sauté the celery, green pepper, and onion until tender, about 5 minutes. Remove from the heat and add the bread crumbs, parsley, cheese, white wine, thyme, oregano, and salt and pepper, mixing well. Wash and stem the mushrooms and fill each cap with stuffing. Lay the filled mushroom caps on a baking sheet coated with nonstick cooking spray and bake for 15 minutes, or until heated throughout.

Makes 60 mushrooms

Nutritional information per 1-mushroom serving

Calories	26	Cal. from Fat (%)	17.3	Sodium (mg)	124
Fat (g)	0.5	Saturated Fat (g)	0.2	Cholesterol (mg)	1

SPINACH AND CHEESE TORTILLA PIZZA ♥

You could also serve a single tortilla for lunch with a bowl of soup or a salad. Then you can eat the whole tortilla without guilt!

2 large (10-inch) flour
　tortillas
2 tablespoons nonfat sour
　cream
1 (10-ounce) package frozen
　chopped spinach, thawed
　and squeezed dry

1 large tomato, chopped
½ cup shredded reduced-fat
　Monterey Jack cheese
¼ cup thinly sliced green
　onions (scallions)

Preheat the oven to 450°F. Place the tortillas on a baking sheet coated with nonstick cooking spray. Bake for 3 minutes, or until golden

brown. Remove from the oven and reduce the temperature to 350°F.
Spread the sour cream evenly over the tortillas. Top with the spinach
and tomato. Next, sprinkle evenly with the Monterey Jack cheese.
Bake for 5 minutes more, or until the cheese is melted. Sprinkle with
the green onions. Cut each tortilla into 6 slices and serve immediately.

Makes 12 slices

Nutritional information per slice

Calories	53	Cal. from Fat (%) 25.5	Sodium (mg)	96
Fat (g)	1.5	Saturated Fat (g) 0.6	Cholesterol (mg)	3

ASPARAGUS AND BRIE PIZZA

*This elegant combination of asparagus and Brie makes a fancy pizza top-
ping, a nice starter for a weekend dinner with friends.*

12 thin asparagus spears, tips only	½ teaspoon dried basil
	½ teaspoon dried oregano
1 red bell pepper, seeded and thinly sliced	Salt and pepper to taste
	3½ ounces Brie cheese, skin
1 teaspoon minced garlic	removed and thinly sliced
1 (10-ounce) can refrigerated pizza crust or 1 (16-ounce) Boboli prepared crust	

Preheat the oven to 425°F. Fill a small saucepan with water and
bring to a boil. Cook the asparagus tips until tender, about 4
minutes. Drain and set aside. Heat a skillet coated with nonstick
cooking spray over medium heat and sauté the red pepper until tender, about 4 minutes. Blend in the garlic.

Coat a 12-inch pizza pan with nonstick cooking spray. Unroll the
dough and place in the prepared pan, starting at the center and
pressing out with your hands. Bake for 5 minutes. Remove and
sprinkle the crust with the basil, oregano, and salt and pepper, if
desired, then evenly distribute the pepper, Brie cheese, and asparagus. Continue baking for 8 to 10 minutes more.

Makes 12 slices

Nutritional information per slice

Calories	94	Cal. from Fat (%) 30.6	Sodium (mg)	184
Fat (g)	3.2	Saturated Fat (g) 1.7	Cholesterol (mg)	8

ITALIAN SQUARES ♥

Italian Squares is a very flexible recipe as these can be served hot, at room temperature, or even out of the refrigerator. They can also be reheated, covered. When a friend asked for this recipe it quickly became her favorite standby. They are a variation of an Italian frittata, which is a type of omelet.

1 cup chopped onion	3 large egg whites, slightly
1 cup chopped red bell	beaten
pepper	2 large eggs, slightly beaten
1 cup chopped green bell	1 teaspoon dried oregano
pepper	1 teaspoon dried basil
1 cup sliced mushrooms	$\frac{1}{4}$ teaspoon cayenne pepper
1 teaspoon minced garlic	$\frac{1}{2}$ cup Italian bread crumbs
2 (14-ounce) cans artichoke	$\frac{3}{4}$ cup shredded reduced-fat
hearts, drained, rinsed,	sharp Cheddar cheese
and chopped	$\frac{1}{4}$ cup Parmesan cheese

Preheat the oven to 350°F. In a medium pan coated with nonstick cooking spray, sauté the onion, red pepper, green pepper, mushrooms, and garlic over medium heat until the vegetables are tender, about 8 minutes. Transfer the sautéed vegetables into a large bowl and add the chopped artichokes, egg whites, eggs, oregano, basil, cayenne, bread crumbs, Cheddar cheese, and Parmesan cheese, mixing with a spoon until well combined. Pour the mixture into a 2-quart oblong dish coated with nonstick cooking spray. Bake for 30 minutes, or until the mixture is set and the top is light brown.

Makes 42 squares

Nutritional information per square

Calories	27	Cal. from Fat (%)	30	Sodium (mg)	108
Fat (g)	0.9	Saturated Fat (g)	0.5	Cholesterol (mg)	12

MUFFINS, BREADS, *and* BRUNCH

EXTRA-SPECIAL HERBED GARLIC BREAD

This bread takes very little effort, but will make every meal special.

1 tablespoon olive oil
2 tablespoons (¼ stick) light
  stick margarine, melted
2 tablespoons minced garlic
1 tablespoon dried rosemary
¼ teaspoon crushed red
  pepper flakes (optional)

2 tablespoons chopped
  parsley
4 tablespoons grated
  Parmesan cheese
1 (16-ounce) loaf French
  bread, cut in half
  lengthwise
Paprika

Preheat the oven to 350°F. Combine the olive oil, margarine, garlic, rosemary, red pepper flakes, if using, parsley, and Parmesan cheese in a small bowl. Brush the mixture over each cut side of the bread. Place the bread, cut side up, on a baking sheet, sprinkle with paprika, and bake for 10 minutes.

Makes 16 slices

Nutritional information per slice

Calories	102	Cal. from Fat (%)	25.3	Sodium (mg)	215
Fat (g)	2.9	Saturated Fat (g)	0.7	Cholesterol (mg)	1

JALAPEÑO CORN BREAD ♥

There's nothing like jalapeño corn bread to spice up your dinner. There are certain special dishes such as chili, barbecue, or simple chicken dishes that I prefer to serve corn bread with rather than bread.

1½ cups yellow cornmeal
1 cup all-purpose flour
2 tablespoons sugar
1½ teaspoons baking
  powder
½ teaspoon baking soda

2 cups plain nonfat yogurt
3 tablespoons canola oil
1 (10-ounce) package frozen
  corn, thawed
2 tablespoons chopped
  seeded jalapeño peppers

Preheat the oven to 400°F. Coat a 9 × 9 × 2-inch baking pan with nonstick cooking spray. In a large bowl, mix the cornmeal, flour, sugar, baking powder, and baking soda until blended. Stir in the yogurt, then the canola oil, corn, and jalapeño peppers. Pour the batter into the prepared baking pan and bake for 30 minutes.

Makes 8 slices

Nutritional information per slice

Calories	273	Cal. from Fat (%)	20.5	Sodium (mg)	244
Fat (g)	6.2	Saturated Fat (g)	0.6	Cholesterol (mg)	1

SPINACH BREAD ♥

This is one of my favorite bread recipes. I like to serve it with soup and pretty much anything else. You can freeze the bread before baking it by wrapping each half in plastic wrap and then foil. Defrost the bread at least partway wrapped, then unwrap and cook as directed.

2 (10-ounce) packages frozen chopped spinach
½ cup chopped onion
1 teaspoon minced garlic
2 tablespoons skim milk
5 ounces light pasteurized processed cheese spread
1 (16-ounce) loaf French bread, split in half lengthwise

Preheat the oven to 350°F. Cook the spinach according to package directions. Drain very well and set aside. In a pot coated with non-stick cooking spray, sauté the onion over medium heat, about 4 minutes, until tender. Add the garlic, milk, cheese spread, and spinach, stirring over medium heat until the cheese is melted, about 3 minutes. Spread the spinach mixture on each cut half side of the French bread. Place the bread, cut side up, on a baking sheet and bake for 10 minutes, or until the bread is crispy.

Makes 16 slices

Nutritional information per slice

Calories	107	Cal. from Fat (%)	15.1	Sodium (mg)	335
Fat (g)	1.8	Saturated Fat (g)	0.8	Cholesterol (mg)	3

CHEESY CORN MUFFINS

This is a super way to dress up a cornmeal mix. I think these muffins go well with barbecue. The recipe makes 42 to 48 dozen miniature muffins.

1 cup chopped onion	2 tablespoons canola oil
1 (8½-ounce) can cream-style corn	2 large egg whites
	1 tablespoon sugar
1 cup shredded reduced-fat sharp Cheddar cheese	1½ cups self-rising cornmeal mix
⅔ cup nonfat sour cream	

Preheat the oven to 400°F. Coat 18 muffin tins with nonstick cooking spray. Sauté the onion in a pan coated with nonstick cooking spray over low heat until tender but not browned, about 8 minutes. Combine the onion with the corn, Cheddar cheese, sour cream, oil, egg whites, and sugar. Add the cornmeal mix and blend well. Fill the muffin tins ¾ full and bake for 20 to 25 minutes. Remove the muffins from the tins and cool on a wire rack.

Makes 18 muffins

Nutritional information per muffin

Calories	38	Cal. from Fat (%)	25.4	Sodium (mg)	97
Fat (g)	1.1	Saturated Fat (g)	0.4	Cholesterol (mg)	2

BEER BREAD MUFFINS

The short ingredients list is appealing but hard to believe after you taste these amazing homemade muffins. Beer bread is frequently requested at my house.

1 (10-ounce) can light beer	2 tablespoons (¼ stick) light stick margarine, melted
2 tablespoons sugar	
3 cups self-rising flour	

Preheat the oven to 350°F. Coat 12 muffin tins with nonstick cooking spray. In a large bowl, mix the beer, sugar, flour, and margarine together. Fill the tins with the batter and bake for 30 to 40 minutes, or until golden brown.

Makes 12 muffins

Nutritional information per muffin

Calories	134	Cal. from Fat (%)	8.6	Sodium (mg)	422
Fat (g)	1.3	Saturated Fat (g)	0.2	Cholesterol (mg)	0

APRICOT BREAD ♥

Munching on this bread was as good as eating cake. My testers demanded this recipe immediately.

1 cup diced dried apricots	2 cups all-purpose flour
1 large egg	1 tablespoon baking powder
1 cup sugar	¼ teaspoon baking soda
2 tablespoons (¼ stick) light stick margarine, melted	¾ cup orange juice

Preheat the oven to 350°F. Coat a 9 × 5 × 3-inch loaf pan with non-stick cooking spray and dust with flour. Pour boiling water over the apricots to cover and let stand 5 minutes. Drain. Meanwhile, in a mixing bowl, beat the egg, then stir in the sugar. Add the melted margarine. In a separate bowl, combine the flour, baking powder, and baking soda. Add alternately with the orange juice to the sugar mixture. Stir in the apricots. Pour the batter into the prepared loaf pan and bake for 1 hour.

Makes 16 slices

Nutritional information per slice

Calories	141	Cal. from Fat (%)	8	Sodium (mg)	145
Fat (g)	1.3	Saturated Fat (g)	0.2	Cholesterol (mg)	13

BUTTERSCOTCH BANANA BREAD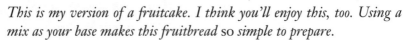

When plain banana bread doesn't seem exciting enough, this variation is just the ticket.

1¾ cups all-purpose flour
2 teaspoons baking powder
½ teaspoon baking soda
½ teaspoon ground
   cinnamon
½ teaspoon ground nutmeg
1 cup mashed bananas
   (2 large bananas)

¾ cup sugar
1 large egg
2 large egg whites
¼ cup canola oil
¼ cup skim milk
½ cup butterscotch chips

Preheat the oven to 350°F. Coat a 9 × 5 × 3-inch loaf pan with non-stick cooking spray. Combine the flour, baking powder, baking soda, cinnamon, and nutmeg in a bowl; set aside. In a mixing bowl, combine the mashed bananas, sugar, egg, egg whites, and oil, blending well. Add the flour mixture alternately with the milk to the banana mixture. Stir in the butterscotch chips. Pour into the prepared loaf pan. Bake for 50 minutes to 1 hour or until a toothpick inserted in the center comes out clean. Cool in pan.

Makes 16 slices

Nutritional information per slice

Calories	167	Cal. from Fat (%) 29.9		Sodium (mg)	119
Fat (g)	5.5	Saturated Fat (g) 1.7		Cholesterol (mg)	13

FRUITBREAD ♥

This is my version of a fruitcake. I think you'll enjoy this, too. Using a mix as your base makes this fruitbread so simple to prepare.

2 (7-ounce) packages
   blackberry muffin mix
1 (6-ounce) package dried
   apricots, chopped
½ teaspoon ground
   cinnamon

¾ cup raisins
1 large egg, beaten
½ cup skim milk
¾ cup applesauce
1 tablespoon brandy
1 teaspoon vanilla extract

Preheat the oven to 350°F. Coat a 9 × 5 × 3-inch loaf pan with non-stick cooking spray and dust with flour. Combine the muffin mix, apricots, cinnamon, raisins, egg, skim milk, applesauce, brandy, and vanilla in a bowl, mixing by hand. Pour into the prepared loaf pan and bake for 45 minutes or until a toothpick inserted in the center comes out clean. Cool in pan.

Makes 16 slices

Nutritional information per slice

Calories	155	Cal. from Fat (%)	16.8	Sodium (mg)	146
Fat (g)	2.9	Saturated Fat (g)	0.5	Cholesterol (mg)	13

LEMON BREAD ♥

The lemon syrup soaks through the bread, enhancing the flavor. Put this bread on top of your "must-try" list. You can add blueberries for a variation.

¼ cup (½ stick) light stick
  margarine, softened
⅔ cup plus ½ cup sugar
1 large egg
2 large egg whites
1 tablespoon grated lemon
  rind

½ teaspoon vanilla extract
2¼ cups all-purpose flour
1 teaspoon baking powder
½ teaspoon baking soda
1 (8-ounce) carton low-fat
  lemon yogurt
½ cup lemon juice

Preheat the oven to 350°F. Coat a 9 × 5 × 3-inch loaf pan with nonstick cooking spray. In a mixing bowl, cream the margarine with ⅔ cup sugar until light and fluffy. Add the egg, egg whites, lemon rind, and vanilla; beat until well blended. In another bowl, combine the flour, baking powder, and baking soda. Add the flour mixture alternately with the yogurt to the creamed mixture, beginning and ending with the flour mixture. Pour the batter into the prepared loaf pan. Bake for 55 minutes, or until a toothpick inserted in the center comes out clean. Remove from the oven and place on a wire rack.

Combine ½ cup sugar and ½ cup lemon juice in a saucepan; bring to a boil and cook 1 minute. Remove from the heat. Pierce the top of the bread several times with a meat fork. Pour the sugar mixture over the bread; cool in the pan 10 minutes. Remove from the pan and cool completely on a wire rack.

Makes 16 slices

Nutritional information per slice

Calories	156	Cal. from Fat (%)	11.8	Sodium (mg)	121
Fat (g)	2.1	Saturated Fat (g)	0.5	Cholesterol (mg)	14

CRANBERRY-PUMPKIN BREAD

The cranberries make tart bursts of flavor in this sweet, spicy pumpkin bread. I'm a fan of mixing other fruits, such as blueberries, with pumpkin.

2 large eggs, slightly beaten	2¼ cups all-purpose flour
1½ cups sugar	1 teaspoon ground
⅓ cup plus 1 tablespoon	cinnamon
canola oil	½ teaspoon ground allspice
1 cup packed unsweetened	1 teaspoon baking soda
pumpkin	1 cup chopped cranberries
1 teaspoon vanilla extract	

Preheat the oven to 350°F. Coat a 9 × 5 × 3-inch loaf pan with non-stick cooking spray and dust with flour. In a large bowl, combine the eggs, sugar, canola oil, pumpkin, and vanilla. In a separate bowl, combine the flour, cinnamon, allspice, and baking soda. Make a well in the center. Pour the pumpkin mixture into the well. Mix just until moistened. Stir in the cranberries. Spoon the batter into the prepared loaf pan. Bake for 1 to 1¼ hours, or until a toothpick inserted in the center comes out clean. Cool in the pan on a wire rack.

Makes 16 slices

Nutritional information per slice

Calories	203	Cal. from Fat (%)	27.8	Sodium (mg)	95
Fat (g)	6.3	Saturated Fat (g)	0.6	Cholesterol (mg)	27

CINNAMON BREAD ♥

This yeast bread is an exception to the rule. It is quick, easy, and a great breakfast.

1 (16-ounce) package hot roll	1 large egg, beaten
mix	2 tablespoons sugar
1 cup light beer, at room	1 teaspoon ground
temperature (never	cinnamon
refrigerated)	¼ cup light brown sugar

Preheat the oven to 375°F. Coat a 9-inch tube pan with nonstick cooking spray and dust with flour. Soften the yeast from the hot roll mix in the beer. Stir in the egg, sugar, and cinnamon. Add the remaining dry ingredients from the package and beat until smooth. Cover the bowl and let rise in a warm place until doubled in bulk, about 45 minutes to 1 hour. Beat the dough again and spread it in the prepared tube pan. Sprinkle the brown sugar over the dough. Let rise again in a warm place until double, about 45 minutes. Bake for 25 to 30 minutes. Remove from the pan.

Makes 16 slices

Nutritional information per slice

Calories	132	Cal. from Fat (%)	8.2	Sodium (mg)	195
Fat (g)	1.2	Saturated Fat (g)	0.1	Cholesterol (mg)	13

GOOEY ROLLS

I made these rolls specifically for my children, but all the adults ate them before the children had a chance. So be sure to make extra!

⅛ cup sugar
½ teaspoon ground
 cinnamon
1 (8-ounce) package large
 marshmallows

1½ tablespoons light stick
 margarine, melted
1 (8-ounce) can quick
 crescent dinner rolls

Preheat the oven to 375°F. Coat 8 muffin cups with nonstick cooking spray. Mix the sugar and cinnamon together in a small bowl. Dip each marshmallow in the melted margarine and roll in the sugar mixture. Separate the dough into triangles. Wrap one triangle around each marshmallow and pinch the dough together. Place each one in a muffin tin. If there is any extra margarine, drizzle over the top of the rolls. Bake for 8 to 12 minutes.

Makes 8 rolls

Nutritional information per roll

Calories	212	Cal. from Fat (%)	28.4	Sodium (mg)	255
Fat (g)	6.7	Saturated Fat (g)	1.5	Cholesterol (mg)	0

MORNING MUFFINS ♥

If you freeze a big batch of these muffins, you can pull them out as needed for a daily morning treat.

1½ cups all-purpose flour
½ cup whole wheat flour
1¼ cups sugar
1 tablespoon ground
  cinnamon
1 teaspoon baking powder
1 teaspoon baking soda
2 cups grated peeled carrots
1 apple, peeled and chopped
  (about 1 cup)

1 cup raisins
1 large egg, lightly beaten
2 large egg whites, lightly
  beaten
½ cup applesauce
¼ cup canola oil
1 tablespoon vanilla extract

Preheat the oven to 375°F. Coat 18 muffin cups with nonstick cooking spray. In a large bowl, stir together the flours, sugar, cinnamon, baking powder, and baking soda. Stir in the carrots, apple, and raisins. In a medium bowl, whisk together the egg, egg whites, applesauce, oil, and vanilla. Add to the dry ingredients and stir just until moistened. Spoon the batter into the muffin cups, filling them about ¾ full. Bake for 15 to 20 minutes.

Makes 18 muffins

Nutritional information per muffin

Calories	177	Cal. from Fat (%) 18.2	Sodium (mg)	121
Fat (g)	3.6	Saturated Fat (g) 0.4	Cholesterol (mg)	12

APPLE MUFFINS ♥

A wonderful way to celebrate autumn, this is another anytime-of-the-day muffin recipe.

2 tablespoons (¼ stick) light
  stick margarine, softened
¼ cup light brown sugar
½ cup sugar
1 large egg, beaten
1 cup buttermilk
1¾ cups all-purpose flour

1 teaspoon ground
  cinnamon
1 teaspoon baking soda
1 apple, peeled and finely
  chopped (approximately
  1 cup)

Preheat the oven to 400°F. Coat 12 muffin cups with nonstick cooking spray. Cream the margarine and sugars until fluffy. Add the egg and mix. Fold in the buttermilk. In a separate bowl, mix the flour, cinnamon, and soda. Add this gradually to the sugar-egg mixture, making sure there are no lumps. Add the chopped apple. Fill the muffin tins almost to the top of each cup. Bake for 15 minutes.

Makes 12 muffins

Nutritional information per muffin

Calories	145	Cal. from Fat (%)	11.1	Sodium (mg)	167
Fat (g)	1.8	Saturated Fat (g)	0.4	Cholesterol (mg)	18

BRAN MUFFINS

This batter keeps in the refrigerator for several weeks in a covered plastic or glass container, so you can bake muffins as you need them. Even those who were not normally bran muffin eaters raved about these, as the flaky cereal gives the muffin a lighter bran taste.

4 cups raisin-bran cereal	**2 teaspoons ground**
1 cup sugar	**cinnamon**
2½ cups all-purpose flour	**2 large eggs, beaten**
2½ teaspoons baking soda	**⅓ cup canola oil**
	2 cups buttermilk

Preheat the oven to 400°F. Line 24 muffin cups with paper liners. In a large bowl, mix the raisin bran, sugar, flour, baking soda, and cinnamon together. Add the eggs, oil, and buttermilk, stirring with a spoon until well combined. Fill each muffin cup ⅔ full of batter. Bake for 15 minutes, or until a toothpick inserted in the center of a muffin comes out clean.

Makes 24 muffins

Nutritional information per muffin

Calories	149	Cal. from Fat (%)	23.8	Sodium (mg)	218
Fat (g)	3.9	Saturated Fat (g)	0.5	Cholesterol (mg)	18

BREAKFAST CASSEROLE

This egg dish is always a hit for my guests and for me since it can be prepared ahead of time. Remember, if you prepare the casserole in a glass dish, place in a cold oven, then turn the oven on and add 10 or 15 minutes longer to the baking time.

8 slices of white bread, crusts removed
3 ounces Canadian bacon, chopped
1 bunch green onions (scallions), chopped
2 cups broccoli florets
5 large eggs, beaten
3 large egg whites
2½ cups skim milk

1 teaspoon dry mustard
1 cup plain nonfat yogurt
½ cup grated Parmesan cheese
½ teaspoon minced garlic
2 tablespoons chopped parsley
1 teaspoon dried basil
1 tablespoon dried rosemary
Salt and pepper to taste

Arrange the bread along the bottom of a 3-quart oblong casserole dish or a 13 × 9 × 2-inch baking pan, overlapping the slices slightly. In a small skillet coated with nonstick cooking spray, sauté the bacon, green onions, and broccoli over medium heat until tender, about 8 minutes. Spread on top of the bread.

In a mixing bowl, blend the eggs, egg whites, skim milk, and mustard; set aside. In a food processor, blend the yogurt, Parmesan cheese, garlic, parsley, basil, rosemary, and salt and pepper. Pour into the egg mixture, stirring until well combined. Pour over the bread and press the bread down to soak up the liquid. Cover with plastic wrap and place in the refrigerator for 6 hours or overnight.

Preheat the oven to 375°F. Bake for 1 hour, or until browned and a knife inserted in the center comes out clean.

Makes 12 servings

Nutritional information per serving

| Calories | 134 | Cal. from Fat (%) | 29.3 | Sodium (mg) | 319 |
| Fat (g) | 4.4 | Saturated Fat (g) | 1.6 | Cholesterol (mg) | 96 |

HOT FRUIT CASSEROLE ♥

I always enjoy serving this dish at a winter brunch when good fresh fruit is not available. You might volunteer to make this simple recipe next time you have to bring a dish to a luncheon. You can put the casserole together ahead of time and bake when ready to serve.

You can make vanilla wafer crumbs by placing vanilla wafers in a food processor or between two sheets of wax paper and crushing them with a rolling pin. The crumbs combined with the brown sugar and margarine thickens the fruit casserole.

1 (20-ounce) can pineapple chunks, in their own juice	4 bananas, peeled and sliced
2 (16-ounce) cans sliced peaches in light syrup	2 tablespoons lemon juice
	⅔ cup light brown sugar
2 (16-ounce) cans pear halves in light syrup, sliced	1 cup vanilla wafer crumbs
	4 tablespoons (½ stick) light stick margarine, cut up
1 (16-ounce) can pitted tart red cherries	⅓ cup crème de banana

Preheat the oven to 350°F. Drain the pineapple chunks, peaches, pears, and cherries. Peel the bananas and sprinkle with the lemon juice. Add the bananas to the fruit. Transfer half of the combined fruit to a 3-quart casserole dish. Sprinkle with half the brown sugar, half the vanilla wafer crumbs, half the light margarine, and half the crème de banana. Cover with the remaining fruit and the remaining brown sugar, vanilla wafer crumbs, margarine, and crème de banana. Bake for 30 to 40 minutes, or until the fruit is bubbly. Stir to combine before serving.

Makes 10 to 12 servings

Nutritional information per serving:

Calories	228	Cal. from Fat (%)	13.5	Sodium (mg)	84
Fat (g)	3.4	Saturated Fat (g)	0.7	Cholesterol (mg)	4

BAKED FRENCH TOAST ♥

With this method of preparing French toast, everything is done ahead of time and you can enjoy your morning. Serve with fruit or confectioners' sugar.

1 cup light maple syrup	2 large egg whites
1 (16-ounce) loaf French bread	1½ cups skim milk
	1 tablespoon vanilla extract
2 large eggs	¼ teaspoon ground nutmeg

Coat a 3-quart oblong baking dish with nonstick cooking spray. Pour the maple syrup into the dish. Slice the French bread into eight 2-inch slices and place over the syrup. In another bowl, beat the eggs, egg whites, skim milk, vanilla, and nutmeg until well blended. Pour the egg mixture over the bread, pressing the bread to soak up the liquid. Cover with plastic wrap and refrigerate overnight. Preheat the oven to 350°F. Bake for 40 to 45 minutes, or until golden brown.

Makes 8 servings

Nutritional information per serving

Calories	262	Cal. from Fat (%)	10.5	Sodium (mg)	477
Fat (g)	3.1	Saturated Fat (g)	0.8	Cholesterol (mg)	54

GOOD MORNING GRITS ♥

Make Good Morning Grits when you have a busy day ahead of you. They'll sustain you until lunch.

¼ cup finely chopped onion	½ cup chopped tomatoes
½ cup chopped green bell pepper	3 cups water
	¾ cup quick-cooking grits
½ cup chopped Canadian bacon	2 slices reduced-fat American cheese, chopped

Coat a skillet with nonstick cooking spray and sauté the onion, green pepper, and bacon over medium heat until tender, about 6 minutes. Stir in the tomatoes; set aside. In a saucepan, bring the water to a boil. Stir in the grits. Cover, reduce the heat, and simmer 5 minutes, or until thickened, stirring occasionally. Stir in the cheese and the reserved tomato mixture.

Makes 4 servings

Nutritional information per serving

Calories	176	Cal. from Fat (%)	17.4	Sodium (mg)	467
Fat (g)	3.4	Saturated Fat (g)	1.5	Cholesterol (mg)	16

SOUPS

CORN SOUP

It is hard to believe this creamy soup is not full of heavy cream. You can garnish it with chopped green onions when serving.

1 onion, chopped
1 green bell pepper, seeded
  and chopped
½ teaspoon minced garlic
1 (16-ounce) bag frozen
  sweet corn
1 (8½-ounce) can cream-style
  corn
1 (10-ounce) can diced
  tomatoes and green chilies

1 (14½-ounce) can fat-free
  chicken broth
1 tablespoon Worcestershire
  sauce
Salt and pepper to taste
2 cups low-fat milk
⅓ cup all-purpose flour

In a pot coated with nonstick cooking spray, sauté the onion, green pepper, and garlic over medium-high heat until tender, about 5 minutes. Add the frozen corn, cream-style corn, diced tomatoes and green chilies, chicken broth, Worcestershire sauce, and salt and pepper. In a separate bowl, blend together the milk and flour. Gradually stir into the corn mixture. Cook for 15 minutes, until hot throughout.

Makes 8 one-cup servings

Nutritional information per serving

Calories	125	Cal. from Fat (%)	2.9	Sodium (mg)	387
Fat (g)	0.4	Saturated Fat (g)	0.1	Cholesterol (mg)	1

QUICK CHEESY POTATO SOUP ♥

You would think this rich soup is a no-no, but it's completely painless to make and eat!

1 large onion
2 carrots, peeled
1 green bell pepper, seeded
2 (10¾-ounce) cans cream of
  potato soup
1 (16-ounce) can fat-free
  chicken broth

2 ounces pasteurized
  processed light cheese
  spread
1 (8-ounce) carton nonfat
  sour cream

Chop the onion, carrots, and green bell pepper in a food processor. In a large pot coated with nonstick cooking spray, sauté the chopped vegetables over medium heat until tender, about 5 minutes. Add the

soup, chicken broth, and cheese, stirring until the cheese is melted
and the soup is well heated. Before serving, stir in the sour cream;
do not boil.

Makes 6 one-cup servings

Nutritional information per serving

Calories	155	Cal. from Fat (%) 17.4	Sodium (mg)	1,152
Fat (g)	3	Saturated Fat (g) 1.7	Cholesterol (mg)	12

ONION SOUP ♥

I love onion soup and actually prefer this version to some of the high-fat recipes I've tried. The soup is full-flavored without being heavy.

1 tablespoon light stick margarine
3 large onions (about 2 pounds), halved and thinly sliced
1 teaspoon sugar
3 tablespoons all-purpose flour
2 cups water
2 (10½-ounce) cans beef broth
1 (10-ounce) can beef consommé
1 teaspoon Worcestershire sauce
2 tablespoons Cognac (optional)
8 (½-inch-thick) slices of French bread, toasted
1 cup shredded part-skim mozzarella cheese

In a large pot coated with nonstick cooking spray, melt the margarine over medium heat. Add the onions and cook 20 minutes, or until golden, stirring frequently. Add the sugar and stir well. Add the flour, stirring constantly for 1 minute. Gradually add the water, beef broth, and beef consommé. Bring to a boil, cover, reduce the heat, and simmer 30 minutes. Stir in the Worcestershire sauce and Cognac, if desired.

Preheat the broiler. Place 8 ovenproof soup bowls on a baking sheet and fill with the soup. Top each with a slice of French bread. Sprinkle the cheese evenly over the bread. Broil several minutes, or until the cheese melts. Serve immediately.

Makes 8 one-cup servings

Nutritional information per serving

Calories	191	Cal. from Fat (%) 19.4	Sodium (mg)	676
Fat (g)	4.1	Saturated Fat (g) 1.8	Cholesterol (mg)	8

CREAM OF SPINACH SOUP

Frozen broccoli can also be used for a cream of broccoli soup. I always enjoy these quickies when I need a soup to serve.

½ pound fresh mushrooms, sliced
1 small onion, chopped
2 (10¾-ounce) cans reduced-fat cream of mushroom soup
1 (14½-ounce) can fat-free chicken broth

2 (10-ounce) packages frozen chopped spinach, cooked according to package directions and drained well
Salt and pepper to taste

In a large pot coated with nonstick cooking spray, sauté the mushrooms and onion until tender over medium heat for 5 minutes. Add the soup, chicken broth, spinach, and salt and pepper, stirring until thoroughly heated. Transfer to a food processor or blender to puree.

Makes 8 one-cup servings

Nutritional information per serving

Calories	75	Cal. from Fat (%)	26.4	Sodium (mg)	483
Fat (g)	2.2	Saturated Fat (g)	0.6	Cholesterol (mg)	6

CREAMY POTATO SOUP

I like to serve this soup as a first course. When the potatoes are pureed they give the soup great body and creaminess but no added fat.

For the deluxe version, serve with reduced-fat shredded Cheddar cheese and a dollop of nonfat sour cream.

2 tablespoons (¼ stick) light stick margarine
1 cup chopped onion
2 large garlic cloves, minced
3 tablespoons all-purpose flour
2 (16-ounce) cans fat-free chicken broth
4 cups peeled diced potatoes (about 3 large)

½ cup sliced green onions (scallions)
Salt and pepper to taste
1 cup liquid nondairy creamer
Chopped parsley or sliced green onions (scallions), to garnish

Melt the margarine in a large pot over medium heat and sauté the onion and garlic until tender, about 5 minutes. Lower the heat and add the flour, stirring until smooth. Cook 1 minute, stirring constantly. Gradually add the broth, stirring constantly. Add the potatoes and green onions. Bring to a boil, cover, reduce the heat, and simmer for 20 minutes, stirring occasionally, or until the potatoes are tender. Transfer the mixture to a blender or food processor and blend until smooth, in batches if necessary. Return to the pot. Add salt and pepper, stir in the nondairy creamer, and heat thoroughly. Garnish with the parsley or green onions.

Makes 8 one-cup servings

Nutritional information per serving ·

Calories	144	Cal. from Fat (%)	28.8	Sodium (mg)	306
Fat (g)	4.6	Saturated Fat (g)	0.9	Cholesterol (mg)	0

CHICKEN SOUP

If you have any soup left, freeze it. My children like me to strain the soup so when I serve it to them there are no "green things." Somehow just the words "Chicken Soup" get kids so excited. To reduce the sodium, you may leave out some or all of the bouillon cubes.

4 quarts water
3 pounds skinless, boneless chicken breasts, cut into pieces
1 large onion, cut into wedges
6 sprigs of parsley
3 bay leaves

2 garlic cloves, halved
1 (16-ounce) package baby carrots
1 cup chopped celery
Salt and pepper to taste
4 chicken bouillon cubes
Cooked rice or noodles (optional)

Place the water, chicken, onion, parsley, bay leaves, garlic, carrots, celery, salt and pepper, and bouillon cubes in a large pot. Bring to a boil, cover, reduce the heat, and simmer 45 minutes, or until the chicken is tender. If desired, remove the chicken and carrots from the broth and strain the soup. Add the rice or noodles, if desired, and heat through.

Makes 8 to 10 one-cup servings

Nutritional information per serving

Calories	204	Cal. from Fat (%)	18.3	Sodium (mg)	585
Fat (g)	4.1	Saturated Fat (g)	1.1	Cholesterol (mg)	89

SHRIMP AND ARTICHOKE SOUP

I got the idea for this soup from a friend's mother who uses potatoes to thicken her soup.

1 pound peeled medium shrimp	3 cups thinly sliced peeled potatoes (about 2 medium)
1 bunch green onions (scallions), chopped (reserve the green stems)	2 (14-ounce) cans artichoke hearts, drained and halved
	Salt and pepper to taste
6 cups canned fat-free chicken broth	½ cup liquid nondairy creamer

In a pan coated with nonstick cooking spray, sauté the shrimp and green onion tops over medium heat until the shrimp are done, about 5 minutes. Set aside. In a pot, bring the chicken broth to a boil. Add the sliced potatoes, artichokes, and salt and pepper to taste. Return to a boil and continue boiling for 10 minutes. Transfer to a food processor and puree. Return to the pot and add the cooked shrimp, green onion stems, and nondairy creamer. Stir and heat through.

Makes 6 to 8 one-cup servings

Nutritional information per serving

Calories	139	Cal. from Fat (%)	13.6	Sodium (mg)	570
Fat (g)	2.1	Saturated Fat (g)	0.4	Cholesterol (mg)	81

SPLIT PEA SOUP ♥

Split Pea Soup is best made the day before so it can have time to refrigerate. Don't rule out the possibility of serving it the day it's made, however, if time is a factor. Serve with crackers or sour black bread.

3 quarts water	1 garlic clove, minced
2 cups dried split peas	1 bay leaf
Beef shank bone with meat	1 teaspoon sugar
½ cup chopped onion	Cayenne pepper to taste
1 cup chopped celery with leaves	¼ teaspoon dried thyme
½ cup chopped peeled carrots	

In a large pot, combine the water, split peas, and beef shank bone with meat. Bring to a boil, reduce the heat, and simmer, covered, 2½ to 3 hours. Add the onion, celery, and carrots. Simmer, covered, for

30 minutes longer. Add the garlic, bay leaf, sugar, cayenne pepper, and thyme. Remove the shank bone and bay leaf, then chill the soup. Skim the grease off the top and reheat to serve.

Makes 8 one-cup servings

Nutritional information per serving

Calories	182	Cal. from Fat (%)	6.5	Sodium (mg)	32
Fat (g)	1.3	Saturated Fat (g)	0.3	Cholesterol (mg)	8

ITALIAN SOUP ♥

This hearty soup is what the expression "everything but the kitchen sink" must mean. Serve it on a cold night and you'll be a hit.

If desired, leave the bacon out for vegetarian approval, and feel free to add and subtract vegetables as needed.

1 (5-ounce) package
  Canadian bacon, chopped
  in pieces
½ teaspoon minced garlic
1 large onion, sliced
⅔ cup chopped peeled
  carrots
2 zucchini, sliced
1 (28-ounce) can no-salt-
  added crushed tomatoes
  with their juice, undrained
½ cup red wine

Salt and pepper to taste
½ teaspoon dried oregano
4 (10¾-ounce) cans beef
  consommé
1½ cups water
1 (15-ounce) can red kidney
  beans, drained and rinsed
2 cups chopped cabbage
1 cup chopped fresh spinach
1 cup shell macaroni
1 teaspoon dried basil

In a large pot coated with nonstick cooking spray, cook the Canadian bacon until brown over medium heat, about 3 minutes. Then stir in the garlic, onion, carrots, zucchini, tomatoes, red wine, salt and pepper, oregano, beef consommé, water, kidney beans, cabbage, and spinach. Bring to a boil, lower the heat, and cook for 10 minutes. Add the macaroni and basil and continue cooking for 20 minutes longer.

Makes 10 to 12 one-cup servings

Nutritional information per serving

Calories	148	Cal. from Fat (%)	8.2	Sodium (mg)	750
Fat (g)	1.3	Saturated Fat (g)	0.3	Cholesterol (mg)	6

CHICKEN AND SAUSAGE GUMBO

The browned flour takes the place of a roux. which is browned flour and oil. This way, you get the toasty, rich flavor of a roux without the fat.

2 cups all-purpose flour
1 teaspoon minced garlic
2 onions, chopped
½ cup chopped celery
16 cups water
1 (15-ounce) can no-salt-added tomato sauce
4 pounds skinless, boneless chicken breasts, cut in big pieces

2 bay leaves
1 teaspoon dried thyme
1 tablespoon Worcestershire sauce
¼ teaspoon cayenne pepper
12 ounces light sausage
1 bunch green onions (scallions), thinly sliced
6 cups cooked rice

Preheat the oven to 400°F. Place the flour on a baking sheet and bake for 30 minutes, or until dark brown, stirring every 10 minutes. Be careful not to let it burn. While the flour is browning, coat a large pot with nonstick cooking spray and sauté the garlic, onions, and celery over medium heat until tender, about 5 minutes. Add the flour, stirring constantly. Gradually add the water, tomato sauce, chicken, bay leaves, thyme, Worcestershire sauce, and cayenne pepper. Bring to a boil, lower the heat, and simmer for 1 hour.

While the gumbo is cooking, boil the sausage in a pot of water for 10 minutes to remove any grease. Remove and slice thinly. Add to the gumbo and continue cooking for 10 minutes. Add the green onions, discard the bay leaves, and serve the gumbo over the rice.

Makes 12 one-cup servings

Nutritional information per serving (with 1/2 cup rice)

Calories	422	Cal. from Fat (%)	13	Sodium (mg)	368
Fat (g)	6.1	Saturated Fat (g)	1.9	Cholesterol (mg)	102

COLD PEACH SOUP ♥

It is hard to believe this outstanding soup gets its fresh taste from canned peaches. Everyone rated it A+ when they had some, and wanted more. Serve with a salad and you have a nice refreshing luncheon.

1 (1-pound 12-ounce) can light peach slices, drained
1 (8-ounce) carton nonfat sour cream

2 tablespoons lemon juice
1 tablespoon Triple Sec
1 tablespoon almond extract
1 tablespoon sugar

Place the peaches, sour cream, lemon juice, Triple Sec, almond extract, and sugar in a food processor and blend well. Transfer to a bowl, refrigerate, and serve chilled.

Makes 4 one-cup servings

Nutritional information per serving

Calories	145	Cal. from Fat (%)	1.2	Sodium (mg)	52
Fat (g)	0.2	Saturated Fat (g)	0	Cholesterol (mg)	5

BEEFY VEGETABLE SOUP ♥

This makes a huge pot of soup. I put it in containers to freeze and have dinner only minutes away when I get a request for vegetable soup. Remember, you can always add your favorite fresh or frozen vegetables to the pot. I always clean out my refrigerator this way, and no one's the wiser.

2 pounds extra-lean stewing
beef, cubed
1 pound cross-cut beef
shank, cubed
6 quarts water
Salt and pepper to taste
1 large onion, chopped
1 cup chopped celery
1 (16-ounce) package frozen
corn

1 (16-ounce) package frozen
cut green beans
1 (16-ounce) package baby
carrots
2 (28-ounce) cans no-salt-
added whole tomatoes,
mashed with their juice
2 bay leaves
1 (8-ounce) package small
shell pasta

In a very large pot, place the stewing beef, beef shank, and 6 quarts of water. Season with salt and pepper. Bring to a boil and boil 1½ hours over medium heat. Add the onion and celery and cook 30 minutes. Add the corn, green beans, carrots, tomatoes, and bay leaves. Continue cooking for 30 minutes. Add the pasta and cook until the pasta is done and meat is tender, about 10 to 15 minutes. Remove the bay leaves before serving. Season to taste.

Makes 16 one-cup servings

Nutritional information per serving

Calories	223	Cal. from Fat (%)	19	Sodium (mg)	81
Fat (g)	4.7	Saturated Fat (g)	1.6	Cholesterol (mg)	41

WILD RICE SOUP ♥

No one will complain about leftovers when they're cleverly disguised in a tempting soup like this one. You can also use leftover cooked rice if you have it on hand.

4 tablespoons (½ stick) light stick margarine
½ cup chopped onion
½ cup finely chopped peeled carrots
½ cup all-purpose flour
3 cups canned fat-free chicken broth

1 (6-ounce) package long-grain and wild rice
1 cup chopped cooked chicken or turkey
3 tablespoons sherry

In a large pot, melt the margarine over medium heat and sauté the onion and carrots until tender, about 5 minutes. Stir in the flour. Gradually add the broth and let the mixture come to a boil, stirring constantly. Meanwhile, prepare the rice according to package directions, omitting any oil and salt. Add the cooked rice and cooked chicken and simmer 5 minutes. Add the sherry. If the soup gets too thick, add more chicken broth or water. Boil 1 minute.

Makes 4 to 6 one-cup servings

Nutritional information per serving

Calories	261	Cal. from Fat (%)	20.7	Sodium (mg)	361
Fat (g)	6	Saturated Fat (g)	1.2	Cholesterol (mg)	21

SALADS

FRUITY TOSSED GREEN SALAD WITH STRAWBERRY DRESSING ♥

The Strawberry Dressing can be used on spinach salad as well. It will keep up to 4 days tightly covered in the refrigerator.

1 head Bibb lettuce, torn into pieces
1 large head romaine lettuce, torn into pieces
2 (11-ounce) cans mandarin orange slices, drained

¼ cup slivered almonds, toasted
½ cup chopped red onion
Strawberry Dressing (recipe follows)

Combine the lettuces, orange slices, almonds, and onion in a large salad bowl. Toss with the Strawberry Dressing.

Makes 10 to 12 servings

Strawberry Dressing

1 (16-ounce) package frozen strawberries, thawed
1½ teaspoons honey
¼ teaspoon dried thyme
¼ teaspoon pepper

3 tablespoons raspberry vinegar
½ cup water
2 teaspoons canola oil
1 teaspoon soy sauce

Combine the strawberries, honey, thyme, pepper, vinegar, water, oil, and soy sauce in a blender or food processor and puree until thoroughly blended. Pour the dressing into a covered container and refrigerate.

Makes 2 cups

Nutritional information per serving (includes dressing)

Calories	69	Cal. from Fat (%) 26.2		Sodium (mg)	38
Fat (g)	2	Saturated Fat (g)	0.2	Cholesterol (mg)	0

SPINACH SALAD ♥

Don't let this combination scare you away! The brown sugar and balsamic vinegar give this interesting salad a spicy, sweet-tart kick.

1 (12-ounce) bag fresh spinach, washed, stemmed, and torn into pieces
½ cup sliced green onions (scallions)
1 (8-ounce) can sliced water chestnuts, drained
2 ounces shredded reduced-fat Monterey Jack cheese

3 tablespoons light brown sugar
⅓ cup fat-free chicken broth
3 tablespoons balsamic vinegar
2 dashes of hot sauce
1 (11-ounce) can mandarin orange slices, drained

Combine the spinach, green onions, water chestnuts, and Monterey Jack cheese. Toss well and set aside. Combine the brown sugar, chicken broth, vinegar, and hot sauce in a small saucepan. Stir well and bring to a boil. Remove from the heat and stir in the mandarin orange slices. Pour the mandarin mixture over the spinach mixture. Toss gently. Serve immediately.

Makes 6 servings

Nutritional information per serving

Calories	110	Cal. from Fat (%)	16.4	Sodium (mg)	154
Fat (g)	2	Saturated Fat (g)	1	Cholesterol (mg)	7

CAESAR SALAD

You may think of Caesar Salad as the forbidden salad because it is normally high in fat. This one is fat-free and and guilt-free as well.

1 head romaine lettuce, torn into pieces	2 tablespoons red wine vinegar
2 tablespoons grated Parmesan cheese	½ teaspoon dry mustard
	½ teaspoon garlic powder
1 teaspoon coarsely ground black pepper	⅓ cup plain nonfat yogurt
	1 cup croutons (optional)
2 tablespoons lemon juice	
1 teaspoon Worcestershire sauce	

Combine the lettuce, cheese, and pepper in a large bowl and toss well. Combine the lemon juice, Worcestershire sauce, vinegar, mustard, and garlic powder and blend well. Add the yogurt; stir well. Add the dressing to the lettuce mixture and toss gently to coat. Add the croutons, if using, to the lettuce mixture and toss gently. Serve immediately.

Makes 6 servings

Nutritional information per serving

Calories	55	Cal. from Fat (%)	18.3	Sodium (mg)	91
Fat (g)	1.1	Saturated Fat (g)	0.4	Cholesterol (mg)	2

TROPICAL ROMAINE SALAD ♥

Your family or guests will certainly be impressed with this unusual salad.

DRESSING	2 tablespoons sugar
Dash of pepper	1 large head romaine lettuce, torn into pieces
1 tablespoon canola oil	
1 tablespoon chopped parsley	1 cup chopped celery
	4 green onions (scallions), chopped
2 tablespoons sugar	
⅓ cup raspberry vinegar	1 (11-ounce) can mandarin orange slices, drained
¼ cup water	
¼ teaspoon hot sauce	½ cup chopped dates
¼ cup sliced almonds	

In a small bowl, mix the pepper, oil, parsley, sugar, vinegar, water, and hot sauce together and chill. The dressing can be made a day ahead. In a small pan over medium heat, cook the almonds and sugar, stirring constantly until the sugar is dissolved and the almonds are coated. Watch carefully as they will burn easily. Cool and store in an airtight container for up to one week if not using right away. In a salad bowl, mix the lettuce, celery, and green onions. Toss with the dressing. Just before serving, add the almonds, oranges, and dates.

Makes 8 servings

Nutritional information per serving

Calories	121	Cal. from Fat (%)	28.4	Sodium (mg)	23
Fat (g)	3.8	Saturated Fat (g)	0.3	Cholesterol (mg)	0

WILD RICE AND FETA SALAD

If you don't have tarragon wine vinegar on hand, don't make a special trip to the store. Just use 2 tablespoons white wine vinegar and add ¹/₂ teaspoon dried tarragon.

1 (6-ounce) package long-grain and wild rice

2 ounces feta cheese, crumbled

¹/₂ cup chopped green bell pepper

¹/₂ cup chopped yellow bell pepper

¹/₂ cup chopped onion

1 (2-ounce) jar diced pimiento, drained

DRESSING

2 tablespoons water

1 tablespoon olive oil

¹/₄ cup tarragon wine vinegar

¹/₈ teaspoon pepper

Cook the rice according to package directions. Cool slightly. In a medium mixing bowl, combine the cheese, peppers, onion, and pimiento. For the dressing, stir together the water, olive oil, vinegar, and pepper. Add to the rice mixture. Toss gently to coat. Cover and chill for 1 hour before serving (this salad can be made a day ahead).

Makes 6 servings

Nutritional information per serving

Calories	153	Cal. from Fat (%)	27.6	Sodium (mg)	417
Fat (g)	4.7	Saturated Fat (g)	1.7	Cholesterol (mg)	8

WALDORF CARROT SALAD

By combining carrots and apples, you have a very colorful salad as well as a delicious one. This salad can be made year-round, and will add to any luncheon buffet or plate.

2 cups peeled shredded
   carrots
2 cups unpeeled chopped
   tart apples
1 cup chopped celery

⅓ cup chopped dates
⅓ cup plain nonfat yogurt
¼ cup fat-free mayonnaise
3 tablespoons orange juice

In a medium bowl, combine the carrots, apples, celery, and dates. In a small bowl, mix together the yogurt, mayonnaise, and orange juice. Pour over the carrot mixture, tossing gently.

Makes 8 servings

Nutritional information per serving

Calories	64	Cal. from Fat (%)	2.8	Sodium (mg)	83
Fat (g)	0.2	Saturated Fat (g)	0	Cholesterol (mg)	0

SEVEN-LAYER SALAD ♥

Even if you're not a feta cheese fan, you'll still want to try this layered salad as the cheese just lends creaminess and flavor to the dressing. This make-ahead side dish is great for a crowd.

DRESSING
½ cup nonfat sour cream
½ cup buttermilk
½ cup crumbled feta cheese
   (about 2 ounces)
1 teaspoon sugar
¼ teaspoon dried dillweed
½ teaspoon dried basil
   leaves
⅛ teaspoon ground white
   pepper
1 (9-ounce) package spinach
   tortellini

6 cups torn fresh spinach
   leaves or romaine lettuce
½ pound fresh mushrooms,
   sliced
2 Roma (plum) tomatoes,
   chopped
4 green onions (scallions),
   chopped
2½ ounces sliced Canadian
   bacon, pan-cooked and cut
   into pieces

In a food processor, blend the sour cream, buttermilk, feta cheese, sugar, dillweed, basil, and pepper until smooth to make the dressing. Chill. Cook the tortellini according to package directions, omitting any oil and salt. Drain and rinse in cold water. In a 3-quart oblong dish, layer the spinach leaves, tortellini, mushrooms, tomatoes, and green onions. Pour the dressing over the salad and sprinkle with the bacon. Cover and chill at least 2 hours to blend the flavors, or until serving time.

Makes 8 to 10 servings

Nutritional information per serving

Calories	158	Cal. from Fat (%)	21.7	Sodium (mg)	441
Fat (g)	3.8	Saturated Fat (g)	2.4	Cholesterol (mg)	27

NEW POTATO SALAD

In my opinion, there's always a place on the table for potato salad.

2 pounds red new potatoes
⅓ cup nonfat sour cream
¼ cup nonfat mayonnaise
Salt and pepper to taste
1 teaspoon Dijon mustard
1 tablespoon minced parsley
½ cup chopped celery

1 bunch green onions
  (scallions), sliced
1 small red bell pepper,
  seeded and chopped
2 tablespoons sweet pickle
  relish

Place the potatoes in a pot and cover with water. Bring to a boil and cook until tender but not mushy, about 20 minutes. Drain and cool. Cut into chunks and place in a large bowl. In another small bowl, combine the sour cream, mayonnaise, salt and pepper, and mustard; blend well. Add the parsley, celery, green onions, red pepper, and relish to the potatoes in the bowl and toss gently with the dressing. Store in a covered bowl in the refrigerator.

Makes 8 servings

Nutritional information per serving

Calories	120	Cal. from Fat (%)	1.5	Sodium (mg)	115
Fat (g)	0.2	Saturated Fat (g)	0	Cholesterol (mg)	1

BEAN AND CORN SALAD

This salad also works well served as a salsa with chips. You'll need a lot of willpower not to eat more than your share.

2 cups frozen whole kernel
corn, thawed
1 red or green bell pepper,
seeded and chopped
1 medium tomato, chopped
1 (15-ounce) can garbanzo
beans or chickpeas,
drained and rinsed
1 (15-ounce) can black
beans, drained and rinsed
1 (15-ounce) can pinto
beans, drained and rinsed
1 bunch green onions
(scallions), sliced

¼ cup red wine vinegar
¼ cup olive oil
2 tablespoons chopped
parsley
2 tablespoons lime juice
½ teaspoon dried cumin
¼ teaspoon pepper
Dash of salt
1 tablespoon chopped
jalapeño pepper
1 teaspoon minced garlic

In a large bowl, combine the corn, pepper, tomato, garbanzo beans, black beans, pinto beans, green onions, vinegar, olive oil, parsley, lime juice, cumin, pepper, salt, jalapeño, and minced garlic; mix well. Serve immediately or cover and refrigerate until serving time.

Makes 12 servings

Nutritional information per serving

Calories	175	Cal. from Fat (%)	29.1	Sodium (mg)	184
Fat (g)	5.7	Saturated Fat (g)	0.8	Cholesterol (mg)	0

MARINATED BROCCOLI AND ARTICHOKES ♥

This tasty dressing works with any number of vegetables.

DRESSING
½ cup fat-free Italian
Parmesan dressing
¼ cup balsamic vinegar
1 tablespoon Dijon mustard
2 tablespoons honey

1 large bunch broccoli, cut
into florets
1 (14-ounce) can artichoke
hearts, drained and cut
into quarters
½ red onion, sliced into rings
2 tablespoons drained capers

Combine the Italian Parmesan dressing, vinegar, mustard, and honey in a bowl, mixing very well. Combine the broccoli, artichoke hearts, onion, and capers in a glass bowl and pour the dressing over. Cover with plastic wrap and refrigerate for several hours or overnight, tossing occasionally.

Makes 8 servings

Nutritional information per serving

Calories	69	Cal. from Fat (%)	6.5	Sodium (mg)	207
Fat (g)	0.5	Saturated Fat (g)	0.1	Cholesterol (mg)	0

TUNA AND WHITE BEAN SALAD

Serve this simple salad as part of a salad buffet or on top of leaf lettuce.

1 (12¼-ounce) can solid white tuna packed in water, drained

1 cup chopped green onions (scallions)

1 (15-ounce) can white beans, rinsed and drained

2 tablespoons chopped parsley

½ cup diced celery

⅓ cup lemon juice

1½ tablespoons olive oil

¼ teaspoon dried rosemary

¼ teaspoon pepper

In a large bowl, combine the tuna, green onions, white beans, parsley, and celery, tossing well. In a small bowl, blend the lemon juice, olive oil, rosemary, and pepper. Pour over the tuna mixture and stir gently to combine. Refrigerate for 2 hours or let stand at room temperature for at least 30 minutes.

Makes 4 to 6 servings

Nutritional information per serving

Calories	171	Cal. from Fat (%)	25.8	Sodium (mg)	311
Fat (g)	4.9	Saturated Fat (g)	0.8	Cholesterol (mg)	19

MACARONI SALAD ♥

My family enjoyed this salad before "pasta salad" became fashionable.

1 (8-ounce) package small
  macaroni shells
½ cup chopped celery
3 large hard-boiled eggs,
  whites only, chopped
½ cup chopped red onion

⅓ cup nonfat Italian
  dressing
Salt and pepper to taste
½ cup dill pickle relish
¼ cup nonfat mayonnaise
1 teaspoon Dijon mustard

Cook the macaroni shells according to package directions, omitting the oil and salt. Drain and set aside. In a large bowl, combine the cooled macaroni, celery, egg whites, and onion. Add the Italian dressing and salt and pepper. In another small bowl, mix the pickle relish, mayonnaise, and mustard together. Add to the macaroni mixture and toss gently but well. Chill before serving.

Makes 10 to 12 servings

Nutritional information per serving

Calories	99	Cal. from Fat (%)	3.6	Sodium (mg)	177
Fat (g)	0.4	Saturated Fat (g)	0.1	Cholesterol (mg)	0

GREEK TORTELLINI SALAD

This salad is always a hit and really convenient because you can make it a day ahead. Leave out the feta cheese to make the salad lower in fat.

1 (6-ounce) package
  tricolored tortellini
1 (6-ounce) package cheese
  tortellini
6 ounces ziti pasta
1 red bell pepper, cut into
  thin strips
1 green bell pepper, cut into
  thin strips
½ red onion, chopped
¼ cup sliced pitted ripe
  black olives
1 (14-ounce) can artichoke
  hearts, drained and
  quartered

⅔ cup balsamic or red wine
  vinegar
2 tablespoons olive oil
2 tablespoons chopped
  parsley
3 tablespoons lemon juice
3 tablespoons dry sherry
1 teaspoon dried oregano
1 teaspoon garlic powder
1 teaspoon pepper
⅛ teaspoon crushed red
  pepper flakes
½ cup crumbled feta cheese

Cook both packages of tortellini and ziti pasta according to package
directions, omitting the oil and salt. Drain. In a large bowl, combine
the cooked pasta, peppers, onion, olives, and artichokes. For the
dressing, in a small bowl, combine the vinegar, olive oil, parsley,
lemon juice, sherry, oregano, garlic powder, pepper, and red pepper
flakes. Pour the dressing over the pasta mixture, add the cheese, and
toss gently. Cover and chill for at least 2 hours or overnight.

Makes 10 to 12 servings

Nutritional information per serving

| Calories | 225 | Cal. from Fat (%) | 24 | Sodium (mg) | 457 |
| Fat (g) | 6 | Saturated Fat (g) | 2.6 | Cholesterol (mg) | 24 |

ITALIAN PASTA SALAD ♥

*This vegetarian salad can be adjusted to your taste and your pantry. Use
your imagination and your favorite kind of pasta.*

8 ounces ziti pasta
4 ounces tricolored rotini
1 green bell pepper, seeded
and chopped
1 red bell pepper, seeded
and chopped
½ cup chopped celery
2 teaspoons drained capers
⅓ cup thinly sliced green
onions (scallions)

2 Roma (plum) tomatoes,
chopped
½ cup red wine vinegar
¼ cup water
1 teaspoon dried basil
1 teaspoon dried oregano
½ teaspoon minced garlic
1 tablespoon Dijon mustard
¼ cup grated Parmesan
cheese

Cook both the pastas together according to package directions,
omitting the oil and salt. Rinse and drain and place in a large bowl.
Add the green pepper, red pepper, celery, capers, green onions, and
tomatoes. Combine the vinegar with the water, basil, oregano, garlic, mustard, and Parmesan cheese in a small bowl, mixing well.
Pour over the pasta mixture and toss well.

Makes 8 to 12 servings

Nutritional information per serving

| Calories | 112 | Cal. from Fat (%) | 9 | Sodium (mg) | 75 |
| Fat (g) | 1.1 | Saturated Fat (g) | 0.4 | Cholesterol (mg) | 1 |

SHRIMP, SPINACH, AND PASTA SALAD WITH POPPY SEED DRESSING

This is a wonderful salad if you're short on time, and if you buy your shrimp already cooked and peeled, it's even quicker. Try the Poppy Seed Dressing over fruit salad.

1 (12-ounce) package
tricolored rotini
1 pound large shrimp,
cooked, peeled, and
deveined
1 bunch green onions
(scallions), thinly sliced

½ (10-ounce) bag fresh
spinach, stemmed and
torn into pieces
Poppy Seed Dressing (recipe
follows)

Cook the pasta according to package directions, omitting the oil and salt. Drain and combine with the shrimp, green onions, and spinach. Toss to coat with the Poppy Seed Dressing.

Makes 6 servings

Poppy Seed Dressing

1 cup nonfat sour cream
1 tablespoon honey

1½ tablespoons lemon juice
1½ teaspoons poppy seeds

In a medium bowl, combine the sour cream, honey, lemon juice, and poppy seeds, mixing well.

Makes 1 cup

Nutritional information per serving (includes dressing)

Calories	366	Cal. from Fat (%)	5.7	Sodium (mg)	226
Fat (g)	2.3	Saturated Fat (g)	0.4	Cholesterol (mg)	151

BROCCOLI VERMICELLI SALAD

You wouldn't think a salad with just pasta and broccoli could be so good. But with a hint of olive oil and cheese, this side dish gets a #1 rating.

2 (10-ounce) packages frozen
chopped broccoli
8 ounces vermicelli, broken
into 1-inch pieces
1 teaspoon minced garlic
2 tablespoons olive oil

2 tablespoons grated
Parmesan cheese
¼ teaspoon crushed red
pepper flakes
Salt and pepper to taste

Cook the broccoli according to package directions, omitting the oil and salt. Drain very well. Cook the vermicelli according to package directions, omitting the oil and salt. Drain. Combine the vermicelli with the broccoli, garlic, olive oil, Parmesan cheese, red pepper flakes, and salt and pepper; toss well. Serve at room temperature.

Makes 6 servings

Nutritional information per serving

Calories	225	Cal. from Fat (%)	24	Sodium (mg)	54
Fat (g)	6	Saturated Fat (g)	1.1	Cholesterol (mg)	1

APRICOT DELIGHT

I like to serve this at lunch along with another salad, such as chicken salad, but you might want to serve it as dessert. If desired, the Topping can be omitted.

2 (3-ounce) packages orange gelatin
2 cups boiling water
2 (16-ounce) cans light apricot halves, drained and chopped, juice reserved
1 (20-ounce) can crushed pineapple in juice, drained, juice reserved
1 cup miniature marshmallows

TOPPING
½ cup sugar
3 tablespoons all-purpose flour
Reserved apricot and pineapple juices (approximately 1 cup)
1 cup light frozen whipped topping, thawed

Dissolve the gelatin in the boiling water. Add 1 cup of the reserved juices, keeping the remaining apricot and pineapple juice for the topping. Chill until slightly firm. Fold in the fruit and marshmallows. Pour into a 7 × 11 × 2-inch oblong dish. Chill until firm. Combine the sugar and flour in a saucepan. Gradually blend in the reserved juice. Cook over low heat until thickened, about 5 to 8 minutes, stirring constantly. Remove from heat. Cool. Fold in the whipped topping. Spread over the chilled gelatin.

Makes 12 servings

Nutritional information per serving

Calories	165	Cal. from Fat (%)	8.2	Sodium (mg)	45
Fat (g)	1.5	Saturated Fat (g)	1.3	Cholesterol (mg)	0

CHERRY GELATIN MOLD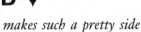

Everyone likes cherry gelatin, and this recipe makes such a pretty side dish for the holidays.

1 (6-ounce) package cherry
  gelatin
1 cup boiling water
1 (16-ounce) can light cherry
  pie filling

1 (20-ounce) can crushed
  pineapple in juice, drained

Place the cherry gelatin in a bowl and pour the boiling water over. Stir until the gelatin is dissolved. Add the cherry pie filling and the pineapple. Pour into a mold and refrigerate until firm.

Makes 10 servings

Nutritional information per serving

Calories	135	Cal. from Fat (%)	1	Sodium (mg)	48
Fat (g)	0.1	Saturated Fat (g)	0	Cholesterol (mg)	0

SALMON SALAD ♥

For a nice change from tuna fish, open a can of salmon and throw together this easy lunch salad. You might even find yourself using it in a sandwich.

½ cup nonfat sour cream
1 tablespoon fat-free
  mayonnaise
1 tablespoon Dijon mustard
1 teaspoon dried dillweed
1 tablespoon grated lemon
  rind
1 tablespoon fresh lemon
  juice

1 (14-ounce) can water-
  packed red salmon,
  drained, bones removed,
  and flaked
1 cup finely chopped celery
⅓ cup chopped red onion
1 tablespoon drained capers
Salt and pepper to taste

In a medium bowl, whisk together the sour cream, mayonnaise, mustard, dillweed, lemon rind, and lemon juice. Stir in the salmon, celery, red onion, and capers. Season with salt and pepper.

Makes 4 servings

Nutritional information per serving

Calories	192	Cal. from Fat (%)	29.5	Sodium (mg)	782
Fat (g)	6.3	Saturated Fat (g)	1.6	Cholesterol (mg)	58

CURRIED CHICKEN SALAD

This chicken salad has just a hint of curry, but, depending on how much you like curry, you can adjust the amount. I can always count on this salad being a hit with luncheon guests whenever I am in a pinch.

4 cooked skinless, boneless
   chicken breasts, diced
¾ cup chopped celery
½ cup chopped onion
¼ cup nonfat mayonnaise
¼ cup plain nonfat yogurt
1 teaspoon lemon juice

1 tablespoon soy sauce
¼ teaspoon curry powder
¼ cup chopped almonds,
   toasted
½ cup thawed frozen green
   peas

Combine the chicken, celery, and onion in a bowl. Blend the mayonnaise, yogurt, lemon juice, soy sauce, and curry powder together. Pour the sauce over the chicken mixture and mix thoroughly. Before serving, fold in the almonds and peas.

Makes 4 servings

Nutritional information per serving

Calories	232	Cal. from Fat (%)	26	Sodium (mg)	484
Fat (g)	6.7	Saturated Fat (g)	1.2	Cholesterol (mg)	73

VEGETABLES
and
STARCHES

SPINACH STROGANOFF ♥

This creamed spinach dish adds color to your plate, and it's also delicious. If desired, you can substitute ½ cup sliced fresh mushrooms for the canned ones. Sauté the mushrooms when you sauté the green onions.

2 (10-ounce) packages frozen chopped spinach
1 bunch green onions (scallions), chopped
1 (10¾-ounce) can 97% fat-free cream of mushroom soup
1 (8-ounce) carton nonfat sour cream
1 tablespoon Worcestershire sauce
1 (4-ounce) can sliced mushrooms, drained
1 tablespoon lemon juice
¼ teaspoon garlic powder
Salt and pepper to taste

Preheat the oven to 350°F. Coat a 2-quart casserole with nonstick cooking spray. Cook the spinach according to package directions and drain. Sauté the green onions in a pan coated with nonstick cooking spray until tender, 4 minutes. Mix together the mushroom soup, sour cream, Worcestershire sauce, mushrooms, lemon juice, garlic powder, and salt and pepper. Combine with the green onions and spinach. Pour into the 2-quart casserole and bake for 30 minutes.

Makes 4 to 6 servings

Nutritional information per serving

Calories	127	Cal. from Fat (%)	29.1	Sodium (mg)	613
Fat (g)	4.1	Saturated Fat (g)	1.1	Cholesterol (mg)	4

VEGETABLES AND STARCHES

CRANBERRY-GLAZED BABY CARROTS

Not only do these carrots look beautiful, but they taste delicious, too. You'll want to prepare these carrots on more than just holiday occasions.

1 pound fresh baby carrots
2 tablespoons light tub margarine
¼ cup light brown sugar

½ cup jellied cranberry sauce
Freshly ground black pepper to taste

Bring a saucepan of water to a boil, add the carrots, and boil gently, covered, until crisp-tender, about 8 to 10 minutes. Drain and set aside. In a large skillet over medium-high heat, combine the margarine, brown sugar, and cranberry sauce, stirring until smooth and dissolved. Simmer for 2 minutes. Add the carrots and cook, stirring occasionally, until glazed and heated through, about 5 minutes. Season with pepper, if desired.

Makes 12 servings

Nutritional information per serving

Calories	50	Cal. from Fat (%) 18.7	Sodium (mg)	47
Fat (g)	1	Saturated Fat (g) 0.2	Cholesterol (mg)	0

TIPSY MUSHROOMS

These mushrooms are a great side dish with beef.

1 tablespoon light stick margarine
1 red bell pepper, seeded and coarsely chopped
1 green bell pepper, seeded and coarsely chopped
1 red onion, coarsely chopped

1 pound fresh mushrooms, halved
⅓ cup Burgundy wine
½ teaspoon garlic salt
Pepper to taste

In a skillet, melt the margarine and sauté the peppers and onion over medium-low heat until tender, about 4 minutes. Stir in the mushrooms, wine, and garlic salt, cooking until tender and the wine is somewhat reduced, about 5 minutes. Season with pepper.

Makes 6 servings

Nutritional information per serving

Calories	44	Cal. from Fat (%) 26.1	Sodium (mg)	220
Fat (g)	1.3	Saturated Fat (g) 0.2	Cholesterol (mg)	0

SPECIAL SPINACH CASSEROLE

I love to make this spinach for two reasons: First, you don't have to defrost or cook the spinach separately, and, second, the topping has a great flavor thanks to the horseradish (the secret ingredient).

1 tablespoon light stick margarine, melted	¼ cup shredded reduced-fat Cheddar cheese
2 (10-ounce) packages frozen chopped spinach	Zesty Topping (recipe follows)
¼ teaspoon ground nutmeg	Paprika
1 (4-ounce) can mushroom stems and pieces, drained	Salt and pepper to taste

Preheat the broiler. In a skillet, melt the margarine and add the frozen spinach. Cover and cook until defrosted, about 3 to 5 minutes. Stir in the salt and pepper, nutmeg, mushrooms, and cheese and cook until the cheese is melted. Pour into a shallow 2-quart casserole dish coated with nonstick cooking spray. Spread the Zesty Topping over the spinach mixture and sprinkle with the paprika. Broil 2 inches from the heat until browned.

Makes 6 servings

Zesty Topping

¾ cup nonfat sour cream	1 tablespoon Dijon mustard
2 tablespoons prepared horseradish	

Mix the sour cream, horseradish, and Dijon mustard together in a small bowl.

Makes ¾ cup

Nutritional information per serving (includes topping)

Calories	85	Cal. from Fat (%)	22.2	Sodium (mg)	232
Fat (g)	2.1	Saturated Fat (g)	0.8	Cholesterol (mg)	6

SQUASH AND ZUCCHINI MEDLEY

This herby side dish can also be served over pasta as a main course.

1 teaspoon minced garlic
1 bunch green onions
(scallions), sliced
4 medium yellow squash
(about 1 pound), sliced
4 medium zucchini (about
1 pound), sliced
½ cup canned fat-free
chicken broth

¼ cup white wine (optional)
1 teaspoon dried basil
1 teaspoon dried oregano
1 teaspoon dried crumbled
rosemary
Salt and pepper to taste

In a pan coated with nonstick cooking spray, sauté the garlic and green onions over medium heat for about 3 minutes. Add the yellow squash, zucchini, chicken broth, and white wine. Sprinkle with the basil, oregano, rosemary, and salt and pepper. Cover and stir occasionally. Cook until the squash is tender, about 5 minutes.

Makes 8 servings

Nutritional information per serving

Calories	28	Cal. from Fat (%)	6.4	Sodium (mg)	34
Fat (g)	0.2	Saturated Fat (g)	0	Cholesterol (mg)	0

CHEESY SPICY SQUASH

This is my favorite squash dish. It forms a creamy sauce with the cheese, and the jalapeños make it spicy. It's great on top of or alongside plain grilled or poached chicken breasts.

2 pounds yellow squash
(about 5), sliced
1 onion, chopped
1 teaspoon sugar

¼ pound light pasteurized
processed cheese spread
1 tablespoon chopped
jalapeño pepper

Preheat the oven to 350°F. In a 2-quart microwave dish, cook the squash, onion, and sugar in a small amount of water, covered, in the microwave until tender, about 8 minutes (or cook the squash mixture in a saucepan with a small amount of water, covered, over medium heat until tender). Drain the water. Mash the squash with a fork and add the cheese and jalapeños, mixing well. Bake for 15 minutes. Remove from the oven, stir, and serve.

Makes 4 to 6 servings

Nutritional information per serving

Calories	75	Cal. from Fat (%) 28.8	Sodium (mg)	286
Fat (g)	2.4	Saturated Fat (g) 1.5	Cholesterol (mg)	7

CAULIFLOWER WITH CREAMY MUSTARD SAUCE ♥

This whole cauliflower dish makes a nice presentation. If desired, the cooked cauliflower can be cut into pieces and mixed with the sauce. My children love broccoli, so I often serve this sauce over broccoli also.

1 whole head cauliflower
⅓ cup skim milk
1 (10¾-ounce) can 97% fat-free cream of mushroom soup

1 teaspoon dry mustard
2 tablespoons Dijon mustard
⅛ teaspoon white pepper
4 ounces fat-free cream cheese

In a covered saucepan, cook the whole cauliflower in a small amount of water over medium heat for 15 to 20 minutes. Meanwhile, in a small saucepan, combine the milk, soup, dry mustard, Dijon mustard, and pepper and blend until smooth. Cook, stirring, over medium-low heat until the mixture is heated. Add the cream cheese and continue to cook over low heat until the cheese is blended. Place the cauliflower on a serving platter. Pour the sauce over the hot whole cauliflower and serve immediately.

Makes 6 servings

Nutritional information per serving

Calories	79	Cal. from Fat (%) 23.9	Sodium (mg)	392
Fat (g)	2.1	Saturated Fat (g) 0.5	Cholesterol (mg)	6

BROCCOLI WITH DIJON SAUCE

By cooking the broccoli in the sauce, plain broccoli becomes full of flavor. My children love this simple recipe.

1 bunch fresh broccoli	1 tablespoon Worcestershire
½ cup canned fat-free	sauce
chicken broth	2 tablespoons Dijon mustard
¼ teaspoon minced garlic	

Cut the broccoli into florets, discarding the stems. In a small bowl, combine the chicken broth, garlic, Worcestershire sauce, and mustard. Place the broccoli in a large microwave dish and pour the sauce over. Cover and cook for 8 minutes, or until the broccoli is tender.

Makes 6 servings

Nutritional information per serving

Calories	40	Cal. from Fat (%) 14.8	Sodium (mg)	160
Fat (g)	0.6	Saturated Fat (g) 0.1	Cholesterol (mg)	0

BROCCOLI CASSEROLE ♥

Fresh broccoli can be used by cutting the florets into small pieces. If the casserole begins to brown, you might want to cover it with foil at the end of cooking. Broccoli is always a favorite vegetable and this will become one of your favorite quick casseroles.

2 (10-ounce) packages frozen	1 (12-ounce) carton low-fat
chopped broccoli, thawed	cottage cheese
and drained	6 ounces light pasteurized
1 large egg	processed cheese spread,
2 large egg whites, slightly	cut in pieces
beaten	
3 tablespoons all-purpose	
flour	

Preheat the oven to 350°F. In a large bowl, mix the broccoli, egg, egg whites, flour, cottage cheese, and cheese spread and pour into a 2-quart baking dish coated with nonstick cooking spray. Bake, uncovered, for 1 hour, or until bubbly.

Makes 8 servings

Nutritional information per serving

Calories	119	Cal. from Fat (%) 26.5	Sodium (mg)	529
Fat (g)	3.5	Saturated Fat (g) 2	Cholesterol (mg)	36

GREEN BEAN CASSEROLE ♥

Green bean casseroles are always welcome at big gatherings.

2 (10-ounce) packages frozen
French-style green beans
1½ tablespoons all-purpose
flour
1 teaspoon onion powder
1 teaspoon garlic powder
Salt and pepper to taste

1 teaspoon sugar
1 (8-ounce) package nonfat
cream cheese
2 tablespoons (¼ stick) light
stick margarine
2 tablespoons lemon juice

Preheat the oven to 350°F. Cook the green beans according to package directions. Drain well. Combine the flour, onion powder, garlic powder, salt and pepper, and sugar in a small dish. Melt the cream cheese and margarine in a saucepan over low heat or in the microwave. Remove from the heat and add the lemon juice. Add to the dry ingredients, stirring until combined. Pour over the green beans and toss until well mixed. Pour into a 1½-quart casserole coated with nonstick cooking spray. Bake for 30 minutes.

Makes 4 servings

Nutritional information per serving

Calories	134	Cal. from Fat (%)	20.8	Sodium (mg)	364
Fat (g)	3.1	Saturated Fat (g)	0.5	Cholesterol (mg)	6

STEWED OKRA ♥

You can find frozen sliced okra in the grocery store if you want to take a shortcut or if okra is not in season.

2 large onions, chopped
2 pounds fresh okra,
trimmed and sliced

1 (10-ounce) can diced
tomatoes and green chilies
Salt and pepper to taste
½ teaspoon sugar

In a pot coated with nonstick cooking spray, sauté the onion over medium heat until tender, about 4 minutes. Add the okra and cook until the okra is not stringy, stirring occasionally, about 9 to 10 minutes. Add the tomatoes, salt and pepper, and sugar, cover, and continue cooking over low heat until the okra is tender, about 30 minutes.

Makes 8 servings

Nutritional information per serving

Calories	53	Cal. from Fat (%)	4.4	Sodium (mg)	148
Fat (g)	0.3	Saturated Fat (g)	0	Cholesterol (mg)	0

LAYERED VEGGIES

It's hard to believe all you have to do is open a few cans to please people. Shh—it's our secret! If you wish to use fresh vegetables, they need to be precooked before putting this dish together.

1 (15-ounce) can sweet peas, drained	1 (10¾-ounce) can 97% fat-free cream of mushroom
1 (10½-ounce) can cut asparagus spears, drained	soup
	⅛ teaspoon cayenne pepper
1 (8-ounce) can sliced water chestnuts, drained	½ cup shredded reduced-fat Cheddar cheese
1 (8-ounce) can mushroom pieces and stems, drained	¼ cup bread crumbs
	1 tablespoon light stick margarine, softened

Preheat the oven to 350°F. Layer the peas, asparagus, water chestnuts, and mushrooms in a 2-quart casserole dish in the order listed. In a small bowl, combine the mushroom soup, cayenne, and cheese. Spread over the layered vegetables. Combine the bread crumbs with the margarine and sprinkle over the top. Bake for 30 to 45 minutes, until bubbly and the top is browned.

Makes 8 servings

Nutritional information per serving

Calories	107	Cal. from Fat (%)	30.3	Sodium (mg)	503
Fat (g)	3.6	Saturated Fat (g)	1.4	Cholesterol (mg)	8

OKRA AND CORN ♥

With these frozen vegetables, this bright and tasty dish can be prepared without any trouble. Okra and tomatoes are always popular in the South, and this recipe offers an extra touch.

1 tablespoon light stick margarine	1 (16-ounce) bag frozen corn
1 onion, chopped	2 (10-ounce) cans diced tomatoes and green chilies
1 (16-ounce) bag frozen cut okra	

In a large pan, heat the margarine over medium heat and sauté the onion until tender, about 4 minutes. Add the okra and cook for 5 minutes, stirring. Add the corn and tomatoes with chilies, cooking and stirring until the okra is tender, about 20 minutes.

Makes 6 servings

Nutritional information per serving

Calories	111	Cal. from Fat (%)	10.7	Sodium (mg)	409
Fat (g)	1.3	Saturated Fat (g)	0.2	Cholesterol (mg)	0

CREAMY CORN CASSEROLE

This is such an easy dish to be so good and the paprika gives it such a pretty color. You can keep these ingredients on hand for an extra-special corn dish.

2 (16-ounce) bags frozen
corn
1 (7-ounce) can chopped
green chilies, drained
1 (8-ounce) package fat-free
cream cheese, cut into
pieces

½ cup skim milk
Salt and pepper to taste
½ teaspoon paprika

Preheat the oven to 350°F. In 2-quart baking dish, combine the corn and green chilies. In a microwaveproof dish, heat the cream cheese and milk until the cream cheese is melted, about 60 seconds. Mix with a fork to blend. Stir into the corn and season with salt and pepper. Sprinkle with the paprika. Bake for 30 minutes, or until bubbly.

Makes 8 to 10 servings

Nutritional information per serving

Calories	111	Cal. from Fat (%)	6.5	Sodium (mg)	119
Fat (g)	0.8	Saturated Fat (g)	0.1	Cholesterol (mg)	2

BAKED CORN IN SOUR CREAM

This dish is so creamy and luxurious that eating healthy is a pleasure.

2 tablespoons (¼ stick) light
stick margarine
2 tablespoons chopped onion
2 tablespoons all-purpose
flour
1 cup nonfat sour cream
2 (16-ounce) packages frozen
whole kernel corn

2 tablespoons finely chopped
celery
2 ounces Canadian bacon,
chopped (optional)
2 tablespoons chopped
parsley

Preheat the oven to 350°F. In a large pot, melt the margarine over medium heat and sauté the onion until tender. Blend in the flour. Gradually stir in the sour cream. Add the corn and celery, stirring until heated through. Add the bacon. Pour into a 2-quart baking dish coated with nonstick cooking spray. Top with the parsley and bake for 30 to 45 minutes or until mixture is bubbly.

Makes 6 to 8 servings

Nutritional information per serving

Calories	160	Cal. from Fat (%) 11.8	Sodium (mg)	169
Fat (g)	2.1	Saturated Fat (g) 0.4	Cholesterol (mg)	7

BROILED TOMATOES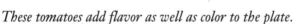

These tomatoes add flavor as well as color to the plate.

1 tablespoon light stick
margarine, melted
1 tablespoon fat-free Italian
dressing
¼ cup chopped parsley
⅓ cup Italian bread crumbs

½ teaspoon minced garlic
½ teaspoon dried basil
1 tablespoon grated
Parmesan cheese
12 (½- to 1-inch) slices
tomato

Preheat the broiler. In a small bowl, blend the melted margarine and Italian dressing with the parsley, bread crumbs, garlic, basil, and cheese. Place the sliced tomatoes on a baking sheet coated with nonstick cooking spray and spoon the topping evenly over the tomatoes. Broil for 10 minutes, until browned.

Makes 12 slices

Nutritional information per slice

Calories	28	Cal. from Fat (%) 25.7	Sodium (mg)	127
Fat (g)	0.8	Saturated Fat (g) 0.2	Cholesterol (mg)	0

SAUTÉED CHERRY TOMATOES WITH BASIL ♥

Who said tomatoes couldn't be special?

1 pound cherry tomatoes	½ teaspoon dried thyme
1 garlic clove, minced	1 teaspoon sugar
1 tablespoon dried basil	Salt and freshly ground
2 tablespoons chopped parsley	pepper to taste

Wash the tomatoes and dry them well. In a small bowl, combine the garlic, basil, parsley, and thyme. Heat a skillet coated with nonstick cooking spray over medium heat and add the tomatoes. Sprinkle with the sugar and salt and pepper and toss briefly until well heated. Stir in the garlic mixture and sauté for 1 minute. Serve immediately.

Makes 6 servings

Nutritional information per serving

Calories	20	Cal. from Fat (%)	12.2	Sodium (mg)	7
Fat (g)	0.3	Saturated Fat (g)	0	Cholesterol (mg)	0

BABY LIMA BEANS ♥

Serve over rice or another starch for a nutritionally complete meal.

1 (1-pound) package dried baby lima beans	½ cup chopped celery
4 garlic cloves, minced	½ cup sliced baby carrots
½ cup chopped green pepper	2 tablespoons chopped parsley
1½ cups chopped onion	2 tablespoons garlic powder
1 tablespoon olive oil	4 bay leaves
10 cups water	Salt and pepper to taste
½ pound lean ham, chopped	

Rinse and sort the beans. Soak the beans in water to cover overnight. Drain. In a large pot, sauté the garlic, green pepper, and onion in the olive oil over medium heat until tender, about 4 minutes. Add the beans, water, ham, celery, carrots, parsley, garlic powder, and bay leaves. Cook over low heat, covered, 1 to 2 hours, or until the beans are tender. Add salt and pepper. Remove the bay leaves before serving.

Makes 8 servings

Nutritional information per serving

Calories	255	Cal. from Fat (%)	16.9	Sodium (mg)	377
Fat (g)	4.8	Saturated Fat (g)	1.1	Cholesterol (mg)	15

BAKED BEANS

This is an easy version of an old-fashioned recipe. If desired, you can leave out the bacon for a vegetarian dish.

1 onion, chopped
1 green bell pepper, seeded
 and chopped
3 ounces Canadian bacon,
 cut in ½-inch pieces
 (optional)
2 (15-ounce) cans red kidney
 beans, drained

2 (19-ounce) cans white
 kidney beans (cannellini),
 drained
⅛ cup Worcestershire sauce
½ cup light brown sugar
⅔ cup barbecue sauce
1 teaspoon dry mustard

Preheat the oven to 350°F. In a large skillet coated with nonstick cooking spray, sauté the onion and green pepper until tender, about 4 minutes. Add the Canadian bacon. Cook for 5 more minutes. Place all the beans in a 2-quart casserole dish and add the sautéed vegetables, Worcestershire sauce, brown sugar, barbecue sauce, and mustard. Mix well. Bake, covered, for 40 minutes.

Makes 12 servings

Nutritional information per serving

Calories	154	Cal. from Fat (%)	6.2	Sodium (mg)	391
Fat (g)	1.1	Saturated Fat (g)	0.3	Cholesterol (mg)	4

FIESTA POTATO CASSEROLE ♥

You can cover the casserole and refrigerate it for a few hours before baking. Bring it to room temperature before putting it in the oven. This recipe takes mashed potatoes to another level.

3 pounds baking potatoes
 (about 8 to 10), peeled and
 quartered
2 tablespoons (¼ stick) light
 stick margarine
1 (8-ounce) package nonfat
 cream cheese, softened
½ cup shredded reduced-fat
 Cheddar cheese

½ cup finely chopped green
 bell pepper
½ cup finely chopped red
 bell pepper
½ cup grated Parmesan
 cheese
½ cup skim milk
Salt and pepper to taste

Preheat the oven to 350°F. Coat an 11 × 7 × 2½-inch baking dish with nonstick cooking spray. Bring a large saucepan of water to a boil. Add the potatoes, cover, and cook for 15 to 20 minutes, or until tender. Drain and mash the potatoes in a large bowl. Add the margarine and cream cheese and beat with a mixer at medium speed until smooth. Stir in the Cheddar cheese, green and red peppers, Parmesan cheese, milk, and salt and pepper. Spoon into the baking dish and bake for 30 to 40 minutes or until well heated through and the cheese is melted.

Makes 10 servings

Nutritional information per serving

Calories	150	Cal. from Fat (%)	15	Sodium (mg)	224
Fat (g)	2.5	Saturated Fat (g)	1	Cholesterol (mg)	5

GARLIC MASHED POTATOES

These smell as good as they taste. Chicken broth makes them light and fluffy without adding any fat. You may want to make extra.

4 pounds red-skinned potatoes, peeled and cut into 1-inch cubes	1 tablespoon dried rosemary
9 large garlic cloves, peeled	⅔ cup (or more) canned fat-free chicken broth
2 tablespoons (¼ stick) light stick margarine	½ cup grated Parmesan cheese
	Salt and pepper to taste

Bring a large pot of salted water to a boil. Add the potatoes and garlic and cook until both are very tender, about 30 minutes. Drain. Transfer the potatoes and the garlic to a large bowl. Using an electric mixer, beat the potatoes and garlic. Add the margarine and rosemary and beat until smooth. Gradually blend the chicken broth into the potato mixture. Stir in the Parmesan cheese. Season with salt and pepper.

Makes 8 to 10 servings

Nutritional information per serving

Calories	160	Cal. from Fat (%)	14.1	Sodium (mg)	488
Fat (g)	2.5	Saturated Fat (g)	1	Cholesterol (mg)	3

DILLY STUFFED POTATOES

Dill gives these potatoes a great flavor. These take a while to bake, but you can pull together the rest of your dinner in the meantime, and maybe even have time for a bath or to help with a homework problem. Sometimes I wrap prepared stuffed potatoes individually and freeze them for a later date.

4 large baking potatoes	1½ teaspoons dried dillweed
¼ cup (½ stick) light stick margarine, softened	1 tablespoon lemon juice
	½ teaspoon garlic powder
⅓ cup nonfat sour cream	⅛ teaspoon pepper
	Paprika

Pierce the potatoes with a fork and microwave on high for 14 to 17 minutes or preheat the oven to 425°F. and bake for 1 hour. Cut the potatoes lengthwise in half and scoop out the flesh. Combine the potato flesh, margarine, sour cream, dillweed, lemon juice, garlic powder, and pepper in a bowl, mixing very well. Restuff the mixture in the potato shells, sprinkle with the paprika, and bake for 20 minutes.

Makes 8 servings

Nutritional information per serving

Calories	124	Cal. from Fat (%)	21.1	Sodium (mg)	84
Fat (g)	2.9	Saturated Fat (g)	0.5	Cholesterol (mg)	1

POTATOES AU GRATIN

This recipe is a wonderful part of a satisfying dinner for a hungry family. The cream cheese makes a wonderful, creamy sauce.

1 (8-ounce) package light cream cheese, softened	2 to 2½ pounds baking potatoes (approximately 4 large), peeled and thinly sliced
2 tablespoons all-purpose flour	
2 cups skim milk	Salt and pepper to taste
3 garlic cloves, minced	1 bunch green onions (scallions), chopped

Preheat the oven to 350°F. Coat a 1½-quart baking dish with nonstick cooking spray. In a small saucepan, combine the cream cheese and flour. Gradually add the milk and the garlic, stirring over low heat until the mixture thickens and is heated, about 3 minutes. Slightly overlap a layer of potato slices in the baking dish. Season with salt and pepper. Pour half of the cheese mixture over the potatoes. Sprinkle with all of the green onions. Repeat the layering with the remaining potato slices, salt, pepper, and cheese mixture. Bake, covered, for 1 hour, or until the potatoes are tender and the top is golden brown.

Makes 8 to 10 servings

Nutritional information per serving

Calories	154	Cal. from Fat (%)	21.6	Sodium (mg)	137
Fat (g)	3.7	Saturated Fat (g)	2.6	Cholesterol (mg)	12

POTATO BAKE ♥

If you're a meat-and-potatoes person, add this recipe to your list. It's a very attractive dish—people can't wait to dig in.

2 pounds baking potatoes (about 3 large), peeled and cut into ⅛-inch-thick slices
1 large red bell pepper, seeded and sliced
1 bunch green onions (scallions), thinly sliced
2 teaspoons dried thyme

1 teaspoon garlic powder
½ teaspoon pepper
⅓ cup grated Parmesan cheese
⅓ cup dry white wine
½ cup canned fat-free chicken broth

Preheat the oven to 350°F. Coat a 2-quart glass baking dish with nonstick cooking spray and arrange ⅓ of the potatoes in overlapping rows in the dish. Top with half of the red bell pepper and green onions. Combine the thyme, garlic powder, and pepper in a small bowl. Sprinkle ⅓ of the seasoning mixture over the green onions. Sprinkle ⅓ of the Parmesan cheese over the casserole. Repeat layering with ⅓ of the potatoes, the remaining red bell peppers and green onions, ⅓ of the seasoning mixture, and ⅓ of the Parmesan cheese. Top with the remaining potatoes.

Combine the wine and chicken broth in a bowl and pour over all. Top with the remaining seasoning mixture and Parmesan cheese. Sprinkle the top with the paprika. Cover and bake for 1 to 1¼ hours, until cooked throughout.

Makes 6 to 8 servings

Nutritional information per serving

Calories	108	Cal. from Fat (%)	10	Sodium (mg)	101
Fat (g)	1.2	Saturated Fat (g)	0.7	Cholesterol (mg)	3

PARMESAN POTATO STICKS

You'll never be able to eat just one of these crispy potatoes! They will complement any meal, so be sure to make plenty.

½ cup seasoned bread
  crumbs
2 tablespoons grated
  Parmesan cheese
2 tablespoons chopped
  parsley
Salt and pepper to taste

¼ teaspoon garlic powder
3 medium baking potatoes,
  peeled and cut into large
  sticks
¼ cup skim milk
1 tablespoon liquid
  margarine

Preheat the oven to 375°F. In a shallow dish, combine the bread crumbs, cheese, parsley, salt and pepper, and garlic powder. Dip the potatoes in the milk and then in the crumb mixture. Lay the sticks on a foil-lined cookie sheet. Drizzle with the margarine. Bake for 45 minutes to 1 hour, until crispy.

Makes 4 to 6 servings

Nutritional information per serving

Calories	95	Cal. from Fat (%)	17	Sodium (mg)	328
Fat (g)	1.8	Saturated Fat (g)	0.6	Cholesterol (mg)	2

SWEET POTATO CASSEROLE WITH PRALINE TOPPING ♥

Sweet potatoes have lots of vitamin A and vitamin C, so include this festive recipe on your table year-round. The Praline Topping makes this dish a true winner!

4 sweet potatoes, peeled
  and halved
⅓ cup light brown sugar
1 large egg white

1½ teaspoons vanilla extract
½ cup orange juice
Praline Topping (recipe
  follows)

Preheat the oven to 350°F. Bring a large saucepan of water to a boil and cook the sweet potatoes for 30 minutes, until very tender. Drain well and mash. In a mixing bowl, combine the potatoes, brown sugar, egg white, vanilla, and orange juice, blending well. Place in a 2-quart casserole coated with nonstick cooking spray and cover with the Praline Topping. Bake for 45 minutes.

Makes 10 to 12 servings

Praline Topping

⅔ cup light brown sugar
1 cup all-purpose flour
½ teaspoon ground
cinnamon

6 tablespoons (¾ stick) light
stick margarine, melted
1 teaspoon vanilla extract

In a bowl, mix together the brown sugar, flour, and cinnamon. Stir in the margarine and vanilla until crumbly.

Nutritional information per serving (includes topping)

Calories	169	Cal. from Fat (%) 16.4	Sodium (mg)	87
Fat (g)	3.1	Saturated Fat (g) 0.5	Cholesterol (mg)	0

CREAMY NOODLE CASSEROLE

If you like cottage cheese, you will enjoy this combination. Of course, you can use noodles or any type of pasta you like. This makes a nice side dish to any entrée.

1 (12-ounce) package
shell pasta
1 (12-ounce) carton low-fat
cottage cheese
1 cup nonfat sour cream
⅓ cup chopped onion

1 tablespoon Worcestershire
sauce
¼ teaspoon hot sauce
¼ teaspoon minced garlic
1 cup shredded reduced-fat
sharp Cheddar cheese

Preheat the oven to 350°F. Cook the pasta according to package directions, omitting any oil and salt. Drain. Combine the cottage cheese, sour cream, onion, Worcestershire sauce, hot sauce, and garlic in a small bowl; mix well. Stir the cottage cheese mixture into the hot pasta and pour into a 3-quart casserole coated with nonstick cooking spray. Top with the shredded cheese. Bake, covered, for 20 minutes, until hot throughout. Remove the cover and bake 10 minutes more, until the cheese is melted.

Makes 6 to 8 servings

Nutritional information per serving

Calories	275	Cal. from Fat (%) 12.1	Sodium (mg)	331
Fat (g)	3.7	Saturated Fat (g) 2.2	Cholesterol (mg)	15

VEGETABLES AND STARCHES

VEGETABLES AND STARCHES

MACARONI AND CHEESE

My version of an old favorite, lightened up. A real family pleaser!

1 (16-ounce) package macaroni shells	1 large egg
2 tablespoons (¼ stick) light stick margarine, melted	2 large egg whites
½ teaspoon garlic powder	⅔ cup skim milk
½ teaspoon paprika	¼ pound light pasteurized processed cheese, cut into pieces
Salt and pepper to taste	¾ pound shredded reduced-fat sharp Cheddar cheese
1 teaspoon hot sauce	

Preheat the oven to 350°F. Cook the pasta according to package directions, omitting any oil and salt. Drain. In a bowl, combine the margarine, garlic powder, paprika, salt, pepper, hot sauce, egg, egg whites, and milk; toss with the macaroni and add the cheeses, mixing well. Transfer to a 2-quart baking dish coated with nonstick cooking spray. Bake for 30 to 40 minutes, or until the liquid is absorbed.

Makes 12 servings

Nutritional information per serving

Calories	270	Cal. from Fat (%) 27.3	Sodium (mg)	411
Fat (g)	8.2	Saturated Fat (g) 4.6	Cholesterol (mg)	41

BARLEY CASSEROLE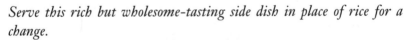

Serve this rich but wholesome-tasting side dish in place of rice for a change.

1 cup medium barley	1 tablespoon light stick margarine
1 envelope onion soup mix	½ pound fresh mushrooms, sliced
4 cups water	

Preheat the oven to 350°F. In a 3-quart casserole dish, combine the barley, onion soup mix, and water. In a small skillet, melt the margarine over medium-low heat and sauté the mushrooms until tender, about 5 minutes. Add to the barley mixture. Cover with a lid or tightly with foil and bake for 1 to 1¼ hours, or until the barley is done and the liquid is absorbed.

Makes 6 to 8 servings

Nutritional information per serving

Calories	102	Cal. from Fat (%) 10.2	Sodium (mg)	99
Fat (g)	1.2	Saturated Fat (g) 0.5	Cholesterol (mg)	0

RED BEANS AND RICE ♥

This traditional Louisiana recipe usually has to be planned ahead because of the time it takes to soak and cook the beans. With this version using canned beans, the recipe is made with little effort. See how easy it is to like Red Beans and Rice now!

⅔ cup chopped onion
½ cup chopped celery
½ cup chopped green pepper
1 teaspoon minced garlic
2 (15-ounce) cans red kidney beans, drained
½ pound fully cooked low-fat sausage, cut into thin ¼-inch slices
1 (8-ounce) can no-salt-added tomato sauce

1 can water
1 teaspoon Worcestershire sauce
⅛ teaspoon cayenne pepper
¼ cup chopped parsley
¼ teaspoon hot pepper sauce
⅓ cup sliced green onions (scallions)
4 cups cooked white rice

In a large pot coated with nonstick cooking spray, sauté the onion, celery, green pepper, and garlic over medium heat until tender, about 4 minutes. Add the beans, sausage, tomato sauce, water, Worcestershire sauce, cayenne, parsley, and hot pepper sauce. Reduce the heat, cover, and simmer for 15 to 20 minutes. Sprinkle with the green onions and serve the red beans with the sauce over the rice.

Makes 6 servings

Nutritional information per serving

Calories	230	Cal. from Fat (%)	23.5	Sodium (mg)	602
Fat (g)	6	Saturated Fat (g)	3.1	Cholesterol (mg)	17

VEGETABLE RICE ♥

This wonderful dish can be a vegetarian meal in itself if you use canned vegetable broth instead of chicken broth. You can change the assortment of vegetables as you like.

2 tablespoons (¼ stick) light
   stick margarine
2 cups diced peeled eggplant
1 yellow squash, diced
1 cup sliced fresh
   mushrooms
2 garlic cloves, minced

1 tomato, chopped
1 (7-ounce) can pimientos,
   minced
Salt and pepper to taste
1¼ cups rice
1 (16-ounce) can fat-free
   chicken broth

In a large pot coated with nonstick cooking spray, melt the margarine and sauté the eggplant, squash, mushrooms, garlic, tomato, and pimientos until just tender, about 4 minutes. Add the salt and pepper, then add the rice and chicken broth. Bring to a boil. Lower the heat, cover, and cook for 20 to 30 minutes, or until the rice is done.

Makes 4 to 6 servings

Nutritional information per serving

Calories	214	Cal. from Fat (%)	10.1	Sodium (mg)	213
Fat (g)	2.4	Saturated Fat (g)	0.4	Cholesterol (mg)	0

POULTRY

CHICKEN SCALOPPINE

This is great served with noodles. Keep chicken breasts in the freezer and you can make this popular dish at home with ease. Another kid pleaser!

⅓ cup all-purpose flour	3 garlic cloves
¼ cup grated fat-free Parmesan cheese	¾ cup canned fat-free chicken broth
Salt and pepper to taste	1 tablespoon lemon juice
6 to 8 skinless, boneless chicken breasts	⅓ cup white wine
2 tablespoons olive oil	1 tablespoon chopped parsley

Mix the flour, Parmesan cheese, and salt and pepper together. Sprinkle the mixture over the chicken breasts, pressing well into the chicken. In a large pan, heat the oil with the garlic over medium heat and brown the chicken lightly on both sides, about 5 minutes in all. Add the broth, lemon juice, and wine. Bring to a boil, lower the heat, and simmer until the chicken is tender, about 15 to 20 minutes. Remove the garlic cloves and sprinkle the chopped parsley over the top.

Makes 4 to 5 servings

Nutritional information per serving

Calories	300	Cal. from Fat (%)	29.1	Sodium (mg)	197
Fat (g)	9.7	Saturated Fat (g)	1.9	Cholesterol (mg)	102

CHICKEN SCAMPI

Cut the chicken into strips and toss with this pasta and you have a super combination. I have always loved shrimp scampi and now you can enjoy the same flavor with chicken.

2 pounds boneless, skinless chicken breasts	¼ teaspoon garlic powder
1 tablespoon olive oil	¼ teaspoon salt
¼ teaspoon pepper	1 tablespoon dried oregano
2 tablespoons grated Parmesan cheese	3 tablespoons lemon juice
1 tablespoon dried parsley flakes	2 tablespoons Worcestershire sauce
	¼ cup dry white wine

Combine the chicken with the olive oil, pepper, Parmesan cheese, parsley, garlic powder, salt, oregano, lemon juice, Worcestershire sauce, and white wine in a shallow bowl. Marinate, covered, in the refrigerator for several hours. Preheat the broiler. Remove the chicken from the marinade, reserving the marinade, and place in a single-layer shallow baking dish. Broil 8 inches from the heat, turning once, until the chicken is done, about 15 minutes. Heat the remaining marinade in a small saucepan or in the microwave, pour over the chicken, and toss and serve.

Makes 6 servings

Nutritional information per serving

| Calories | 217 | Cal. from Fat (%) 27.6 | Sodium (mg) | 262 |
| Fat (g) | 6.7 | Saturated Fat (g) 1.7 | Cholesterol (mg) | 90 |

CHICKEN BREASTS WITH LEMON AND CAPERS

If you've never had capers before, try this recipe for a pleasant surprise. The paprika gives the chicken a nice color.

½ cup all-purpose flour
¼ teaspoon pepper
1 teaspoon paprika
8 to 10 skinless, boneless
  chicken breasts
2 tablespoons (¼ stick) light
  stick margarine

⅔ cup canned fat-free
  chicken broth
2 tablespoons lemon juice
2 tablespoons drained capers

Combine the flour, pepper, and paprika. Press the chicken breasts in the mixture, coating them evenly. In a heavy skillet coated with non-stick cooking spray, heat the margarine over medium heat and cook the breasts 3 to 4 minutes on each side, in batches if necessary. Add the broth to the skillet. Stir in the lemon juice and capers. Bring to a boil, reduce the heat, and cook until the liquid is reduced and thickened and the chicken is done, about 20 to 25 minutes.

Makes 8 servings

Nutritional information per serving

| Calories | 201 | Cal. from Fat (%) 21.5 | Sodium (mg) | 249 |
| Fat (g) | 4.8 | Saturated Fat (g) 1.2 | Cholesterol (mg) | 82 |

CHICKEN AND PEPPERS

Chinese takeout never tasted so good! And you have the added pleasure of knowing there are no preservatives or additives in your dinner.

¼ cup reduced-sodium soy sauce
¼ cup sherry
1 teaspoon ground ginger
2 pounds skinless, boneless chicken breasts, cut into 1-inch slices
1 tablespoon olive oil
1 onion, coarsely chopped
4 garlic cloves, minced

2 red bell peppers, seeded and sliced ¼ inch thick
2 green bell peppers, seeded and sliced ¼ inch thick
⅔ cup peeled sliced carrots
1 pound fresh Chinese bean sprouts
1 teaspoon cornstarch
½ cup water, if needed

In a medium bowl, combine the soy sauce, sherry, ginger, and chicken. Marinate, covered, in the refrigerator for several hours. In a large skillet coated with nonstick cooking spray, heat the oil over medium heat. Add the onion and garlic and cook 3 minutes, stirring frequently. Add the peppers, carrots, and sprouts and cook for 5 minutes. Add the chicken, stirring frequently until the chicken is tender, about 5 minutes. To the remaining marinade, stir in the cornstarch, then add to the chicken mixture. Reduce the heat to low. Cover and cook for 15 minutes and, if needed, add the water, stirring occasionally.

Makes 4 to 6 servings

Nutritional information per serving

Calories	268	Cal. from Fat (%)	21.4	Sodium (mg)	466
Fat (g)	6.4	Saturated Fat (g)	1.4	Cholesterol (mg)	89

LEMON-FETA CHICKEN

Keep this in mind for those last-minute dinners. I like feta cheese a lot and think it's a nice addition to a dish.

8 skinless, boneless chicken breasts (about 2½ pounds)
¼ cup lemon juice, divided
1 tablespoon dried oregano, divided

¼ teaspoon pepper
3 ounces crumbled feta cheese
3 tablespoons chopped green onions (scallions)

Preheat the oven to 350°F. Place the chicken in a 13 × 9 × 2-inch baking dish and drizzle with half of the lemon juice. Sprinkle with half of the oregano and the pepper. Top with the cheese and green onions. Drizzle with the remaining lemon juice and oregano. Bake, covered, for 45 minutes, or until cooked through.

Makes 8 servings

Nutritional information per serving

Calories	174	Cal. from Fat (%)	28	Sodium (mg)	183
Fat (g)	5.4	Saturated Fat (g)	2.5	Cholesterol (mg)	83

PAPRIKA CHICKEN

My family ate this so quickly—and talk about easy! The kids liked the color, and the sherry gives the sauce a wonderful flavor.

8 skinless, boneless chicken
  breast
Salt and pepper to taste
4 tablespoons lemon juice,
  divided
1 tablespoon paprika

4 garlic cloves, minced
1 tablespoon soy sauce
¾ cup dry sherry
5 green onions (scallions),
  sliced

Pound the chicken breasts to a ½-inch thickness. Season with salt and pepper, 3 tablespoons of the lemon juice, and the paprika. Coat a large skillet with nonstick cooking spray and place over medium heat. Cook the chicken breasts 2 minutes on each side. Add the garlic, the remaining tablespoon lemon juice, soy sauce, and sherry to the pan. Cook for 5 minutes. Sprinkle the green onions into the pan and cook 3 to 5 minutes more, until the chicken is done.

Makes 8 servings

Nutritional information per serving

Calories	179	Cal. from Fat (%)	16.1	Sodium (mg)	196
Fat (g)	3.2	Saturated Fat (g)	0.9	Cholesterol (mg)	73

CHICKEN IN CREAM SAUCE

One of the most exciting things about low-fat cooking is that you don't have to give up most of your favorite foods—just cook them differently!

8 skinless, boneless chicken breasts	1 (10¾-ounce) can fat-free cream of mushroom soup
½ envelope dry Italian dressing mix	⅓ cup chopped green onion (scallion) stems (green part only)
4 ounces fat-free cream cheese	⅓ cup dry white wine

Preheat the oven to 350°F. Lay the chicken breasts in a 2-quart baking dish coated with nonstick cooking spray. In a microwave or small pot, heat the Italian dressing mix, cream cheese, and soup, stirring until well blended. Add the green onion stems and wine. Pour the sauce over the chicken and bake for 1 hour.

Makes 8 servings

Nutritional information per serving

Calories	189	Cal. from Fat (%)	19.5	Sodium (mg)	453
Fat (g)	4.1	Saturated Fat (g)	1.2	Cholesterol (mg)	78

INDOOR BARBECUED CHICKEN

When it's too cold to grill outside, I use this recipe. Of course, this sauce can certainly be used to barbecue outdoors, too!

⅔ cup ketchup	2 tablespoons honey
2 tablespoons lemon juice	1 teaspoon minced garlic
2 tablespoons Worcestershire sauce	8 (6-ounce) skinless, boneless chicken breast halves

Preheat the broiler. Combine the ketchup, lemon juice, Worcestershire sauce, honey, and garlic in a saucepan. Bring to a boil, stirring frequently, then reduce the heat and simmer 2 minutes. Remove from the heat and set aside. Place the chicken on a foil-lined broiler pan and coat both sides with the barbecue sauce. Broil 10 to 15 minutes, then turn and baste and continue cooking 10 to 15 minutes longer, until the chicken is done.

Makes 8 servings

Nutritional information per serving

Calories	215	Cal. from Fat (%)	17.8	Sodium (mg)	227
Fat (g)	4.2	Saturated Fat (g)	1.2	Cholesterol (mg)	100

OLD-FASHIONED BAKED CHICKEN

This recipe reminds me of going to my grandmother's house. For extra flavor, marinate the chicken in fat-free Italian dressing before baking.

8 skinless, boneless chicken
  breasts (skinless thighs can
  be used)
1 tablespoon paprika
1 tablespoon garlic powder
½ teaspoon pepper
Salt to taste

1 onion, sliced in rings
1 (16-ounce) package
  carrots, peeled and cut
  into chunks
4 red potatoes, peeled and
  cut in fourths
1 cup water

Preheat the oven to 350°F. In a large baking dish, place the chicken and sprinkle with the paprika, garlic powder, pepper, and salt. Add the onion rings, carrots, potatoes, and water. Cover with foil and bake for 40 minutes. Uncover and bake for 20 minutes longer to let the chicken brown and the vegetables get tender.

Makes 8 servings

Nutritional information per serving

Calories	215	Cal. from Fat (%)	13.9	Sodium (mg)	95
Fat (g)	3.3	Saturated Fat (g)	0.9	Cholesterol (mg)	73

GLAZED CHICKEN STRIPS

These work great on a grill, too. Horseradish gives this dish a real kick!

¾ cup orange marmalade
¼ cup steak sauce
¼ cup prepared horseradish
¼ cup honey
3 tablespoons lime juice

1 teaspoon hot pepper sauce
1 tablespoon grated lemon
  rind
3 pounds skinless, boneless
  chicken strips

Preheat the broiler. Combine the orange marmalade, steak sauce, horseradish, honey, lime juice, pepper sauce, and lemon rind in a small bowl. Dip the chicken strips in the glaze and place on a baking sheet or broiler pan lined with foil. Broil 8 inches away from the heat for 5 to 8 minutes on one side. Turn the strips over, brush the chicken with the glaze, and continue cooking for another 5 to 8 minutes, or until done. Watch carefully so they don't burn.

Makes 10 servings

Nutritional information per serving

Calories	235	Cal. from Fat (%)	16.6	Sodium (mg)	130
Fat (g)	4.3	Saturated Fat (g)	1.2	Cholesterol (mg)	80

GRILLED TERIYAKI CHICKEN

This marinade takes no time to prepare and will make your grilled chicken or beef extra-special.

¼ cup reduced-sodium soy sauce	¼ cup cider vinegar
1 cup pineapple juice	⅓ cup sherry
2 tablespoons sugar	2 pounds skinless, boneless chicken breasts

Preheat the grill. Combine the soy sauce, pineapple juice, sugar, vinegar, and sherry and pour over the chicken. Marinate, covered, in the refrigerator 2 hours or overnight if time permits. Cook the chicken on the grill for 45 minutes, or until tender, turning to cook evenly.

Makes 6 servings

Nutritional information per serving

Calories	259	Cal. from Fat (%)	28.9	Sodium (mg)	358
Fat (g)	8.3	Saturated Fat (g)	2.3	Cholesterol (mg)	100

CHICKEN AND DUMPLINGS

This comforting dish is just the ticket for a cold night. If the soup needs thickening, put a little soup in a bowl and mix with a tablespoon or two of flour, then return to the pot. I added the chicken bouillon cubes for that extra flavor, however, if you're watching your sodium intake, you may leave them out.

2½ pounds skinless, boneless chicken breasts, cut into small serving pieces	3 tablespoons all-purpose flour
3 quarts water	1 celery stalk
Salt and pepper to taste	1 onion, quartered
2 (10-ounce) cans reduced-fat cream of mushroom soup	
	DUMPLINGS
6 chicken bouillon cubes	1½ cups self-rising flour
	¾ cup skim milk

Place the chicken in a large pot with the water, salt and pepper, cream of mushroom soup, bouillon cubes, flour, celery, and onion. Bring to a boil. Reduce the heat to medium and cook 30 minutes, or until the chicken is tender. Meanwhile, make the dumplings. In a small bowl, combine the flour and milk with a fork. Add more milk if necessary to make the dough the right consistency. Turn onto a floured surface and roll the dough ⅛ inch thick. Cut into thin strips and drop into the broth one at a time. You should have 30 to 36 dumplings. Remove the celery and onion, bring the broth to a boil, and add the dumplings. Cook 10 minutes on medium heat.

Makes 8 to 10 servings

Nutritional information per serving (approximately 3 dumplings)

Calories	257	Cal. from Fat (%) 16.1		Sodium (mg)	1,281
Fat (g)	4.6	Saturated Fat (g)	1.3	Cholesterol (mg)	73

CHICKEN POT PIE

Once you've made this recipe, you won't ever buy frozen pot pies again.

1 cup diced peeled carrot
1 cup sliced fresh
  mushrooms
½ cup chopped celery
½ cup frozen English peas
¼ cup minced onion
2 (10¾-ounce) cans 98% fat-
  free cream of chicken soup
¾ cup water

Pepper to taste
½ teaspoon dried thyme
3 to 4 cups diced cooked
  skinless, boneless chicken
  breast
1 cup self-rising flour
1½ tablespoons light stick
  margarine
¼ cup skim milk

Preheat the oven to 425°F. In a large skillet coated with nonstick cooking spray, sauté the carrot, mushrooms, celery, peas, and onion over medium heat until tender, about 5 minutes. In a large bowl, combine the soup, water, pepper, and thyme; stir well. Add the vegetables and cooked chicken, stirring well. Spoon the chicken mixture evenly into a 9 × 9 × 2-inch baking dish coated with nonstick cooking spray. Place the flour in a small bowl; cut in the margarine with a pastry blender until the mixture is crumbly. Add the milk 1 tablespoon at a time, stirring with a fork until the dry ingredients are moistened. Drop the dough evenly by spoonfuls onto the chicken mixture. Bake for 15 to 18 minutes, or until the crust is golden.

Makes 6 servings

Nutritional information per serving

Calories	317	Cal. from Fat (%) 19.3		Sodium (mg)	796
Fat (g)	6.8	Saturated Fat (g)	1.9	Cholesterol (mg)	78

TEQUILA CHICKEN

Be careful when flaming any dish—make sure the area is clear, tie back long hair and loose clothing, use a long match, and keep your face away. The dish is quick and the homemade salsa baked with the chicken really adds a fabulous something extra. For the salsa, I chop my tomatoes in the food processor.

1¾ pounds skinless, boneless chicken breasts	⅛ cup Triple Sec
	⅛ cup tequila
2 teaspoons ground cumin	Salsa (recipe follows)

Preheat the oven to 350°F. Coat the chicken breasts on both sides with the cumin. In a large skillet coated with nonstick cooking spray, sauté the breasts over medium heat until brown on both sides, 5 minutes in all. In a small bowl, combine the Triple Sec and tequila. Remove the pan from the heat, add the liqueur, and ignite very carefully with a match as a high flame will arise. When the flame goes out, add the Salsa. Transfer to a baking dish and bake for 15 minutes. Sprinkle with the shredded cheese and continue baking until the cheese is melted, about 5 more minutes.

Makes 6 servings

Salsa

2 tomatoes, chopped	1 teaspoon chopped jalapeño
2 tablespoons chopped fresh cilantro	pepper
	⅓ cup chopped onion
1 tablespoon lime juice	

Combine the tomatoes, cilantro, lime juice, jalapeño, and onion in a small bowl.

Makes 1 cup

Nutritional information per serving (includes salsa)

| Calories | 232 | Cal. from Fat (%) | 22.1 | Sodium (mg) | 179 |
| Fat (g) | 5.7 | Saturated Fat (g) | 2.2 | Cholesterol (mg) | 85 |

CHICKEN FAJITAS

Fajitas are always welcome in my house. I load my fajitas with salsa, green peppers, and onions while my kids like theirs plain. You can please every-one at the same time and with little effort. Add-ons can include: nonfat sour cream, salsa, reduced-fat Cheddar cheese, and chopped jalapeños . . . it's your choice! The chicken can be grilled or broiled instead of sautéed.

2 pounds skinless, boneless chicken breasts
½ cup fat-free honey-Dijon dressing
1 tablespoon minced garlic
1 tablespoon Worcestershire sauce

¼ cup lime juice
1 teaspoon ground cumin
1 green bell pepper, seeded and thinly sliced
1 onion, thinly sliced
12 flour tortillas

Trim any excess fat and cut the chicken breasts into strips. In a large bowl or oblong glass dish, combine the dressing, garlic, Worcester-shire sauce, lime juice, and cumin, stirring well. Add the chicken strips and marinate for 2 hours or overnight. Drain the marinade from the chicken and in a large skillet coated with nonstick cooking spray, cook the chicken over medium heat until done, about 8 to 10 minutes.

Just before serving, in a small skillet coated with nonstick cook-ing spray, sauté the green pepper strips and onion slices over medium heat until tender, about 5 minutes. Serve the chicken, onions, and peppers together with the flour tortillas that have been heated in the microwave or in the oven wrapped in foil.

Makes 6 servings

Nutritional information per serving

| Calories | 225 | Cal. from Fat (%) | 16 | Sodium (mg) | 322 |
| Fat (g) | 4 | Saturated Fat (g) | 1.1 | Cholesterol (mg) | 91 |

ORIENTAL CHICKEN AND MUSHROOMS

The seasonings for this dish form a tasty glaze on the chicken. Serve this wonderful recipe with rice.

1¼ pounds boneless chicken parts, skin removed
1 tablespoon minced onion flakes
¼ cup reduced-sodium soy sauce

2 teaspoons honey
Dash of garlic powder
½ cup chopped green bell pepper
2½ cups sliced fresh mushrooms

Preheat the oven to 350°F. Place the chicken in a 2-quart baking dish coated with nonstick cooking spray. Sprinkle with the onion flakes. In a small bowl, combine the soy sauce, honey, and garlic powder and pour the mixture evenly over the chicken. Cover and bake for 30 minutes. Spread the green pepper and mushrooms evenly over the chicken and continue to bake, covered, 20 minutes more, or until the mushrooms are tender.

Makes 4 servings

Nutritional information per serving

Calories	197	Cal. from Fat (%) 20.8	Sodium (mg)	573
Fat (g)	4.6	Saturated Fat (g) 1.1	Cholesterol (mg)	99

OVEN-FRIED CHICKEN TENDERS

I couldn't decide between oven-fried chicken recipes, so I included both of them. The kids love this one since the chicken tenders can be picked up and dunked in their favorite sauce. Honey mustard or sweet-and-sour sauces are a step up from just using ketchup as a sauce.

1⅔ cups reduced-fat buttermilk baking and pancake mix
¼ teaspoon pepper
¼ teaspoon salt (optional)
1½ teaspoons paprika

2 to 2½ pounds skinless, boneless chicken tenders (chicken strips)
½ cup buttermilk
2 tablespoons (¼ stick) light stick margarine, melted

Preheat the oven to 350°F. Combine the baking mix, pepper, salt, if using, and paprika in a shallow bowl. Dunk the chicken tenders in the buttermilk and coat with the dry mixture. Place the chicken tenders on a baking sheet coated with nonstick cooking spray and drizzle the melted margarine over the chicken. Bake for 30 to 45 minutes, or until the chicken is tender or lightly browned.

Makes 6 servings

Nutritional information per serving

Calories	326	Cal. from Fat (%) 21.3	Sodium (mg)	597
Fat (g)	7.7	Saturated Fat (g) 1.9	Cholesterol (mg)	115

OVEN-FRIED CHICKEN BREASTS SUPREME

This is the granddaddy of the fried chickens, crisp and tender with lots of seasoning. If you like dark meat, you can use skinless, boneless thighs.

2 cups nonfat sour cream
1/4 cup lemon juice
2 tablespoons Worcestershire sauce
1/2 teaspoon celery salt
2 teaspoons paprika
1/2 garlic clove, finely chopped

1/2 teaspoon pepper
1/8 teaspoon cayenne pepper
12 (6-ounce) skinless chicken breasts
1 3/4 cups dry bread crumbs
1/2 cup (1 stick) light stick margarine, melted

In a large bowl, combine the sour cream, lemon juice, Worcestershire sauce, celery salt, paprika, garlic, pepper, and cayenne. Add the chicken to the mixture, turning to coat well. Let stand, covered, in the refrigerator overnight. Preheat the oven to 350°F. Remove the chicken from the mixture and roll in the bread crumbs, coating evenly. Arrange in a single layer in a large shallow baking pan lined with foil. Drizzle the margarine over the chicken. Bake for 45 minutes to 1 hour, or until the chicken is tender and nicely browned.

Makes 10 to 12 servings

Nutritional information per serving

Calories	276	Cal. from Fat (%) 24.5	Sodium (mg)	310
Fat (g)	7.5	Saturated Fat (g) 1.7	Cholesterol (mg)	77

PAELLA STEW

If the stew gets too thick, you can always add more water. If you have left-over cooked chicken, just add it at the end with the seafood. You can be creative with this recipe and include any seafood or poultry you enjoy eating.

1 onion, chopped
1 green bell pepper, seeded
and chopped
1 teaspoon minced garlic
1 (28-ounce) can no-salt-
added whole tomatoes,
coarsely chopped, with
their juice
1 (16-ounce) can fat-free
chicken broth
1 whole skinless, boneless
chicken breast
(approximately 8 ounces),
cut into cubes

⅔ cup rice
3 cups water
¼ teaspoon paprika
¼ teaspoon ground cumin
¾ cup frozen peas
1 pound bay scallops, rinsed
and drained
1 pound medium shrimp,
peeled and deveined
½ cup thinly sliced green
onions (scallions) stems
(green part only)

In a large pot coated with nonstick cooking spray, sauté the onion, green pepper, and garlic over medium heat until tender, about 5 minutes. Add the tomatoes, broth, chicken, rice, water, paprika, and cumin. Bring to a boil, then reduce the heat. Cover and cook for 30 minutes. Add the peas, scallops, and shrimp. Cook for approximately 10 minutes, or until the shrimp are done. Stir in the green onions before serving.

Makes 6 to 8 servings

Nutritional information per serving

Calories	213	Cal. from Fat (%)	8.5	Sodium (mg)	294
Fat (g)	2	Saturated Fat (g)	0.4	Cholesterol (mg)	75

HONEY-GLAZED TURKEY BREAST

My family loves this tasty turkey breast, and then I use the leftover turkey for sandwiches the next day. Remember, turkey can be enjoyed all year long—don't save it just for holiday dinners.

1 (5-pound) turkey breast	3 tablespoons Dijon mustard
Salt and pepper to taste	1½ teaspoons dried
⅓ cup honey	rosemary

Preheat the oven to 325°F. Remove the skin from the turkey breast and discard; place the breast in a roaster pan. Season with salt and pepper. In a small bowl, mix together the honey, Dijon mustard, and rosemary. Pour half of the glaze over the turkey breast and bake, uncovered, for about 2 hours, or until the meat thermometer registers 170°F. to 175°F. in the thickest part of the breast. You may want to add a little water to the bottom of pan, if needed. During the final 15 minutes of baking, brush the remaining glaze over the turkey breast.

Makes 12 servings

Nutritional information per serving

Calories	180	Cal. from Fat (%)	22.8	Sodium (mg)	110
Fat (g)	4.6	Saturated Fat (g)	1.5	Cholesterol (mg)	66

CORNISH HENS WITH WILD RICE STUFFING

When a dear friend made this attractive dish for dinner at her home in Florida, I immediately knew I had to include the recipe in my book. You might want to save them for a special occasion or a holiday dinner. You can purchase smaller hens and use one per serving, if desired, or cut the recipe in half.

8 Cornish game hens (about 1½ pounds each)
1 tablespoon paprika
1 tablespoon garlic powder
Salt and pepper to taste
2 onions, chopped
2 green bell peppers, seeded and chopped
4 celery stalks, chopped
1 tablespoon minced garlic
1 bunch green onions

(scallions), chopped
3 (6-ounce) packages long-grain and wild rice
1 (16-ounce) jar peach preserves
3 tablespoons honey
3 tablespoons light brown sugar
⅔ cup golden raisins
4 baking apples, cored and sliced

Preheat the oven to 350°F. Clean and rinse the Cornish game hens. Lay the hens in a large casserole dish and pat dry. Season with the paprika, garlic powder, and salt and pepper; set aside. In a large pan coated with nonstick cooking spray, sauté the onions, green peppers, celery, garlic, and green onions until tender, about 7 minutes. Add all the long-grain and wild rice mix and water according to package directions, omitting any oil and salt. Cook until the rice is done and the liquid is absorbed, about 35 to 40 minutes.

Stuff each of the Cornish game hens equally with the wild rice mixture. In another saucepan, heat the peach preserves, honey, and brown sugar over medium-low heat until the mixture is bubbly, about 4 minutes. Pour over the stuffed Cornish game hens. Sprinkle with the raisins and sliced apples. Bake for 1½ to 2 hours, or until the hens are done. You might have to cover them with foil during the last 30 minutes if the hens get too brown. To serve, cut each hen in half and serve with the dressing.

Makes 16 servings

Nutritional information per serving

Calories	570	Cal. from Fat (%)	29.2	Sodium (mg)	486
Fat (g)	18.5	Saturated Fat (g)	5.1	Cholesterol (mg)	118

MEATS

PAN-SAUTÉED STEAK WITH GARLIC-MUSTARD SAUCE

You'll find yourself preparing this quick, rich sauce for all your favorite meats. The sauce seems to be even more popular than the steak . . . how about that! Of course, you can also grill your meat. However, in winter months, I like to have the indoor option.

3 pounds sirloin steak, trimmed of fat	½ cup dry red wine
	½ cup canned beef broth
Salt and pepper	2 tablespoons Dijon mustard
2 tablespoons minced garlic	3 tablespoons minced parsley

Heat a large skillet coated with nonstick cooking spray over medium-high heat and sauté the steak on both sides until done, about 5 to 7 minutes. Season with salt and pepper. With a fork, transfer to a plate. To the pan, add the garlic and sauté 30 seconds. Add the wine and boil until reduced by half, stirring well. Add the beef broth and mustard, stirring until blended. Boil until slightly thickened. Spoon over the cooked sirloin and sprinkle with the parsley.

Makes 6 to 8 servings

Nutritional information per serving

Calories	237	Cal. from Fat (%)	30.4	Sodium (mg)	173
Fat (g)	8	Saturated Fat (g)	3.1	Cholesterol (mg)	102

SMOTHERED ROUND STEAK

This braised steak forms a gravy with a terrific flavor, which is just great served over rice. If the gravy gets too thick, just add more water.

2 pounds round steak, trimmed of fat	2 garlic cloves, chopped
Salt and pepper to taste	1 (10-ounce) can diced tomatoes and green chilies
¼ cup all-purpose flour	¾ cup water
1 medium onion, chopped	

Season the steak with salt and pepper and dust both sides with the flour. In a large skillet coated with nonstick cooking spray, brown the steak over medium-high heat on both sides, about 6 minutes in all. Add the onion, garlic, tomatoes and green chilies, and water and bring to a boil. Reduce the heat and simmer for 1 hour, or until the steak is tender.

Makes 4 to 6 servings

| Calories | 211 | Cal. from Fat (%) 20.2 | Sodium (mg) | 261 |
| Fat (g) | 4.7 | Saturated Fat (g) 1.7 | Cholesterol (mg) | 77 |

MEATS

POLYNESIAN FLANK STEAK WITH RICE

This marinade can also be used for chicken. With the colorful rice, this becomes an attractive as well as tasty dish.

1½ cups unsweetened
 pineapple juice
¼ cup plus 1 tablespoon
 reduced-sodium soy sauce,
 divided
1½ teaspoons garlic powder
1 teaspoon ground ginger
⅓ cup fat-free Italian
 dressing
2½ pounds flank steak,
 trimmed of fat

1 red bell pepper, seeded
 and chopped
1 green bell pepper, seeded
 and chopped
½ pound fresh mushrooms,
 sliced
1 (8-ounce) can sliced water
 chestnuts, drained
6 cups cooked rice

Combine the pineapple juice, ¼ cup soy sauce, garlic powder, ginger, and Italian dressing in a 3-quart oblong baking dish, mixing well. Add the flank steak and turn to coat all sides. Cover and marinate in the refrigerator for 8 hours, if possible, or overnight, turning the steak occasionally. Preheat the grill or broiler. Grill over a hot fire approximately 7 minutes on each side, or place in a pan and broil for about 5 minutes on each side for rare steak. In a large skillet coated with nonstick cooking spray, sauté the red pepper, green pepper, and mushrooms until tender. Add the water chestnuts, rice, and the remaining 1 tablespoon soy sauce, tossing well. To serve, slice the flank steak diagonally against the grain and place over the rice.

Makes 6 servings

Nutritional information per serving

| Calories | 572 | Cal. from Fat (%) 28.6 | Sodium (mg) | 501 |
| Fat (g) | 18.2 | Saturated Fat (g) 7.6 | Cholesterol (mg) | 94 |

SPICY MEAT LOAF

The barbecue sauce and jalapeños give this super-easy meat loaf extra pizzazz. This meat loaf will knock your socks off!

2 pounds ground sirloin	½ cup chopped onion
⅓ cup barbecue sauce	1 green bell pepper, seeded
1½ tablespoons chopped	and chopped
jalapeño pepper	1 large egg white
1 teaspoon garlic powder	½ cup Italian bread crumbs
1 teaspoon dried oregano	Salt and pepper to taste
1 teaspoon dried basil	

Preheat the oven to 375°F. Combine the sirloin, barbecue sauce, jalapeño pepper, garlic powder, oregano, basil, onion, green pepper, egg white, bread crumbs, and salt and pepper and place in a 9 × 5 × 3-inch loaf pan coated with nonstick cooking spray. Bake for 1 hour. Drain off any excess grease before serving.

Makes 8 servings

Nutritional information per serving

Calories	194	Cal. from Fat (%)	29.7	Sodium (mg)	223
Fat (g)	6.4	Saturated Fat (g)	2.4	Cholesterol (mg)	68

QUICK BEEF STEW

On a cold night, nothing beats a steaming bowl of stew. No one will know the secret ingredient—beer—which enhances the flavor.

2 pounds lean boneless top	½ pound fresh mushrooms,
round steak, trimmed of	quartered
fat and cut into 1-inch	3 garlic cloves, minced
cubes	¼ cup chopped parsley
⅓ cup all-purpose flour	½ teaspoon dried thyme
2 cups carrots, peeled and	Salt and pepper to taste
sliced (1-inch)	1 (14½-ounce) can no-salt-
1¾ pounds red potatoes,	added beef broth
scrubbed and cubed	1 cup lite beer
1 large onion, sliced	

Combine the meat and flour in a plastic bag; close the bag and shake. Coat a large pot with nonstick cooking spray and place over high heat until hot. Add the meat and cook until browned, about 8 minutes, stirring often. Add the carrots, potatoes, onion, mushrooms, garlic, parsley, thyme, salt and pepper, beef broth, and beer. Cover and cook approximately 1 hour, or until the meat is tender and the vegetables are done.

Makes 6 servings

Nutritional information per serving

Calories	374	Cal. from Fat (%) 14.7		Sodium (mg)	88
Fat (g)	6.1	Saturated Fat (g) 2.1		Cholesterol (mg)	80

ITALIAN-STYLE POT ROAST

This recipe can also be made in a slow cooker. Everyone loves a pot roast and your family will especially enjoy this flavorful one. Serve this with rice or potatoes.

4- to 5-pound round roast
2 cups canned beef broth
½ cup Burgundy wine
3 tablespoons no-salt-added tomato paste
1 (28-ounce) can no-salt-added whole tomatoes, chopped, with their juice
2 garlic cloves, pressed
1 tablespoon dried basil
1 tablespoon dried oregano
2 bay leaves
1 pound carrots, peeled and cut into 1-inch pieces
3 onions quartered
1 pound fresh mushrooms, halved
1 tablespoon light stick margarine
2 tablespoons all-purpose flour

Preheat the oven to 350°F. Place the roast in a large pot or a Dutch oven. Pour in the beef broth and wine. Add the tomato paste and stir. Add the tomatoes with their juice. Blend in the garlic, basil, oregano, and bay leaves. Cover and cook in the oven for 1½ hours. Turn the meat over and add the carrots, onions, and mushrooms. Cover and continue cooking for 1 to 1½ hours or until the meat is tender.

Transfer the meat to a carving board. Mash the margarine and flour together to form a paste. Place the Dutch oven over medium-high heat and bring the liquid to a boil. Whisk in the paste to thicken the sauce. Slice the meat against the grain. Serve with the vegetables and the sauce, from which the bay leaves have been removed and discarded.

Makes 8 to 10 servings

Nutritional information per serving

Calories	407	Cal. from Fat (%)	29	Sodium (mg)	388
Fat (g)	13.1	Saturated Fat (g)	4.5	Cholesterol (mg)	158

MEATS

BEEF AND RICE

This simple, hearty dish is a comforting favorite of everyone.

1 cup chopped celery	1 tablespoon dried oregano
1 cup sliced green onions (scallions)	1 tablespoon dried basil
	1 tablespoon Worcestershire
3 large garlic cloves, minced	sauce
½ cup chopped green bell pepper	Salt and pepper to taste
	3 cups cooked rice
1 pound lean ground sirloin	1 cup shredded reduced-fat
1 (15-ounce) can no-salt- added tomato sauce	sharp Cheddar cheese (optional)
⅔ cup canned beef consommé	

Preheat the oven to 350°F. In a large skillet coated with nonstick cooking spray, sauté the celery, green onions, garlic, and green pepper until tender, about 5 minutes. Add the meat and cook until browned, about 6 minutes, stirring until it crumbles. Drain off any excess grease. Add the tomato sauce, consommé, oregano, basil, Worcestershire sauce, and salt and pepper and cook for 5 minutes. Mix in the cooked rice and pour into a 3-quart casserole coated with nonstick cooking spray. Sprinkle with the cheese, if desired. Bake, covered, about 30 minutes.

Makes 8 servings

Nutritional information per serving (includes rice)

Calories	249	Cal. from Fat (%) 24.2		Sodium (mg)	287
Fat (g)	6.7	Saturated Fat (g)	3.4	Cholesterol (mg)	44

STUFFED PEPPERS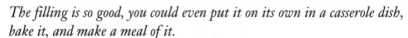

The filling is so good, you could even put it on its own in a casserole dish, bake it, and make a meal of it.

6 medium green bell peppers	1 tablespoon minced garlic
	1 tablespoon dried basil
¾ pound ground sirloin	1 teaspoon dried oregano
1 cup chopped fresh mushrooms	Salt and pepper to taste
	2 cups cooked rice
¾ cup chopped onion	½ cup (2 ounces) shredded
1 cup no-salt-added tomato sauce	part-skim mozzarella cheese

Preheat the oven to 350°F. Cut the tops off the green peppers and remove the core and seeds. Trim the stem from the tops and discard. Chop the remaining tops; set aside. Arrange the pepper shells in a steamer over boiling water, cover, and steam 5 minutes. Drain the shells and set aside.

Combine the ground sirloin, mushrooms, onion, and reserved chopped green pepper in a large skillet coated with nonstick cooking spray. Cook over medium heat until the beef is brown and crumbly, about 8 minutes. Drain off any excess grease. Add the tomato sauce, garlic, basil, oregano, and salt and pepper. Bring to a boil; reduce the heat and simmer 5 minutes. Add the rice. Spoon the mixture into the pepper shells, then place the peppers upright in an 8-inch-square baking dish. Sprinkle with the mozzarella. Bake for 15 minutes.

Makes 6 servings

Nutritional information per serving

Calories	212	Cal. from Fat (%) 20.9	Sodium (mg)	78
Fat (g)	4.9	Saturated Fat (g) 2.2	Cholesterol (mg)	39

BEEF STROGANOFF

If you want to make this classic ahead, prepare the recipe to the point where you add the sour cream. Serve the stroganoff over wild rice or noodles.

½ teaspoon minced garlic
½ pound fresh mushrooms, sliced
2 pounds sirloin steak, cut into 1-inch strips
3 tablespoons all-purpose flour

1 (14½-ounce) can beef broth
1 tablespoon Dijon mustard
4 green onions (scallions), stems only, sliced
¼ cup sherry
½ cup nonfat sour cream

In a pan coated with nonstick cooking spray, sauté the garlic and mushrooms until they begin to get tender, about 4 minutes. Add the sirloin strips and brown, stirring constantly. Sprinkle the meat with the flour and gradually add the broth. Add the mustard and bring to a boil. Add the green onions. Lower the heat and simmer for 20 minutes, or until the meat is tender. Add the sherry and cook for 15 minutes. Before serving, stir in the sour cream; do not boil.

Makes 6 servings

Nutritional information per serving

Calories	269	Cal. from Fat (%) 24.1	Sodium (mg)	365
Fat (g)	7.2	Saturated Fat (g) 2.5	Cholesterol (mg)	94

ORANGE PORK TENDERLOIN

I love tenderloins because they are easy. The orange sauce is wonderful; however, if you're in a pinch, this tenderloin is very tasty without it.

2 (1-pound) pork
tenderloins, trimmed of fat
¼ cup Dijon mustard
¼ cup sliced green onions
(scallions)
1 teaspoon dried rosemary
1 teaspoon dried tarragon

⅛ teaspoon pepper
½ teaspoon minced garlic
½ cup orange marmalade,
divided
½ cup water
⅓ cup canned fat-free
chicken broth

Preheat the oven to 400°F. Cut the tenderloins lengthwise down the center, cutting halfway through the meat but not cutting all the way through. In a small bowl, combine the mustard, green onions, rosemary, tarragon, pepper, and garlic. Spread the mustard mixture on the cut surfaces of the tenderloin. Reshape the tenderloin and tie, if desired. Place it on a rack in a shallow roasting pan and brush with 4 tablespoons of the marmalade.

Bake for 40 to 50 minutes, until tender, or until a meat thermometer registers 160°F. For the sauce, in a small saucepan, combine the remaining 4 tablespoons marmalade, water, and broth. Bring to a boil, then reduce the heat. Simmer 5 to 10 minutes, or until thickened. To serve, slice the tenderloin and spoon the sauce over.

Makes 8 servings

Nutritional information per serving

Calories	207	Cal. from Fat (%)	24.8	Sodium (mg)	177
Fat (g)	5.7	Saturated Fat (g)	1.9	Cholesterol (mg)	67

PORK TENDERLOIN WITH MUSTARD SAUCE

The Mustard Sauce is a wonderful complement to the tenderloin, making this a sophisticated main course.

¼ cup reduced-sodium
soy sauce
¼ cup bourbon
2 tablespoons light brown
sugar

2½ pounds pork tenderloins
Mustard Sauce (recipe
follows)

Combine the soy sauce, bourbon, and brown sugar in an 11 × 7 × 1½-inch baking dish and add the tenderloins. Cover and refrigerate

at least 2 hours, turning occasionally. Preheat the oven to 325°F.
Remove the meat from the marinade, discarding the marinade; place
the tenderloins on a rack in a shallow roasting pan. Bake for 45 minutes, or until a meat thermometer inserted into the thickest portion
registers 160°F. Serve with the Mustard Sauce.

Makes 6 servings

Mustard Sauce

⅔ cup nonfat sour cream   ½ cup thinly sliced green
⅔ cup nonfat mayonnaise   onions (scallions)
2 tablespoons dry mustard

Combine the sour cream, mayonnaise, dry mustard, and green
onions. Cover and chill in the refrigerator until ready to serve.

Makes about 1½ cups

Nutritional information per serving

Calories	258	Cal. from Fat (%) 25.1		Sodium (mg)	426
Fat (g)	7.2	Saturated Fat (g)	2.3	Cholesterol (mg)	86

SMOTHERED PORK CHOPS

*If you need gravy for any dish, try this recipe—my kids love gravy over
rice. If the gravy is too thick, just add more chicken broth.*

1 onion, finely chopped   1½ cups fat-free canned
4 garlic cloves, minced   chicken broth
6 boneless pork chops   1 teaspoon browning and
½ cup water   seasoning sauce
⅓ cup all-purpose flour

In a skillet coated with nonstick cooking spray, sauté the onion and
garlic over medium heat until tender, about 4 minutes. Add the pork
chops and brown on both sides. Add the water and bring to a simmer. Dissolve the flour in the chicken broth and stir into the skillet.
Add the browning sauce to give the gravy a nice color. Cook, covered, over low heat for 1 hour, or until the meat is tender.

Makes 6 servings

Nutritional information per serving

Calories	192	Cal. from Fat (%) 29.5		Sodium (mg)	169
Fat (g)	6.3	Saturated Fat (g)	2.3	Cholesterol (mg)	63

PORK AND PEPPER STIR-FRY

If you enjoy Chinese food, put this stir-fry on your list. The soy sauce is very tasty with the plum jam and pork is very lean. Serve with hot cooked rice.

2 pounds pork tenderloin,
cut in slices
¾ cup plum jam
3 tablespoons reduced-
sodium soy sauce
2 tablespoons lemon juice
1 tablespoon prepared
horseradish
1 tablespoon cornstarch
¼ teaspoon crushed red
pepper flakes

1½ teaspoons ground ginger
1 red bell pepper, seeded
and thinly sliced
1 yellow bell pepper, seeded
and thinly sliced
1 green bell pepper, seeded
and thinly sliced
4 green onions (scallions),
sliced
1 (8-ounce) can sliced water
chestnuts, drained

Trim the pork and cut into bite-size strips about ½ inch thick; set aside. To make the sauce, in a small bowl, stir together the jam, soy sauce, lemon juice, horseradish, cornstarch, red pepper flakes, and ginger; set aside.

In a skillet coated with nonstick cooking spray, sauté all the peppers and green onions over medium heat until crisp-tender, about 4 minutes. Remove the vegetables. Add the pork to the skillet and stir-fry for 2 to 3 minutes, or until no longer pink. Stir the sauce and add it to the skillet. Cook and stir until bubbly. Add the water chestnuts. Return the vegetables to the skillet and stir to coat. Cook until heated through, about 4 minutes.

Makes 8 servings

Nutritional information per serving (not including rice)

| Calories | 261 | Cal. from Fat (%) | 19.2 | Sodium (mg) | 259 |
| Fat (g) | 5.6 | Saturated Fat (g) | 1.9 | Cholesterol (mg) | 80 |

VEAL MARENGO ♥

This delicious veal dish cooks in no time at all. The fresh tomatoes and seasonings add to this Italian favorite. Serve this over pasta to complete your meal.

½ cup white wine, divided
1½ to 2 pounds lean
   scaloppine-style veal
1 onion, chopped
½ pound fresh mushrooms,
   sliced
½ teaspoon minced garlic
1 teaspoon dried basil

1 teaspoon dried oregano
1 bay leaf
1 cup chopped Roma (plum)
   tomatoes
1 bunch green onions
   (scallions), chopped
2 tablespoons chopped
   parsley

In a large skillet coated with nonstick cooking spray, bring ¼ cup white wine to a simmer. Add the veal and brown on both sides. Add the onion, mushrooms, garlic, basil, oregano, bay leaf, tomatoes, and the remaining ¼ cup white wine. Cook, stirring, until the mushrooms and onions are tender and the veal is cooked through. Add the green onions and parsley and continue cooking for 5 more minutes. Remove and discard the bay leaf before serving.

Makes 6 to 8 servings

Nutritional information per serving

Calories	123	Cal. from Fat (%)	23.7	Sodium (mg)	43
Fat (g)	3.2	Saturated Fat (g)	0.9	Cholesterol (mg)	52

SEAFOOD
and
FISH

BARBECUE SHRIMP

Serve Barbecue Shrimp with French bread to dip in the sauce. This wonderful shrimp dish is worth messing up your hands to eat. I also like to serve Barbecue Shrimp with pasta I made this dish on the NBC Weekend Today Show and received 3,000 letters in the mail requesting the recipe. I guess Barbecue Shrimp is everyone's favorite!

4 tablespoons olive oil	1 teaspoon dried oregano
½ cup fat-free Italian dressing	1 tablespoon dried rosemary
1 tablespoon minced garlic	1 teaspoon dried thyme
1 teaspoon hot pepper sauce	1 lemon
⅓ cup Worcestershire sauce	2 pounds headless large shrimp, unpeeled
4 bay leaves	⅓ cup white wine (optional)
1 tablespoon paprika	

In a large, heavy skillet, place the olive oil, Italian dressing, garlic, hot sauce, Worcestershire sauce, bay leaves, paprika, oregano, rosemary, and thyme and cook over medium heat until the sauce begins to boil. Squeeze the lemon into the sauce and then place both halves in the sauce. Add the shrimp and cook approximately 10 to 15 minutes. Add the wine, if using, and cook another 10 minutes, or until the shrimp are done. Serve the shrimp with the sauce, from which the bay leaves have been removed and discarded.

Makes 4 to 6 servings

Nutritional information per serving

Calories	160	Cal. from Fat (%)	29.3	Sodium (mg)	510
Fat (g)	5.2	Saturated Fat (g)	1	Cholesterol (mg)	168

SHRIMP JAMBALAYA

Jambalaya is a Spanish-Cajun-influenced rice dish seasoned with chili powder as well as cayenne and made with chicken, ham, or shellfish.

4 tablespoons (½ stick) light stick margarine	1 (14½-ounce) can no-salt-added chopped tomatoes
1 cup chopped onion	1 cup canned fat-free chicken broth
1 green bell pepper, seeded and chopped	⅛ teaspoon cayenne pepper
1 teaspoon minced garlic	1 teaspoon chili powder
2 tablespoons chopped parsley	Salt and pepper to taste
2 ounces Canadian bacon, chopped	1½ pounds medium shrimp, peeled
1 tablespoon all-purpose flour	4 cups cooked rice
	1 bunch green onions (scallions), thinly sliced

In a large pot, melt the margarine and sauté the onion, green pepper, garlic, parsley, and bacon over medium heat until the vegetables are tender, about 6 minutes. Stir in the flour. Add the chopped tomatoes, chicken broth, cayenne, chili powder, salt and pepper, and shrimp. Cook, stirring occasionally, until the shrimp are done and the mixture begins to thicken, about 10 to 15 minutes. Stir in the cooked rice and green onions, mixing well.

Makes 6 servings

Nutritional information per serving

Calories	297	Cal. from Fat (%)	17.9	Sodium (mg)	510
Fat (g)	5.9	Saturated Fat (g)	1.2	Cholesterol (mg)	131

SHRIMP BASIL

I'm always thrilled when my family requests Shrimp Basil as I know it will be an extra-quick dinner and an extra-special one.

2 tablespoons (¼ stick) light stick margarine	2 tablespoons chopped chives
1 pound medium shrimp, peeled	1 (12-ounce) package angel hair pasta
2 garlic cloves, minced	¼ cup grated Parmesan cheese
1 tablespoon dried basil	
¼ cup chopped parsley	

In a pan coated with nonstick cooking spray, melt the margarine over medium heat and cook the shrimp until done, about 5 minutes. Add the garlic, basil, parsley, and chives. Meanwhile, cook the pasta according to package directions, omitting any oil and salt. Toss with the shrimp mixture and add the cheese, tossing until mixed.

Makes 4 to 6 servings

Nutritional information per serving

Calories	305	Cal. from Fat (%)	13.4	Sodium (mg)	210
Fat (g)	4.5	Saturated Fat (g)	1.2	Cholesterol (mg)	87

BROILED MARINATED SHRIMP

This is for people who aren't crazy about spicy food but want big taste.

2 pounds large shrimp, unpeeled
Salt and pepper to taste
2 tablespoons (¼ stick) light stick margarine, melted
1 lemon, sliced
¼ cup lemon juice
¼ cup Worcestershire sauce
1 teaspoon minced garlic
2 bay leaves
1 teaspoon dried oregano

Spread the shrimp in a 13 × 9 × 2-inch baking pan coated with nonstick cooking spray. Sprinkle with the salt and pepper. Combine the melted margarine, sliced lemon, lemon juice, Worcestershire sauce, garlic, bay leaves, and oregano in a bowl. Stir to mix well and pour over the shrimp. Refrigerate and marinate at least 1 hour, preferably 3 or 4. Before serving, preheat the broiler. Place the pan under the broiler for 15 minutes, until the shrimp are done, turning the shrimp once.

Makes 4 servings

Nutritional information per serving

Calories	120	Cal. from Fat (%)	29.8	Sodium (mg)	504
Fat (g)	4	Saturated Fat (g)	0.8	Cholesterol (mg)	170

QUICK SHRIMP WITH WILD RICE

People will ooh *and* aah *when you set this pretty dish on the table.*

1 (6-ounce) package long-
  grain and wild rice mix
1 green bell pepper, seeded
  and chopped
1 bunch green onions
  (scallions), chopped
¼ pound fresh mushrooms,
  sliced

2 cups cooked, peeled
  shrimp
¼ cup white wine
1 (10¾-ounce) can cream of
  shrimp soup

Cook the rice mix according to package directions, omitting any oil and salt. Meanwhile, in a saucepan coated with nonstick cooking spray, sauté the green pepper and green onions over medium heat until tender, about 5 minutes. Stir in the mushrooms, cooking 3 minutes more. Add the shrimp, wine, and shrimp soup. Heat until bubbly. Arrange the cooked rice in a ring around the outer edge of a 2-quart casserole and pour the shrimp mixture in the center. Serve immediately.

Makes 4 servings

Nutritional information per serving

Calories	330	Cal. from Fat (%)	12.4	Sodium (mg)	770
Fat (g)	4.5	Saturated Fat (g)	2.3	Cholesterol (mg)	157

SHRIMP CASSEROLE ♥

Here's another irresistible shrimp casserole. I like this pasta recipe because with only one pan used to cook a whole meal, the cleanup is a pleasure.

1 large onion, chopped
1 green bell pepper, seeded
  and chopped
2 pounds medium shrimp,
  peeled
1 cup sliced fresh
  mushrooms
1 teaspoon minced garlic
1 tablespoon chopped
  parsley

1 (10¾-ounce) can golden
  mushroom soup
1 (8-ounce) package fat-free
  cream cheese
1 teaspoon hot sauce
½ cup sliced green onions
  (scallions)
1 (12-ounce package) rotini
  pasta

In a large pan coated with nonstick cooking spray, sauté the onion and green pepper over medium heat until tender, about 5 minutes.

Add the shrimp, mushrooms, and garlic, sautéing until the shrimp are done and the vegetables are tender, about 5 minutes. Add the parsley, the golden mushroom soup, and cream cheese, stirring until the cream cheese is melted. Add the hot sauce and green onions. Meanwhile, cook the rotini according to package directions, omitting any oil and salt. Drain and add the pasta to the shrimp mixture, tossing to mix well.

Makes 6 to 8 servings

Nutritional information per serving

Calories	443	Cal. from Fat (%)	8.1	Sodium (mg)	961
Fat (g)	4.0	Saturated Fat (g)	1.0	Cholesterol (mg)	61.2

CRAB AND SPINACH CASSEROLE

This is kind of like a crabmeat cocktail in a casserole. You can serve it as a luxurious side dish to a fish dinner, or as a first course or main course.

2 (10-ounce) packages frozen chopped spinach, thawed
Salt and pepper to taste
1 cup finely chopped onion
1 pound lump crabmeat

1 cup shredded reduced-fat sharp Cheddar cheese
⅔ cup nonfat sour cream
3 tablespoons cocktail sauce

Preheat the oven to 325°F. Squeeze the spinach dry and add the salt and pepper. In a casserole dish coated with nonstick cooking spray, spread a single layer of spinach, onion, crabmeat, and cheese in that order. In a small bowl, combine the sour cream and cocktail sauce and spread on top. Bake for 45 minutes.

Makes 4 servings

Nutritional information per serving

Calories	297	Cal. from Fat (%)	22.7	Sodium (mg)	753
Fat (g)	7.5	Saturated Fat (g)	3.8	Cholesterol (mg)	137

PAN-FRIED FISH ♥

To really make this dish special, top the fish with toasted almonds and parsley. My neighbor deep-fries fish, which we love as a special treat. However, this is the closest I've come to fried fish without the guilt.

2 pounds fish fillets (such as trout, snapper, or your favorite)	1 cup self-rising flour
	1 teaspoon paprika
	1 cup buttermilk
Salt and black pepper to taste	3 tablespoons light stick margarine

Season the fish with the salt and pepper. Combine the flour and paprika in a small, shallow bowl. Dip the fish in buttermilk, then roll in the flour mixture and coat well. In a large skillet coated with non-stick cooking spray, heat the margarine over medium heat and sauté the fish until lightly brown on both sides, about 2 to 3 minutes on each side. *Do not overcook!* Drain on paper towels and serve.

Makes 6 servings

Nutritional information per serving

Calories	215	Cal. from Fat (%)	15.8	Sodium (mg)	341
Fat (g)	3.8	Saturated Fat (g)	0.8	Cholesterol (mg)	48

SPECIAL FISH

This is an easy way to cook up the catch of the day . . . or whatever looks good in the fish department of your supermarket.

⅓ cup all-purpose flour	1 teaspoon minced garlic
Salt and pepper to taste	½ cup white wine
2 pounds firm fish fillets (such as red snapper, catfish, or grouper)	2 tablespoons lemon juice
	1 tomato, chopped
2 tablespoons (¼ stick) light stick margarine	2 tablespoons chopped jalapeños peppers
	1 teaspoon dried dillweed

Preheat the oven to 350°F. Combine the flour and salt and pepper in a shallow bowl. Coat the fish with the flour mixture. In a 3-quart oblong baking dish coated with nonstick cooking spray, heat the margarine in the oven until melted. Stir in the garlic. Place the fish in the dish and sprinkle with wine, lemon juice, tomato, jalapeños, and dillweed. Bake for 20 minutes, or until the fish is done.

Makes 4 servings

| Calories | 298 | Cal. from Fat (%) | 18 | Sodium (mg) | 234 |
| Fat (g) | 6 | Saturated Fat (g) | 1.1 | Cholesterol (mg) | 77 |

CRAWFISH-EGGPLANT BAKE

This well-seasoned dish will be a hit for those who delight in crawfish and eggplant. Of course, shrimp can be substituted in this and most crawfish dishes.

2 tablespoons (¼ stick) light
stick margarine
1 large eggplant, peeled and
cubed
1 large onion, chopped
½ cup chopped celery
1 green bell pepper, seeded
and chopped
1 teaspoon minced garlic

½ teaspoon dried thyme
Salt and pepper to taste
½ teaspoon dried basil
1 pound crawfish tails,
rinsed
Topping (recipe follows)

Preheat the oven to 350°F. In a large pan, melt the margarine and sauté the eggplant, onion, celery, green pepper, and garlic until tender, about 8 minutes. Add the thyme, salt and pepper, basil, and crawfish, cooking 5 more minutes. Transfer to a 9 × 9 × 2-inch-square baking pan coated with nonstick cooking spray. Spread the Topping over the mixture and bake for 20 minutes.

Topping

2 tablespoons (¼ stick) light
stick margarine
1 bunch green onions
(scallions), chopped
¼ cup all-purpose flour

1 cup canned fat-free
chicken broth
1 teaspoon lemon juice
Dash of nutmeg

Melt the margarine in a skillet over medium heat and sauté the green onions for 3 minutes. Add the flour and stir. Gradually add the chicken broth, stirring until thick. Add the lemon juice and nutmeg.

Makes 6 to 8 servings

Nutritional information per serving

| Calories | 126 | Cal. from Fat (%) | 27.9 | Sodium (mg) | 159 |
| Fat (g) | 3.9 | Saturated Fat (g) | 0.7 | Cholesterol (mg) | 78 |

STUFFED CATCH OF THE DAY

Try crabmeat instead of shrimp in the stuffing. I made this recipe years ago on a special date. He's now my husband. It was a great catch!

2 garlic cloves, minced
1 onion, chopped
1 large green bell pepper, seeded and chopped
1 bunch green onions (scallions), chopped
1½ cups herb-seasoned stuffing mix

½ cup plus ⅓ cup white wine
½ teaspoon pepper
½ pound shelled, chopped, and cooked shrimp
4 pounds large trout fillets or your favorite fish
3 tablespoons lemon juice

Preheat the oven to 350°F. In a skillet coated with nonstick cooking spray over medium heat, sauté the garlic, onion, green pepper, and green onions until tender, about 5 minutes. Add the stuffing mix, ½ cup white wine, pepper, and the cooked shrimp, mixing well. Place the fish fillets in a single layer in a baking dish coated with nonstick cooking spray. Put a mound of stuffing on top of each fillet, dividing the stuffing evenly. In a small bowl, mix the ⅓ cup white wine and lemon juice; pour over the fish. Cover the pan with foil and bake 10 minutes, until almost done. Uncover and bake 10 minutes more.

Makes 6 servings

Nutritional information per serving

Calories	338	Cal. from Fat (%)	21.5	Sodium (mg)	404
Fat (g)	8.1	Saturated Fat (g)	1.5	Cholesterol (mg)	118

TUNA STEAKS WITH HORSERADISH SAUCE

This gourmet-tasting tuna can be made ahead and only takes minutes to cook when ready to serve—very impressive! You will want to serve the sauce with other recipes because it is wonderful.

1½ to 2 pounds tuna steaks, ½ to 1 inch thick
3 tablespoons finely chopped blanched almonds
¼ cup all-purpose flour
1 teaspoon minced garlic
1 tablespoon dried basil
1 tablespoon dried thyme

1 tablespoon dried rosemary
1 teaspoon coarsely ground pepper
2 tablespoons water
2 tablespoons white wine (optional)
Horseradish Sauce (recipe follows)

Rinse and trim the tuna steaks. In a food processor or with a fork, combine the almonds, flour, garlic, basil, thyme, rosemary, pepper, and water to make a paste. Spread the paste on both sides of the tuna steaks and refrigerate until ready to use. Heat a skillet coated with nonstick cooking spray over medium heat until hot and cook the tuna steaks 3 to 5 minutes on each side, depending on thickness, until done. If desired, wine can be added to the pan when cooking. Serve with Horseradish Sauce.

Makes 4 servings

Horseradish Sauce

⅔ cup fat-free mayonnaise
1½ tablespoons prepared horseradish

1½ tablespoons Creole or other spicy mustard

Combine the mayonnaise, horseradish, and mustard together in a small bowl.

Makes 1 cup

Nutritional information per serving with about 1/4 cup horseradish sauce

Calories	378	Cal. from Fat (%) 29.8		Sodium (mg)	463
Fat (g)	12.5	Saturated Fat (g)	2.7	Cholesterol (mg)	71

SUPERB SALMON STEAKS

This fast and easy recipe never fails to "wow" guests.

1 tablespoon Dijon mustard
1 tablespoon honey
1 pound 1-inch-thick salmon steaks

½ teaspoon dried tarragon
1 Roma (plum) tomato, sliced
1 tablespoon drained capers

Preheat the oven to 400°F. In a small bowl, combine the mustard and honey. Place the salmon steaks in a baking dish and coat with the mustard mixture. Sprinkle with the tarragon, sliced tomato, and capers. Pour the wine in the dish. Bake for 18 to 25 minutes, or until done as desired.

Makes 2 servings

Nutritional information per serving

Calories	363	Cal. from Fat (%) 22.6		Sodium (mg)	442
Fat (g)	9.1	Saturated Fat (g)	1.4	Cholesterol (mg)	129

PASTA

PASTA PRIMAVERA ♥

Feel free to play with the assortment of vegetables, making changes depending on the season, your preferences, and whatever is lurking in your vegetable bin.

1 (12-ounce) package angel hair (capellini) pasta
⅛ cup olive oil
1 tablespoon minced garlic
1 cup chopped red onion
½ pound asparagus, tips only
2 cups broccoli florets
½ cup sliced fresh mushrooms

1 cup chopped tomato
½ cup dry white wine
⅛ teaspoon red pepper flakes
1 tablespoon dried basil
1 tablespoon dried oregano
1 tablespoon dried thyme
¼ cup grated Parmesan cheese

Cook the pasta according to package directions, omitting any oil and salt. Drain, set aside, and keep warm. Meanwhile, heat the olive oil in a large skillet over high heat. Add the garlic and red onion, stirring constantly until tender, about 5 minutes. Add the asparagus, broccoli, mushrooms, and tomato. Stir in the wine, scraping up the particles that cling to the bottom of skillet if necessary. Add the red pepper, basil, oregano, and thyme. Cook until the vegetables are tender, about 6 minutes. Add the pasta and Parmesan cheese, toss gently, and serve immediately.

Makes 4 to 6 servings

Nutritional information per serving

Calories	329	Cal. from Fat (%)	19.2	Sodium (mg)	130.6
Fat (g)	7.1	Saturated Fat (g)	1.5	Cholesterol (mg)	2.7

EXCELLENT EGGPLANT PASTA

This is a filling vegetarian pasta dish, using the best of the summer vegetables. I love these one-pan dinners!

1 (12-ounce) package
vermicelli
1½ tablespoons olive oil
1 small (1-pound) eggplant,
peeled and sliced ¼ inch
thick
1 teaspoon minced garlic
1 green bell pepper, seeded
and cut into small strips

½ pound fresh mushrooms,
sliced
1 tablespoon dried basil
½ teaspoon crushed red
pepper flakes
1 large tomato, chopped
2 tablespoons grated
Parmesan cheese

Cook the vermicelli according to package directions, omitting any oil and salt. Drain, set aside, and keep warm. While the pasta is cooking, in a large skillet heat the olive oil. Add the eggplant and garlic, cover, and cook about 5 minutes, or until the eggplant is just tender, stirring occasionally. Stir in the pepper strips, mushrooms, basil, and crushed red pepper flakes; cook until tender, about 6 minutes. Stir in the chopped tomato and cook until the mixture is heated through. Toss with the cooked pasta and Parmesan cheese.

Makes 4 to 6 servings

Nutritional information per serving

Calories	303	Cal. from Fat (%)	16.8	Sodium (mg)	48
Fat (g)	5.7	Saturated Fat (g)	1.1	Cholesterol (mg)	2

PICANTE PEPPER PASTA

This is a great vegetarian dish. Serve this pasta with salad and bread and you have a delicious meal. You can use any combination of bell peppers.

8 ounces mostaccioli, bow-
tie, rotini, or your favorite
tubular pasta
1 large onion, halved and
thinly sliced
1 large green bell pepper,
seeded and cut into thin
strips
1 large red bell pepper,
seeded and cut into thin
strips

1 large yellow bell pepper,
seeded and cut into thin
strips
1 tablespoon minced garlic
2 tablespoons olive oil
1 teaspoon dried basil
1 teaspoon dried oregano
1 cup picante sauce
¼ cup grated Parmesan
cheese

Cook the pasta according to package directions, omitting any oil and salt. Drain, set aside, and keep warm. While the pasta is cooking, sauté the onion, peppers, and garlic in the oil in a large skillet over medium-high heat, stirring frequently, about 5 minutes, or until crisp-tender. Sprinkle the basil and oregano over the vegetables. Continue cooking, stirring frequently, until the vegetables are tender, 2 more minutes. Add the picante sauce and stir until heated. Spoon the pepper mixture over the pasta and toss with the cheese.

Makes 4 to 6 servings

Nutritional information per serving

Calories	221	Cal. from Fat (%)	26.6	Sodium (mg)	227
Fat (g)	6.5	Saturated Fat (g)	1.4	Cholesterol (mg)	3

MEDITERRANEAN CAPELLINI

Here is another vegetarian pasta that is very tasty. It can be served either as a main dish or a side dish.

1 (12-ounce) package
  capellini pasta
2 tablespoons olive oil
1 tablespoon minced garlic
1 red onion, chopped
1 red bell pepper, seeded
  and minced
1 (14½-ounce) can no-salt-
  added whole tomatoes,
  chopped, with their juice

1 (10-ounce) can diced
  tomatoes and green chilies
1 teaspoon drained capers
2 teaspoons dried basil
1 teaspoon dried oregano
½ teaspoon crushed red
  pepper flakes
¼ cup grated Parmesan
  cheese

Cook the capellini according to package directions, omitting any oil and salt. Drain, set aside, and keep warm. While the pasta is cooking, in a large pan, heat the oil and sauté the garlic, onion, and red pepper over medium heat until tender, about 5 minutes. Add all the tomatoes, capers, basil, oregano, and red pepper flakes. Simmer for 20 minutes. Serve over the pasta and toss with the Parmesan cheese.

Makes 4 to 6 servings

Nutritional information per serving

Calories	305	Cal. from Fat (%)	21.5	Sodium (mg)	301
Fat (g)	7.3	Saturated Fat (g)	1.7	Cholesterol (mg)	3

GARDEN PASTA ♥

This is great to make in the summer when lots of fresh vegetables are available. You don't have to be a farmer to enjoy this one.

1 tablespoon olive oil	1 tablespoon red wine
4 garlic cloves, minced	vinegar
1 green bell pepper, seeded	¼ teaspoon pepper
and thinly sliced	1 (16-ounce) package
1 yellow bell pepper, seeded	fettuccine or your favorite
and thinly sliced	noodle pasta
2 large tomatoes, cut in	¾ cup shredded part-skim
eighths, or 8 Roma (plum)	mozzarella cheese
tomatoes, quartered	¼ cup grated Parmesan
1 tablespoon dried basil	cheese
¼ teaspoon crushed red	
pepper flakes	

Heat the olive oil in a skillet. Add the garlic and sauté 1 minute. Add the peppers, tomatoes, basil, red pepper flakes, vinegar, and pepper. Cook the pasta according to package directions, omitting any oil and salt. Drain and toss with the mozzarella cheese. Add the tomato mixture and mix well. Place on serving plates and top with the Parmesan cheese.

Makes 6 to 8 servings

Nutritional information per serving

Calories	274	Cal. from Fat (%) 22.5		Sodium (mg)	126
Fat (g)	6.8	Saturated Fat (g) 2.4		Cholesterol (mg)	58

FETTUCCINE FLORENTINE ♥

This pasta recipe is fabulous and quickly took a place on my preferred list. If you're a spinach person, mark this one as special.

1 (12-ounce) package	1 onion, chopped
fettuccine noodles	1 cup reduced-fat ricotta
1 (10-ounce) package frozen	cheese
chopped spinach, thawed	1 cup skim milk
1 tablespoon olive oil	Salt and pepper to taste

Prepare the fettuccine according to package directions, omitting any oil and salt. Drain and set aside. While the pasta cooks, squeeze the spinach of any liquid. In a large skillet, heat the olive oil and sauté the onion over medium heat until tender, about 5 minutes, stirring occasionally. Add the spinach and cook, stirring, until the mixture is heated, about 5 minutes. Stir in the ricotta cheese and milk, mixing well. Season with the salt and pepper. Add the cooked fettuccine to the pan and toss.

Makes 4 to 6 servings

Nutritional information per serving

Calories	332	Cal. from Fat (%)	18.5	Sodium (mg)	105
Fat (g)	6.8	Saturated Fat (g)	2.5	Cholesterol (mg)	13.3

GARLIC PASTA

Grate Parmesan cheese over this pasta and it will be even better. Cooking garlic mellows its sharp, spicy flavor, so don't get nervous as you peel all the cloves. Garlic and pasta go perfectly together, especially as a sidedish, and remember, garlic is good for you.

1 large head garlic (containing approximately 14 cloves)	1 bunch green onions (scallions), sliced
2 tablespoons olive oil	Salt and pepper to taste
	1 (8-ounce) package fettuccine

Peel all the garlic cloves and slice them thinly. In a pan, heat the olive oil over medium-low heat and sauté the garlic about 4 minutes. Add the green onions and continue sautéing until the garlic is golden brown and the green onions are tender, about 4 minutes. Season with the salt and pepper. Meanwhile, cook the fettuccine according to package directions, omitting any oil and salt. Drain and add to the garlic mixture in the pan. Toss and serve.

Makes 3 to 4 servings

Nutritional information per serving

Calories	283	Cal. from Fat (%)	29.5	Sodium (mg)	16
Fat (g)	9.3	Saturated Fat (g)	1.4	Cholesterol (mg)	49

ANGEL HAIR AND
SUN-DRIED TOMATOES ♥

If you like the distinctive taste of sun-dried tomatoes, you'll enjoy this dish. You can add chicken to this for a one-dish meal.

⅔ cup sherry
1 tablespoon minced garlic
1 cup chopped green onions
   (scallions)
1 cup boiling water
3 ounces sun-dried tomatoes
1 tablespoon dried basil

1 tablespoon finely chopped
   jalapeño peppers
1 (8-ounce) package angel
   hair (capellini) pasta
2 tablespoons chopped
   parsley

In a large skillet, heat the sherry over medium heat and sauté the garlic and green onions until tender, about 5 minutes. Pour the boiling water over the sun-dried tomatoes in a bowl to reconstitute. Let sit for 5 minutes. Drain, chop, and add to the skillet. Add the basil and jalapeños, sautéing for a few minutes. Meanwhile, cook the pasta according to package directions, omitting any oil and salt. Drain and add to the skillet, tossing with the mixture. Add the parsley, tossing well.

Makes 3 to 4 servings

Nutritional information per serving

Calories	358	Cal. from Fat (%)	4.6	Sodium (mg)	512
Fat (g)	1.8	Saturated Fat (g)	0.3	Cholesterol (mg)	0

SENSATIONAL MEATLESS SPAGHETTI SAUCE ♥

This is a classic red sauce that you can put on the stove late in the afternoon and get other things done while it's cooking. It also reheats and freezes beautifully, so feel free to make a big batch the day before you need it, and be sure to put some in the freezer for another day.

1 onion, chopped
1 teaspoon minced garlic
¼ cup chopped parsley
1 green bell pepper, seeded and chopped
1 pound fresh mushrooms, chopped
2 (6-ounce) cans no-salt-added tomato paste
1 (28-ounce) can no-salt-added whole Italian tomatoes, chopped, with liquid

1 (15-ounce) can no-salt-added tomato sauce
1 cup water
1 tablespoon Worcestershire sauce
1 tablespoon sugar
½ cup dry red wine
1 tablespoon dried basil
2 bay leaves
1 (16-ounce) package spaghetti
Grated Parmesan cheese (optional)

In a large, heavy pot coated with nonstick cooking spray, sauté the onion and garlic over medium heat until tender, about 5 minutes. Add the parsley, green pepper, mushrooms, tomato paste, tomatoes, tomato sauce, water, Worcestershire sauce, sugar, wine, basil, and bay leaves. Simmer over low heat for at least 1 hour. It can simmer longer.

Cook the spaghetti according to package directions, omitting any oil and salt. Drain and serve with the sauce, from which the bay leaves have been removed and discarded. Sprinkle with the Parmesan cheese, if desired.

Makes 6 to 8 servings

Nutritional information per serving

Calories	334	Cal. from Fat (%)	5.5	Sodium (mg)	83
Fat (g)	2	Saturated Fat (g)	0.3	Cholesterol (mg)	0

MEATBALLS WITH TOMATO SAUCE

There's lots of the tangy sauce, which is great over pasta and freezes well.
A great standby family pleaser.

4 slices of whole wheat
   bread
½ cup water
2 pounds ground sirloin
2 tablespoons grated
   Parmesan cheese
2 large egg whites
½ teaspoon minced garlic

1 tablespoon chopped
   parsley or parsley flakes
1 teaspoon dried oregano
1 teaspoon dried basil
Tomato Sauce (recipe
   follows)
1 (16-ounce) package
   spaghetti

Preheat the broiler. Place the bread in the water in a small bowl for 2 minutes. Remove the bread and squeeze out the excess water. In a bowl, combine the sirloin, Parmesan cheese, egg whites, garlic, parsley, oregano, and basil with the softened bread. Mix well with a fork to combine. With moistened hands, shape the meat into balls. Place on a sheet coated with nonstick cooking spray and broil the meatballs for 5 to 7 minutes on each side. Add the meatballs to the Tomato Sauce in a saucepan on the stove. Meanwhile, cook the pasta according to package directions, omitting any oil and salt. Drain and serve with the meatballs and sauce.

Tomato Sauce

1 (14-ounce) can no-salt-
   added tomato puree
1 (28-ounce) can no-salt-
   added tomato sauce
1 (6-ounce) can no-salt-
   added tomato paste

¾ cup water
1 (0.7-ounce) package dry
   Italian dressing mix
1 teaspoon dried oregano
1 teaspoon dried basil

Combine the tomato puree, tomato sauce, tomato paste, water, Italian dressing mix, oregano, and basil in a large pot. Heat over medium heat until it begins to boil, about 5 to 7 minutes, and add the cooked meatballs.

Makes 6 to 8 servings

Nutritional Information per serving

Calories	562	Cal. from Fat (%)	17.3	Sodium (mg)	548
Fat (g)	10.8	Saturated Fat (g)	3.7	Cholesterol (mg)	74

MEAT SAUCE

*Meat Sauce freezes very well, so double the recipe and put it in contain-
ers. I always serve Meat Sauce over spaghetti, but be creative and use
your favorite type of pasta or whatever you happen to have on hand.
Serve with salad and bread and your meal is complete.*

1 celery stalk with leaves,
  finely chopped
1 carrot, peeled and finely
  chopped
1 onion, finely chopped
2 garlic cloves, minced
2 pounds ground sirloin
1 tablespoon dried oregano
½ cup dry red wine
1 (28-ounce) can no-salt-
  added plum tomatoes,
  roughly chopped, with
  their juices

2 tablespoons no-salt-added
  tomato paste
1 cup canned fat-free
  chicken broth
1 teaspoon sugar
Salt and pepper to taste
1 (16-ounce) package pasta
  of your choice (spaghetti,
  spirals, bow-ties)

In a heavy pot coated with nonstick cooking spray, sauté the celery,
carrot, onion, and garlic until tender, about 5 minutes. Add the
ground sirloin and oregano. Cook, stirring, until the meat begins to
brown, about 4 minutes. Add the wine and simmer for about 10
minutes. Then add the tomatoes, tomato paste, chicken broth, and
sugar. Simmer over medium heat for 30 minutes (it can simmer
longer). Add the salt and pepper. Meanwhile, cook the pasta according to package directions, omitting any oil and salt. Drain and serve
with the Meat Sauce.

Makes 6 to 8 servings

Nutritional information per serving

Calories	199	Cal. from Fat (%)	24.4	Sodium (mg)	150
Fat (g)	5.4	Saturated Fat (g)	1.8	Cholesterol (mg)	69

CHICKEN VERMICELLI

I always seem to make Chicken Vermicelli when I need to take a casserole to someone's home for a big group. You can always freeze the extra one so you have a delicious meal to pull out one night. For me, peace of mind is having a casserole in the freezer!

6 pounds skinless chicken pieces
Salt and pepper to taste
2 celery stalks, cut in half
2 onions, 1 halved and 1 chopped
1 (16-ounce) package vermicelli
1 tablespoon light stick margarine
1 green bell pepper, seeded and chopped
2 cups chopped celery
2 garlic cloves, minced
1 (8-ounce) can mushrooms, drained

1 cup all-purpose flour
4 cups reserved chicken broth
1 (10-ounce) can diced tomatoes and green chilies
¼ teaspoon cayenne pepper
Salt and pepper to taste
1 tablespoon Worcestershire sauce
½ cup grated Parmesan cheese
¼ cup chopped parsley
1 cup chopped green onions (scallions)

Preheat the oven to 300°F. Place the chicken in a large pot and add water to cover. Add the salt and pepper, celery, and halved onion and bring to a boil. Cook for 25 to 30 minutes, or until the chicken is done. Reserve the broth, discarding the celery and onion. Cool slightly, then debone the chicken and cut into bite-size pieces.

Meanwhile, cook the vermicelli according to package directions, omitting any oil and salt. Drain and set aside. In a large pot, melt the margarine over medium heat and sauté the chopped onion, green pepper, celery, and garlic until tender, about 5 minutes. Add the mushrooms. Gradually stir in the flour, mixing for 30 seconds. Gradually add the chicken broth, stirring. Add the tomatoes and green chilies, cayenne, salt and pepper, and Worcestershire sauce. Add the chicken and vermicelli, mixing well.

Divide the mixture into two 2-quart shallow casseroles coated with nonstick cooking spray. Top each casserole with the Parmesan cheese, parsley, and green onions and bake for 30 minutes.

Makes 16 servings

| Calories | 373 | Cal. from Fat (%) | 17.1 | Sodium (mg) | 319 |
| Fat (g) | 7.1 | Saturated Fat (g) | 1.9 | Cholesterol (mg) | 121 |

RIGATONI WITH ROASTED TOMATO SAUCE ♥

Even my sister, who doesn't really like to cook, prepared this pasta easily, so don't let roasting the tomatoes scare you. They give the sauce a rich, smoky flavor and a beautiful color.

1 (16-ounce) package
  rigatoni (tubular) pasta
8 to 10 Roma (plum)
  tomatoes
1 tablespoon minced garlic
½ cup sliced fresh
  mushrooms

¼ cup green peas
Salt and pepper to taste
1 tablespoon dried basil
¼ cup grated Parmesan
  cheese

Cook the rigatoni according to package directions, omitting any oil and salt. Drain and set aside. Meanwhile, preheat the broiler or grill and broil or grill the tomatoes until black on the outside, turning occasionally, about 15 minutes. Do not peel! Place in a food processor and puree; set aside.

In a large skillet coated with nonstick cooking spray, sauté the garlic over medium heat until light brown, about 2 minutes. Add the mushrooms and green peas and continue cooking until the mushrooms are tender, about 4 minutes. Add the tomato puree and cook 3 minutes. Add the salt and pepper, basil, and Parmesan cheese, mixing well. Toss with the rigatoni and serve.

Makes 6 servings

Nutritional information per serving

| Calories | 296 | Cal. from Fat (%) | 8.5 | Sodium (mg) | 81 |
| Fat (g) | 2.8 | Saturated Fat (g) | 0.9 | Cholesterol (mg) | 3 |

PASTA WITH CHICKEN AND VEGETABLES ♥

The bit of sugar used here balances the sourness of the vinegar. This is a great selection and one of my family's favorite pasta and chicken dishes.

1 tablespoon olive oil
2 large red bell peppers, seeded and cut into ½-inch slices
1 pound fresh mushrooms, halved
1 medium onion, chopped
1½ pounds skinless, boneless chicken breasts, cut into ¾-inch slices

¼ cup balsamic or red wine vinegar
1 teaspoon dried basil
½ teaspoon sugar
Pepper to taste
1 (14-ounce) can artichoke hearts, halved
1 (16-ounce) package rigatoni (tubular) pasta

In a large skillet, heat the olive oil and sauté the red peppers, mushrooms, and onion over medium heat until tender, about 6 minutes. Add the chicken slices, cooking and stirring until the chicken is done, about 6 minutes. Add the balsamic vinegar, basil, sugar, and pepper, stirring. Add the artichoke hearts. Meanwhile, cook the pasta according to package directions, omitting any oil and salt. Drain and toss with the chicken mixture.

Makes 6 to 8 servings

Nutritional information per serving

Calories	332	Cal. from Fat (%)	13.7	Sodium (mg)	147
Fat (g)	5	Saturated Fat (g)	1	Cholesterol (mg)	49

PASTA WITH STEAMED SHRIMP AND GREEN ONIONS

Covering the shrimp to steam with the other ingredients allows all of the flavors to mix together. If desired, toss with Parmesan cheese.

¼ cup olive oil
2 pounds large shrimp, peeled and deveined
2 tablespoons minced garlic
2 cups chopped green onions (scallions)

1 teaspoon hot sauce
Salt and pepper to taste
1 (16-ounce) package vermicelli

In a large pan, heat the olive oil over medium heat and add the shrimp, garlic, green onions, hot sauce, and salt and pepper. Cook,

stirring, until the shrimp are almost done, about 4 minutes. Cover,
turn the heat off, and let stand 20 minutes. Meanwhile, cook the
pasta according to package directions, omitting any oil and salt.
Drain and serve with the steamed shrimp and sauce.

Makes 6 to 8 servings

Nutritional information per serving

Calories	360	Cal. from Fat (%)	21.4	Sodium (mg)	151
Fat (g)	8.6	Saturated Fat (g)	1.3	Cholesterol (mg)	126

CHICKEN MEDITERRANEAN PASTA ♥

*My mother-in-law came over and enjoyed this dish for dinner, then
again cold the next day as a chicken pasta salad. You can always leave the
chicken out for a vegetarian dish or make it with leftover chicken if you
have it. To reduce the sodium, you can use less of the capers or black olives.*

2 tablespoons olive oil
1 cup chopped onion
2 tablespoons minced garlic
Salt and pepper to taste
1 tablespoon dried basil
1 teaspoon dried thyme
1 (10-ounce) can diced green
chilies and tomatoes
1 (8-ounce) can no-salt-
added tomato sauce
4 skinless, boneless chicken
breast halves

1 (3½-ounce) bottle capers,
drained
1 (2¼-ounce) can chopped
black olives, drained
1 (16-ounce) package
linguine pasta
¼ cup grated Parmesan
cheese
½ cup finely minced parsley

Heat the olive oil in a saucepan over medium heat. Sauté the onion
and garlic over medium heat until transparent, about 4 minutes. Add
the basil, thyme, chilies and tomatoes, tomato sauce, and chicken.
Season with the salt and pepper. Simmer slowly for 15 to 20 minutes,
stirring occasionally. Add the capers and olives. Meanwhile, cook the
pasta according to package directions, omitting any oil and salt.
Drain and toss with the Parmesan cheese. Pour the sauce over the
pasta, toss, sprinkle with the parsley, and serve immediately.

Makes 6 servings

Nutritional information per serving

Calories	503	Cal. from Fat (%)	18.6	Sodium (mg)	880
Fat (g)	10.4	Saturated Fat (g)	2.2	Cholesterol (mg)	51

SHRIMP AND ZITI PASTA

I know you have to use an extra saucepan, but it's really not much trouble; I promise—it's well worth the effort! This pasta has a creamy sauce but, happily, no cream.

1 (16-ounce) package ziti pasta	2 cups canned fat-free chicken broth
3 ounces Canadian bacon, chopped	½ cup white wine (optional)
2 pounds medium shrimp, peeled	¼ teaspoon crushed red pepper flakes
1 onion, chopped	½ tablespoon dried basil
2 tablespoons (¼ stick) light stick margarine	1 tablespoon chopped garlic
3 tablespoons all-purpose flour	1 teaspoon dried rosemary
	1 bunch green onions (scallions), thinly sliced

Cook the pasta according to package directions, omitting any oil and salt. Drain and keep warm. While the pasta is cooking, in a large pan coated with nonstick cooking spray, sauté the Canadian bacon, shrimp, and onion over medium heat until the shrimp begins to turn pink, about 4 minutes.

While the shrimp is cooking, melt the margarine in a saucepan over medium heat. Add the flour and gradually stir in the chicken broth to make a white sauce. Cook until thickened and set aside. If the shrimp has formed a lot of liquid, drain. To the shrimp add the wine, if using, and cook 1 minute. Add the red pepper flakes, basil, garlic, rosemary, green onions, and the white sauce and cook for 5 minutes, until thickened. Toss with the cooked pasta.

Makes 6 to 8 servings

Nutritional information per serving

Calories	354	Cal. from Fat (%)	10.5	Sodium (mg)	467
Fat (g)	4.1	Saturated Fat (g)	0.8	Cholesterol (mg)	142

FETTUCCINE WITH SHRIMP, TOMATOES, AND ARTICHOKE HEARTS

Since the tomatoes are drained, a light, delicate sauce is formed when you combine the chopped tomatoes with the chicken broth and white wine.

½ cup chopped onion
⅓ cup finely chopped celery
4 teaspoons minced garlic
⅓ cup all-purpose flour
1 (28-ounce) can no-salt-added Italian plum tomatoes, drained and coarsely chopped
1 (16-ounce) can fat-free chicken broth
1 (16-ounce) can no-salt-added Italian plum tomatoes, drained and coarsely chopped

1 cup dry white wine
1 tablespoon dried basil
2 (14-ounce) cans artichoke hearts, drained and halved
2 pounds large shrimp, peeled and deveined
1 (16-ounce) package fettuccine

In a large pot coated with nonstick cooking spray, sauté the onion and celery over medium heat until tender, about 5 minutes. Add the garlic and sauté 1 more minute. Sprinkle the flour over the vegetables. Stir in all the chicken broth, chopped canned tomatoes, white wine, and basil and bring to a boil. Reduce the heat to medium and cook until slightly thickened, stirring frequently, about 45 minutes. Add the artichoke hearts and shrimp, cooking until the shrimp are done, about 5 minutes.

Meanwhile, cook the pasta according to package directions, omitting any oil and salt. Drain and toss the sauce with the pasta.

Makes 6 to 8 servings

Nutritional information per serving

Calories	397	Cal. from Fat (%)	5.2	Sodium (mg)	491
Fat (g)	2.3	Saturated Fat (g)	0.4	Cholesterol (mg)	136

GREEK SHRIMP AND PASTA

You can always substitute chicken for the shrimp or skip it altogether and serve it plain as a side dish.

1 (8-ounce) package
   tricolored rotini
1 bunch green onions
   (scallions), chopped
1 teaspoon minced garlic
¼ cup white wine (optional)
1 (28-ounce) can no-salt-
   added whole tomatoes,
   drained and chopped

1 tablespoon dried basil
½ teaspoon dried oregano
1 pound medium shrimp,
   peeled
1 tablespoon chopped
   parsley
¼ cup crumbled feta cheese

Cook the pasta according to package directions, omitting any oil and salt. Drain, set aside, and keep warm. Meanwhile, in a large skillet coated with nonstick cooking spray over medium-high heat, sauté the green onions and garlic for 1 minute, stirring frequently. Stir in the wine, if using, tomatoes, basil, and oregano. Cook for several minutes, stirring occasionally. Add the shrimp and cook until the shrimp are done, about 5 minutes; then add the parsley. To serve, place the pasta on plates or a serving dish and top with the shrimp sauce and crumbled feta cheese.

Makes 4 servings

Nutritional information per serving

| Calories | 383 | Cal. from Fat (%) | 10.6 | Sodium (mg) | 214 |
| Fat (g) | 4.5 | Saturated Fat (g) | 1.9 | Cholesterol (mg) | 132 |

TUNA PASTA CASSEROLE ♥

I usually do not like cooked canned tuna, but I love this recipe! The dill-weed complements the flavor and the peas make it very eye-appealing.

1 cup sliced fresh
   mushrooms
1 cup chopped onions
⅓ cup chopped celery
¼ teaspoon minced garlic
¾ cup skim milk
¼ cup reduced-fat
   mayonnaise
1 teaspoon dried dillweed
Salt and pepper to taste

1 (10¾-ounce) can reduced-
   fat cream of celery soup
1 (8-ounce) package rotini
   pasta
1 cup frozen green peas
1 (6¼-ounce) can tuna fish,
   packed in water, drained
1 (2-ounce) jar diced
   pimiento, drained

Preheat the oven to 350°F. In a large skillet coated with nonstick cooking spray, sauté the mushrooms, onions, celery, and garlic over medium heat until tender, about 5 minutes. Set aside. In a large bowl, combine the milk, mayonnaise, dillweed, salt and pepper, and cream of celery soup. Meanwhile, cook the rotini according to package directions, omitting any oil and salt. Drain and add to the soup mixture. Fold the mushroom mixture, peas, tuna fish, and pimiento into the rotini mixture. Transfer the mixture into a 2-quart casserole dish coated with nonstick cooking spray and bake, covered, for 40 minutes.

Makes 6 servings

Nutritional information per serving

Calories	264	Cal. from Fat (%)	17.7	Sodium (mg)	421
Fat (g)	5.2	Saturated Fat (g)	1.1	Cholesterol (mg)	10

SCALLOPS WITH PASTA ♥

This scallop recipe with its creamy sauce is one of my father's favorites.

⅓ cup plus ¼ cup dry white
  wine
1 tablespoon lemon juice
¾ pound bay scallops
2 tablespoons (¼ stick) light
  stick margarine
½ pound fresh mushrooms,
  thickly sliced
½ cup sliced green onions
  (scallions)

2 tablespoons all-purpose
  flour
1 (5-ounce) can evaporated
  skimmed milk
Salt and pepper to taste
1 (8-ounce) package rotini
  pasta

In a small pot, combine the ⅓ cup white wine, lemon juice, and scallops. Cook about 5 minutes, or until the scallops are opaque. Drain and set aside. In another pan, melt the margarine and sauté the mushrooms and green onions over medium heat until tender, about 5 minutes. Stir in the flour. Gradually add the evaporated skimmed milk. Season with salt and pepper. Return the cooked scallops to the pan. Stir in the remaining ¼ cup white wine. Meanwhile, cook the rotini according to package directions, omitting any oil and salt. Drain and toss with the scallops and sauce.

Makes 4 servings

Nutritional information per serving

Calories	359	Cal. from Fat (%)	11.9	Sodium (mg)	261
Fat (g)	4.7	Saturated Fat (g)	0.8	Cholesterol (mg)	30

SOUTHWESTERN DISHES

BAKED MEXICAN SPINACH DIP ♥

Serve this tasty dip with reduced-fat chips or crackers or as a side dish.

1 onion, chopped
3 garlic cloves, minced
3 medium tomatoes, chopped
2 tablespoons chopped jalapeño peppers
3 (10-ounce) packages frozen chopped spinach, cooked according to package directions and drained well

½ cup shredded reduced-fat Monterey Jack cheese
4 ounces fat-free cream cheese, cut into ½-inch cubes
1 cup skim milk
Salt and pepper to taste

In a 12-inch skillet coated with nonstick cooking spray, sauté the onion over medium heat until tender, about 5 minutes. Add the garlic, chopped tomatoes, and jalapeño peppers, sautéing for 3 minutes. Add the cooked spinach and cheeses, stirring until the cheeses are melted. Gradually add the skim milk, stirring. Add the salt and pepper.

Makes 8 servings (2 cups)

Nutritional information per serving (approximately ¼ cup)

Calories	105	Cal. from Fat (%)	24.9	Sodium (mg)	271
Fat (g)	2.9	Saturated Fat (g)	1.6	Cholesterol (mg)	13

SOUTHWESTERN DISHES

CORN AND ZUCCHINI SALSA

This salsa is great over chicken or fish, as well as served with crackers or chips for scooping. It's colorful, full of texture, and tastes great.

1 zucchini, thinly sliced	1 (15-ounce) can black
1 teaspoon minced garlic	beans, rinsed and drained
2 teaspoons finely chopped	1 cup chopped tomato
jalapeño pepper	½ cup thinly sliced green
1 teaspoon ground cumin	onions (scallions)
¼ teaspoon pepper	1 tablespoon chopped
1 (11-ounce) can Mexicorn,	parsley or cilantro
drained	

In a skillet coated with nonstick cooking spray, sauté the zucchini over medium heat until tender, about 4 minutes. Add the garlic, jalapeño pepper, cumin, pepper, corn, black beans, tomato, green onions, and parsley. Serve warm.

Makes 6 four-cup servings

Nutritional information per serving (approximately 1 cup)

Calories	117	Cal. from Fat (%)	5.9	Sodium (mg)	325
Fat (g)	0.8	Saturated Fat (g)	0.1	Cholesterol (mg)	0

TEX-MEX DIP ♥

Whenever you serve this recipe at a party, there will be a crowd around the bowl. This is one of those dips that is hard to quit eating; it's one of my all-time favorites!

1 cup nonfat sour cream	1 bunch green onions
½ cup fat-free mayonnaise	(scallions), chopped
1 (1¼-ounce) package taco	1 (3½-ounce) can pitted ripe
seasoning mix	olives, drained and
1 (16-ounce) can fat-free	coarsely chopped
refried beans	1 cup shredded reduced-fat
1 large tomato, chopped	sharp Cheddar cheese

Combine the sour cream, mayonnaise, and taco seasoning mix in a bowl. To assemble, spread the refried beans on a large shallow serving plate, then spread the sour cream–taco mixture over the beans. Sprinkle with the tomato, chopped green onions, and olives. Top with the shredded Cheddar cheese. Serve chilled.

Makes 15 to 20 servings

| Calories | 60 | Cal. from Fat (%) 19.5 | Sodium (mg) | 206 |
| Fat (g) | 1.3 | Saturated Fat (g) 0.7 | Cholesterol (mg) | 5 |

TAMALES ♥

I was so excited that my tamales came out so well. In fact, I thought they tasted like the ones you get at a restaurant. They are not difficult but do take a little time to make. The good news is this recipe makes a lot and freezes very well. I froze mine in zip-top plastic bags. You can find tamale papers in many grocery stores today.

2 pounds ground sirloin	Tamale papers, soaked in
1 (14-ounce) can enchilada	water for 30 minutes
sauce	2 (46-ounce) cans 100%
3 cups self-rising yellow	vegetable juice (V-8)
cornmeal mix	2 (2.12-ounce) bottles mild
2 cups water	chili powder

Preheat the oven to 325°F. In a large bowl, combine the ground sirloin and enchilada sauce, cover with plastic wrap, and refrigerate overnight. The next day, mix the cornmeal mix and water, stirring well. Take about 1½ tablespoons meat and mold the cornmeal mixture around to coat the outside. Then wrap each prepared tamale in a tamale paper, folding the ends. Lay, seam side down, in a very large roasting pan. You can place a second layer of tamales on top of the bottom layer in the pan.

Pour the vegetable juice and sprinkle the chili powder over all the prepared tamales, using half on the bottom layer, if needed. Cover tightly and bake for 2 hours. Do not open while cooking.

Makes 36 to 48 tamales

Nutritional information per tamale

| Calories | 70 | Cal. from Fat (%) 28.1 | Sodium (mg) | 267 |
| Fat (g) | 2.2 | Saturated Fat (g) 0.6 | Cholesterol (mg) | 11 |

SOUTHWESTERN DISHES

MEXICAN TAMALE DIP ♥

If you don't have homemade tamales in the freezer, try to locate some in the freezer section of the grocery store or in a specialty store. You can use canned tamales, but your fat content will be higher. Serve this dip with reduced-fat chips.

1 onion, chopped
2 garlic cloves, minced
1 (14½-ounce) can diced
   tomatoes and green chilies
1 (14-ounce) can no-salt-
   added whole tomatoes,
   chopped
1 (6-ounce) can no-salt-
   added tomato paste

1 (1¼-ounce) package taco
   seasoning mix
6 homemade tamales,
   chopped (page 131)
1 cup shredded reduced-fat
   sharp Cheddar cheese

Heat the onion, garlic, tomatoes and chilies, tomatoes, and tomato paste in a saucepan coated with nonstick cooking spray for 20 minutes, stirring. Add the taco seasoning mix and tamales, stirring until heated. Place in a serving dish and sprinkle with cheese. Allow the cheese to melt or run it under the broiler, watching carefully.

Makes 8 to 10 servings

Nutritional information per ½-cup serving

Calories	25	Cal. from Fat (%)	21.6	Sodium (mg)	92
Fat (g)	0.6	Saturated Fat (g)	0.3	Cholesterol (mg)	1

BLACK BEAN SOUP ♥

In Florida, Black Bean Soup is served thick over cooked rice with chopped onion on top, Cuban style. I enjoy it this way very much and it makes a complete meal.

1 (1-pound) package black
   beans
1½ cups chopped onion
4 garlic cloves, minced
½ cup chopped green bell
   pepper
½ cup chopped celery
4 ounces lean ham, chopped

8 cups water
1 teaspoon Worcestershire
   sauce
1 teaspoon sugar
1 teaspoon ground cumin
4 bay leaves
Salt and pepper to taste

Rinse and sort the beans, then soak the beans, overnight in water. Drain the beans. In a large pot coated with nonstick cooking spray, sauté the onion, garlic, green pepper, celery, and ham over medium-low heat until tender, about 5 minutes. Add the beans, water, Worcestershire sauce, sugar, cumin, and bay leaves. Cook over low heat for 2 hours, or until beans are tender, adding water if needed. Add the salt and pepper. Discard the bay leaves before serving.

Makes 6 to 8 one-cup servings

Nutritional information per serving

Calories	219	Cal. from Fat (%)	6.6	Sodium (mg)	222
Fat (g)	1.6	Saturated Fat (g)	0.4	Cholesterol (mg)	7

TORTILLA SOUP

This wonderful Tortilla Soup will become a quick favorite, with or without the smoked turkey breast.

1 large onion, chopped
½ cup chopped celery
1 green bell pepper, seeded and chopped
1 tablespoon minced garlic
1 (4-ounce) can chopped green chilies
1 (28-ounce) can no-salt-added Italian plum tomatoes, drained and chopped
1 teaspoon ground cumin
1 teaspoon chili powder
1 teaspoon dried oregano

2 (14½-ounce) cans fat-free chicken broth
2 (14-ounce) cans vegetable broth
1 cup chopped smoked turkey breast
5 (6-inch) flour tortillas, cut into ¼-inch strips
½ cup chopped green onion stems (scallions) (white part reserved for another use)
⅔ cup shredded reduced-fat Monterey Jack cheese

Preheat the oven to 350°F. In a heavy pot coated with nonstick cooking spray, sauté the onion, celery, green pepper, garlic, and green chilies over medium-low heat until tender. Gradually add the tomatoes, cumin, chili powder, oregano, chicken broth, vegetable broth, and turkey. Bring the soup to a boil, lower the heat, and cook for 15 minutes. While the soup is cooking, place the tortilla strips on a baking sheet and bake for 10 to 15 minutes, until crisp. Serve the soup in bowls, topped with the green onions, cheese, and tortilla strips.

Makes 10 one-cup servings

Nutritional information per serving

Calories	140	Cal. from Fat (%)	22.5	Sodium (mg)	1,017
Fat (g)	3.5	Saturated Fat (g)	1.1	Cholesterol (mg)	11

CHILI

On a cold night, we love a chili dinner, so I make a big pot and freeze the extra. Serve the chili with shredded reduced-fat Cheddar cheese, chopped fresh cilantro, and nonfat sour cream for the deluxe version.

2 onions, chopped
1 red bell pepper, seeded
    and finely chopped
1 tablespoon minced garlic
3 pounds ground sirloin
2 (15-ounce) cans black
    beans, rinsed and drained
1 (28-ounce) can no-salt-
    added whole tomatoes,
    chopped, with their juice
1 (12-ounce) can no-salt-
    added tomato paste

1 (14-ounce) can no-salt-
    added Italian-style
    tomatoes, chopped, with
    their juice
1 (7-ounce) can chopped
    green chilies, undrained
1 (12-ounce) can light beer
⅓ to ½ cup chili powder
1 tablespoon dried basil
1 tablespoon dried oregano
1 tablespoon ground cumin
Salt and pepper to taste

In a large pot coated with nonstick cooking spray, sauté the onions, red pepper, and garlic over medium-high heat, stirring constantly until the vegetables are tender, about 5 minutes. Add the ground sirloin, cooking until the meat is browned, about 6 minutes. Drain off any excess grease. Stir in the black beans, tomatoes, Italian-style tomato paste, tomatoes, green chilies, beer, chili powder, basil, oregano, cumin, and salt and pepper and bring to a boil. Cover, reduce the heat, and simmer 30 minutes.

Makes 8 to 10 one-cup servings

Nutritional information per serving

Calories	353	Cal. from Fat (%)	22.9	Sodium (mg)	702
Fat (g)	9	Saturated Fat (g)	2.9	Cholesterol (mg)	81

MEXICAN LASAGNE

Mexican Lasagne is a popular recipe for my family. It serves a crowd easily and I sometimes serve it with extra salsa on the side.

1½ pounds ground sirloin
1 large onion, chopped
2 garlic cloves, minced
2 tablespoons chili powder
1 (10-ounce) can enchilada
  sauce, divided
1 (10-ounce) can diced
  tomatoes and green chilies
1 (15-ounce) container fat-
  free ricotta cheese

1 large egg white
8 ounces reduced-fat
  Monterey Jack cheese,
  shredded
8 flour tortillas, quartered
½ cup chopped green onions
  (scallions)

Preheat the oven to 350°F. In a large pot, brown the meat, onion, and garlic over medium heat until the meat is cooked, about 7 minutes. Drain off any excess fat. Sprinkle the chili powder over the meat and mix well. Add ½ cup enchilada sauce and the green chilies and tomatoes and simmer 15 minutes. In a bowl, beat the ricotta cheese and egg white together; set aside.

Spread ⅓ of the meat mixture in the bottom of a deep 3-quart casserole coated with nonstick cooking spray. Cover with half of the Monterey Jack cheese, half of the ricotta cheese mixture, half of the tortillas, and half of the remaining enchilada sauce. Repeat the layers, finishing with a final layer of meat. Bake for 30 minutes, or until bubbly. Sprinkle with the chopped green onions. The casserole can be prepared a day ahead and refrigerated.

Makes 8 to 10 servings

Nutritional information per serving

Calories	343	Cal. from Fat (%)	29.9	Sodium (mg)	967
Fat (g)	11.4	Saturated Fat (g)	0.9	Cholesterol (mg)	57

SOUTHWESTERN ROUND STEAK

Unbelievable, fantastic, full of flavor, and sure to win friends—I can't think of enough good things to say about this recipe. Don't let the term "butterfly" scare you—just ask your butcher to do it for you. He or she will split the meat in half to fill with stuffing. Flank steak can also be used.

¾ cup lemon juice
1 teaspoon ground cumin, divided
⅓ cup Worcestershire sauce
1 teaspoon minced garlic
1 teaspoon liquid smoke
½ teaspoon pepper
1 (1¾- to 2-pound) top round steak, butterflied (*brociolini* steak)
1 (10-ounce) package frozen chopped spinach, thawed and well drained

1 red bell pepper, seeded and cut into thin strips
½ cup finely chopped onion
1 (4-ounce) can chopped green chilies, drained
1 garlic clove, minced
½ teaspoon chili powder
¼ cup shredded reduced-fat Monterey Jack cheese

Preheat the oven to 350°F. Combine the lemon juice, ½ teaspoon cumin, Worcestershire sauce, garlic, liquid smoke, and pepper in a bowl; stir well. Place the steak in a large heavy-duty, zip-top plastic bag. Pour the marinade mixture over the steak. Seal the bag securely and place in the refrigerator to marinate for 8 hours, turning occasionally.

Remove the steak from the marinade, discarding the marinade. Open the steak and spread the spinach in the inside to within ½ inch of the edges; top with the red pepper and onion. In a small bowl, combine the chilies, garlic, remaining ½ teaspoon cumin, and chili powder; spread the chile mixture over the pepper and onion layer. Sprinkle with the cheese. Roll the steak up jelly-roll fashion, starting at the long side. Place, seam side down, in a baking dish and bake for 45 minutes. Let stand 5 minutes before slicing into pinwheels.

Makes 6 servings

Nutritional information per serving

Calories	239	Cal. from Fat (%)	29.8	Sodium (mg)	473
Fat (g)	7.9	Saturated Fat (g)	3.2	Cholesterol (mg)	71

SOUTHWESTERN CHICKEN LASAGNE ♥

This is an exciting twist on lasagne. It's a snap to put together because you don't have to cook the noodles separately. This freezes very well. It's great served with extra salsa, too.

SAUCE
½ medium onion
1 (28-ounce) can no-salt-added whole tomatoes with juice
1 (14-ounce) jar picante sauce or salsa
1 (1¼-ounce) package taco seasoning mix
1 (16-ounce) can black beans, rinsed and drained
2 large egg whites
1 cup reduced-fat ricotta cheese

1 (8-ounce) package lasagna noodles
4 skinless, boneless chicken breast halves (about 1 pound), cut in 1-inch pieces
1 (4-ounce) can chopped green chilies
1 (8-ounce) package reduced-fat Monterey Jack cheese, shredded

Preheat the oven to 350°F. In a food processor with the metal blade, chop the onion. Add the tomatoes with their juice, salsa, and taco seasoning and pulse until the tomatoes are in small pieces, 3 or 4 times. Remove to a medium bowl and stir in the beans to make the sauce. In a small bowl, mix the egg whites with the ricotta cheese; set aside.

Spread 1 cup of the bean sauce over the bottom of a 13 × 9 × 2-inch casserole dish coated with nonstick cooking spray. Top with 5 noodles, overlapping slightly. Sprinkle with half the chicken, half the chilies, and 2 more cups of the sauce. Spoon out the ricotta cheese mixture and spread it out lightly. Top with half the shredded cheese, 5 more remaining noodles, and the remaining chicken, chilies, sauce, and cheese. Bake, uncovered, for 40 minutes, or until the noodles are tender when pierced with a sharp knife. Cool at least 20 minutes before serving.

Makes 12 servings

Nutritional information per serving

Calories	244	Cal. from Fat (%)	22.9	Sodium (mg)	717
Fat (g)	6.2	Saturated Fat (g)	3	Cholesterol (mg)	56

CHICKEN CHILI CON QUESO

I always think cheese just makes a recipe even better, so this recipe is pretty near perfect. Serve with sliced green onions (scallions) and chopped cilantro to sprinkle on at the table.

1 pound skinless, boneless chicken breasts, cut into ¾-inch pieces
1 large onion, chopped
1 large green bell pepper, seeded and coarsely chopped
1 large red bell pepper, seeded and coarsely chopped
1 tablespoon chili powder

2 teaspoons ground cumin
2 (15-ounce) cans kidney beans, rinsed and drained
1 (28-ounce) can no-salt-added whole tomatoes, coarsely chopped, with their juice
1 (10-ounce) can diced tomatoes and green chilies
8 ounces light pasteurized processed cheese spread

In a large pot coated with nonstick cooking spray, cook the chicken, onion, and green and red peppers over medium heat until the chicken loses its pink color, about 4 minutes. Sprinkle the chili powder and cumin over the chicken and vegetables. Add the beans, tomatoes, and chopped tomatoes and green chilies. Bring to a boil. Reduce the heat, cover, and simmer 20 minutes. Add the cheese spread and stir until melted and well blended.

Makes 8 to 10 one-cup servings

Nutritional information per serving

Calories	212	Cal. from Fat (%)	18.3	Sodium (mg)	634
Fat (g)	4.3	Saturated Fat (g)	2	Cholesterol (mg)	34

SOUTHWESTERN QUICHE

If you're in the Southwestern mode, you can even enjoy a regional break-fast. This could also be a light dinner or lunch.

4 (8½-inch) flour tortillas
½ cup shredded reduced-fat Cheddar cheese
1 (4-ounce) can chopped green chilies, drained
¼ cup sliced green onions (scallions)

⅓ cup picante sauce
3 large eggs
3 large egg whites
⅓ cup nonfat plain yogurt
½ teaspoon chili powder
¼ teaspoon pepper

Preheat the oven to 350°F. In a pie plate coated with nonstick cooking spray, layer all 4 tortillas, overlapping to cover the pie plate. Sprinkle the cheese, chilies, and green onions over the tortillas, then cover with the picante sauce. Combine the eggs, egg whites, yogurt, chili powder, and pepper in a small bowl and pour into the dish. Bake for 40 to 45 minutes. Let stand 5 minutes, then cut into wedges and serve hot.

Makes 8 servings

Nutritional information per serving

Calories	178	Cal. from Fat (%) 28.8		Sodium (mg)	481
Fat (g)	5.7	Saturated Fat (g)	1.9	Cholesterol (mg)	13

SOUTHWESTERN RICE SALAD

This is a full-flavored rice salad that is hearty enough to eat on its own, but it also makes an outstanding side dish to grilled chicken and other meals. Another make-ahead lifesaver!

1 (16-ounce) can black
  beans, rinsed and drained
2 cups cooked rice
1 medium tomato, seeded
  and chopped
1 red bell pepper, seeded
  and chopped
½ cup chopped fresh
  cilantro leaves

1 bunch green onions
  (scallions), sliced
1 small jalapeño pepper,
  seeded
¼ cup olive oil
¼ cup lime juice
½ teaspoon ground cumin
1 cup shredded reduced-fat
  mild Cheddar cheese

In a large bowl, combine the beans, rice, tomato, bell pepper, cilantro, and green onions. Drop the jalapeño through the feed tube of a food processor while the machine is running and process until minced. Pour in the oil, lime juice, and cumin and process until well blended. Toss the dressing with the bean mixture. Cover and chill at least 2 hours or overnight. Just before serving, toss the cheese with the salad.

Makes 10 to 12 servings

Nutritional information per serving

Calories	291	Cal. from Fat (%) 22.6		Sodium (mg)	296
Fat (g)	7.3	Saturated Fat (g)	2.7	Cholesterol (mg)	10

SPICY SOUTHWESTERN PASTA

I'm a fan of Southwestern recipes, as you've probably figured out. Vegetarians as well as pasta lovers will put this recipe high on their lists.

½ teaspoon ground cumin
1 (28-ounce) can no-salt-
  added whole tomatoes,
  pureed, with their juice
1 onion, chopped
1½ teaspoons chili powder
1 teaspoon dried oregano
½ teaspoon minced garlic
½ teaspoon sugar
¼ teaspoon ground
  cinnamon
¼ teaspoon red pepper
  flakes

Salt and pepper to taste
1 (16-ounce) package rotini
1 (16-ounce) can black
  beans, drained and rinsed
1 (10-ounce) package
  frozen corn
1 (4½-ounce) can chopped
  green chilies, drained
1 cup shredded reduced-fat
  Cheddar cheese (optional)

Heat a large pot coated with nonstick cooking spray to medium heat, and add the cumin, stirring for 1 minute. Add the tomato puree, onion, chili powder, oregano, garlic, sugar, cinnamon, red pepper flakes, and salt and pepper. Bring to a boil, reduce the heat, and simmer, covered, to blend the flavors, 20 to 25 minutes. Meanwhile, cook the pasta according to package directions, omitting any oil and salt. Drain well and keep hot. Stir the black beans, corn, and green chilies into the sauce. Cook until the corn is crisp-tender, about 5 minutes. Remove from the heat. To serve, toss the black bean mixture with the pasta. If desired, serve with shredded reduced-fat Cheddar cheese.

Makes 6 to 8 servings

Nutritional information per serving

Calories	362	Cal. from Fat (%)	10.4	Sodium (mg)	491
Fat (g)	4.2	Saturated Fat (g)	2.1	Cholesterol (mg)	10

SOUTHWESTERN GRITS

Depending on how hot you like your grits, use more or less green chilies.

1 cup grits
4 ounces light pasteurized
  processed cheese spread
½ cup shredded reduced-fat
  sharp Cheddar cheese

1 teaspoon dry mustard
¼ cup picante sauce
2 tablespoons chopped,
  drained canned green
  chilies

Cook the grits according to package directions in a large saucepan; remove from the heat. Add the cheese spread and Cheddar cheese; mix until melted. Add the dry mustard, picante sauce, and green chilies and mix well. Serve immediately.

Makes 8 servings

Nutritional information per serving

Calories	126	Cal. from Fat (%)	22.9	Sodium (mg)	336
Fat (g)	3.2	Saturated Fat (g)	2	Cholesterol (mg)	10

SOUTHWESTERN PASTA SALAD

The small amount of chili powder used here gives this pasta salad a great flavor. Since this is a plain pasta salad, it's great to serve with a salad medley featuring lots of different kinds.

4 cups pasta spirals
¾ cup finely chopped red
  bell pepper
½ cup finely chopped
  red onion
2 tablespoons chopped
  jalapeño pepper
2 tablespoons fat-free
  mayonnaise

2 tablespoons nonfat sour
  cream
¼ teaspoon chili powder
1 tablespoon red wine
  vinegar
Salt and pepper to taste
2 tablespoons chopped fresh
  cilantro (optional)

Cook the pasta according to package directions, omitting any oil and salt. Drain and cool. Combine the pasta, red pepper, onion, and jalapeños in a large bowl. In a small bowl, combine the mayonnaise, sour cream, chili powder, and vinegar. Toss with the pasta and season with the salt and pepper. Add the cilantro, if desired.

Makes 4 servings

Nutritional information per serving

Calories	433	Cal. from Fat (%)	4.2	Sodium (mg)	127
Fat (g)	2	Saturated Fat (g)	0.3	Cholesterol (mg)	1

VEGETARIAN ENTRÉES

This is a wonderful recipe and I will gladly make a meal out of this dish any night. You can even use the sauce with pasta—it's a fantastic tomato sauce. This dish can be doubled and half of the recipe can be frozen in the baking dish for a quick dinner at a later date. This recipe appeared in Cooking Light Magazine *in the "Make It Light" section of the October 1995 issue.*

SAUCE
1 (28-ounce) can no-salt-added peeled tomatoes, coarsely chopped, with their juice
2 (15-ounce) cans no-salt-added tomato sauce
1 (6-ounce) can no-salt-added tomato paste
½ cup white wine
1 teaspoon minced garlic

1 tablespoon dried basil
1 tablespoon dried oregano

2 eggplants, peeled and cut into ½-inch slices
3 large egg whites
¼ cup water
1½ cups seasoned bread crumbs
3 cups shredded reduced-fat mozzarella cheese

Preheat the broiler. In a large saucepan, make the sauce by combining the tomatoes with juice, tomato sauce, tomato paste, white wine, garlic, basil, and oregano. Bring to a boil, lower the heat, and cook 20 minutes. Meanwhile, soak the eggplant slices in water to cover for 30 minutes. Pat dry.

In a bowl, mix the egg whites and ¼ cup water together with a fork. Dip the eggplant slices in the egg white mixture and roll in the bread crumbs. Place on a baking sheet coated with nonstick cooking spray and broil 5 minutes on each side, until lightly browned. Watch closely. Remove and set aside. Lower the oven temperature to 350°F. In a 2-quart oblong baking dish, layer half the sauce, half the eggplant, and half the mozzarella cheese. Repeat the layers. Bake for 30 minutes, or until bubbly and the cheese is melted.

Makes 8 servings

Nutritional information per serving

Calories	293	Cal. from Fat (%)	25.2	Sodium (mg)	741
Fat (g)	8.2	Saturated Fat (g)	4.6	Cholesterol (mg)	25

EGGPLANT AND PEPPER BAKE

This dish is so good that it is hard to believe it is just veggies. And nothing could be faster to throw together. Leftovers are yummy at room temperature.

1 tablespoon olive oil
1 tablespoon minced garlic
1 onion, chopped
1 red bell pepper, seeded
   and sliced into strips
1 yellow bell pepper, seeded
   and sliced into strips
1 green bell pepper, seeded
   and sliced into strips

1 pound fresh mushrooms,
   sliced
1 large eggplant, peeled and
   cubed
¼ cup grated fat-free
   Parmesan cheese
Salt and pepper to taste

Preheat the oven to 350°F. In a large skillet, heat the olive oil and sauté the garlic, onion, peppers, mushrooms, and eggplant until tender, about 5 minutes. Add the Parmesan cheese and salt and pepper. Transfer to a baking dish coated with nonstick cooking spray and bake, covered, for 1 hour, until cooked through.

Makes 4 to 6 servings

Nutritional information per serving

Calories	91	Cal. from Fat (%)	28.7	Sodium (mg)	70
Fat (g)	2.9	Saturated Fat (g)	0.4	Cholesterol (mg)	0

ITALIAN SPINACH PIE

This is the perfect type of dish to serve when you have vegetarians and meat eaters at one table. It is a special spinach side dish, too, for any chicken or beef main course and a delicious main dish in its own right.

½ cup chopped onions
2 (10-ounce) packages frozen
   chopped spinach
1 (14½-ounce) can artichoke
   hearts, quartered
1 cup fat-free ricotta cheese
¼ cup skim milk
2 large egg whites, beaten
   with a fork

½ teaspoon garlic powder
1 (8-ounce) can no-salt-
   added tomato sauce
½ teaspoon dried oregano
½ teaspoon dried basil
½ cup shredded part-skim
   mozzarella cheese

Preheat the oven to 350°F. In a skillet coated with nonstick cooking spray, sauté the onions over medium heat until tender, about 5 minutes. Meanwhile, cook the spinach according to package direc-

tions; drain very well. In a large bowl, combine the onions, artichoke hearts, spinach, ricotta cheese, milk, egg whites, and garlic
powder, mixing well. Spoon the mixture into a 9-inch pie plate
coated with nonstick cooking spray. Mix the tomato sauce with the
oregano and basil and spread evenly over the spinach. Bake for 15
minutes. Sprinkle with the mozzarella cheese and continue baking
for 5 to 10 minutes longer, until the cheese is melted.

Makes 6 servings

Nutritional information per serving

Calories	119	Cal. from Fat (%)	14.4	Sodium (mg)	207
Fat (g)	1.9	Saturated Fat (g)	1	Cholesterol (mg)	6

SPEEDY BEAN SOUP ♥

*Why in the world would you serve bean soup from a can when this
scrumptious homemade soup can be on the table in about twenty minutes?
And fifteen of those minutes require no attention from you—what a
lovely bonus!*

½ cup chopped onion
1 green bell pepper, seeded
and chopped
1 garlic clove, minced
1 (15-ounce) can Great
Northern beans, drained
and rinsed

1 (15-ounce) can garbanzo
beans, drained and rinsed
1 (14½-ounce) can vegetable
broth
1 tablespoon chili powder
Grated Parmesan cheese
(optional)

In a large saucepan coated with nonstick cooking spray, sauté the
onion, bell pepper, and garlic over medium heat for about 5 minutes, stirring until tender. Add the Great Northern beans, garbanzo
beans, vegetable broth, and chili powder. Mix well and bring to a
boil. Reduce the heat, cover, and simmer 10 to 15 minutes, or until
thoroughly heated. Before serving, sprinkle with Parmesan cheese,
if desired.

Makes 4 servings

Nutritional information per serving

Calories	219	Cal. from Fat (%)	11.9	Sodium (mg)	787
Fat (g)	2.9	Saturated Fat (g)	0.3	Cholesterol (mg)	0

BAKED MACARONI AND CHEESE PRIMAVERA ♥

Everyone loves macaroni and cheese and everyone loves pasta primavera, so what's not to love about this cheesy combination?

2 tablespoons (¼ stick) light
   stick margarine
⅓ cup all-purpose flour
2 cups skim milk
1 cup shredded reduced-fat
   Monterey Jack cheese
1 cup shredded reduced-fat
   Cheddar cheese
3 cups broccoli florets

1 (12-ounce) package cooked
   elbow macaroni
1 (10-ounce) package frozen
   peas
1 red bell pepper, seeded
   and chopped
Salt and pepper to taste
Paprika

Preheat the oven to 350°F. Melt the margarine in a medium saucepan, stir in the flour, and cook, stirring, for 1 minute. Gradually stir in the milk and heat to boiling, stirring constantly, until thickened. Remove from the heat and add the cheeses, stirring until melted.

Meanwhile, cook the broccoli florets in a microwaveproof bowl with a little water in the microwave, about 4 minutes, until crisptender. Combine the cooked macaroni, broccoli, peas, red pepper, and cheese sauce in a large bowl. Season with salt and pepper. Spoon the mixture into a 2-quart casserole coated with nonstick cooking spray. Sprinkle with paprika. Bake, covered, for 20 minutes. Uncover and continue baking for 10 minutes, until golden.

Makes 6 main-dish or 10 to 12 side-dish servings

Nutritional information per serving

Calories	223	Cal. from Fat (%) 20.6	Sodium (mg)	218
Fat (g)	5.1	Saturated Fat (g) 2.5	Cholesterol (mg)	15

CHEESE-STUFFED SHELLS ♥

The name of this recipe sounds decadent, the taste is pure indulgence, but the fat count is completely within the guidelines! This is one of those dishes you'll have a hard time convincing people is low-fat.

1 (12-ounce) carton low-fat cottage cheese
1 cup nonfat ricotta cheese
1 large egg, slightly beaten
2 tablespoons chopped parsley
½ teaspoon minced garlic
2 teaspoons dried basil, divided
2 teaspoons dried oregano, divided

⅓ cup grated Parmesan cheese
1 cup chopped onion
½ teaspoon minced garlic
1 (14½-ounce) can no-salt-added whole tomatoes, chopped, with their juice
1 (8-ounce) can no-salt-added tomato sauce
1 (12-ounce) package jumbo pasta shells

Preheat the oven to 375°F. Blend the cottage cheese and ricotta cheese in a large bowl. Add the egg, parsley, garlic, 1 teaspoon of the basil, 1 teaspoon of the oregano, and the Parmesan cheese; set aside. In a saucepan coated with nonstick cooking spray, sauté the onion and garlic over medium heat, until tender, about 5 minutes. Stir in the tomatoes, tomato sauce, and the remaining teaspoons of basil and oregano. Bring to a boil, reduce the heat, and simmer 15 minutes.

Meanwhile, cook the pasta according to package directions, omitting any oil and salt; drain well. Spoon the cheese mixture evenly into the shells and arrange the shells in a 2-quart baking dish coated with nonstick cooking spray. Pour the tomato mixture over the shells. Bake, covered, for 25 to 30 minutes.

Makes 8 servings

Nutritional information per serving

Calories	269	Cal. from Fat (%)	10.4	Sodium (mg)	292
Fat (g)	3.1	Saturated Fat (g)	1.3	Cholesterol (mg)	31

VEGETABLE LASAGNE

Don't turn the page because the instructions look slightly longer than the other lasagne recipes. It takes only a few more minutes and the spinach white sauce gives it a rich flavor.

2 cups chopped fresh broccoli florets
1½ cups thinly sliced peeled carrots
1 cup sliced green onions (scallions)
½ cup chopped red bell pepper
3 garlic cloves, minced
½ cup all-purpose flour
3 cups skim milk
Dash of nutmeg

¼ cup grated Parmesan cheese
Salt and pepper to taste
1 (10-ounce) package frozen chopped spinach, thawed and squeezed dry
1½ cups nonfat cottage cheese
1 cup shredded part-skim mozzarella cheese
12 lasagna noodles

Preheat the oven to 375°F In a large pot coated with nonstick cooking spray, sauté the broccoli, carrots, onions, red bell pepper, and garlic over medium heat until tender, about 7 minutes; set aside. Place the flour in a medium saucepan. Gradually add the milk, stirring with a wire whisk until blended. Bring to a boil over medium heat and cook 5 minutes, or until thickened, stirring constantly. Add the nutmeg, Parmesan cheese, and salt and pepper. Cook 1 more minute, stirring constantly. Remove from the heat and stir in the spinach. Reserve ½ cup of the mixture and set aside.

Combine the cottage cheese and mozzarella; stir well. Meanwhile, cook the lasagna noodles according to package directions, omitting any oil and salt. Drain. Spread a thin layer of the spinach mixture in the bottom of a 13 × 9 × 2-inch baking dish coated with nonstick cooking spray. Arrange 4 lasagna noodles over the spinach mixture; top with half of the cottage cheese mixture, half of the vegetable mixture, and half of the remaining spinach mixture. Repeat the layers, ending with the remaining noodles. Spread the reserved ½ cup spinach mixture over the noodles. Cover and bake for 35 minutes, until bubbly. Let stand 5 minutes before serving.

Makes 12 servings

Nutritional information per serving

Calories	174	Cal. from Fat (%)	15.5	Sodium (mg)	145
Fat (g)	3	Saturated Fat (g)	1.5	Cholesterol (mg)	23

EGGPLANT AND ZUCCHINI LASAGNE ♥

If you don't tell your family this rich lasagne is meatless, they probably won't think to ask.

½ cup chopped onion	1 teaspoon dried oregano
½ teaspoon minced garlic	1 teaspoon dried basil
2 cups peeled diced eggplant	¼ teaspoon pepper
½ cup chopped green bell pepper	8 lasagna noodles
1 small zucchini, diced	2 large egg whites, beaten
1 cup sliced fresh mushrooms	1 (12-ounce) carton nonfat cottage cheese
1 (16-ounce) can no-salt-added whole tomatoes, chopped, with their juice	2 tablespoons chopped parsley
	1 cup shredded part-skim mozzarella cheese

Preheat the oven to 350°F. In a large pan coated with nonstick cooking spray, sauté the onion and garlic over medium-high heat for 2 minutes. Stir in the eggplant, green pepper, zucchini, mushrooms, tomatoes with juice, oregano, basil, and pepper. Cover, reduce the heat, and simmer for 10 minutes, or until the vegetables are tender. Set the vegetable mixture aside. Cook the lasagna noodles according to package directions, omitting any oil and salt. Drain the noodles and cut in half crosswise; set aside. Combine the egg whites, cottage cheese, and parsley; set aside.

Coat a 9-inch-square baking dish with nonstick cooking spray. Place half the lasagna noodle halves on the bottom. Spoon half of the cottage cheese mixture over the noodles. Spread half of the vegetable mixture over the cottage cheese mixture and sprinkle half of the mozzarella over the vegetable mixture. Repeat the layers. Cover and bake for 20 to 25 minutes, until bubbly.

Makes 6 servings

Nutritional information per serving

Calories	221	Cal. from Fat (%)	17.9	Sodium (mg)	295
Fat (g)	4.4	Saturated Fat (g)	2.2	Cholesterol (mg)	39

ITALIAN LINGUINE CASSEROLE

A tomatoey twist on baked macaroni and cheese, this is the perfect recipe to make for a hungry crowd, especially a bunch of kids.

2 tablespoons (¼ stick) light
stick margarine
1 onion, chopped
1 (15-ounce) can no-salt-
added tomato sauce
1 teaspoon dried basil
1 teaspoon dried oregano
1 teaspoon dried thyme

Salt and pepper to taste
1 (1-pound) package
linguine
2 cups shredded part-skim
mozzarella cheese
1 cup shredded reduced-fat
Cheddar cheese

Preheat the oven to 350°F. In a saucepan, melt the margarine over medium-low heat. Add the onion and sauté until soft, about 5 minutes. Add the tomato sauce, basil, oregano, thyme, and salt and pepper. Bring to a boil, then lower the heat and simmer 5 minutes. Cook the linguine according to package directions, omitting any oil and salt. Drain and toss with the tomato sauce, mixing well. Transfer the linguine to a 13 × 9 × 2-inch casserole coated with nonstick cooking spray. Sprinkle with both cheeses and bake for 20 minutes.

Makes 8 to 10 servings

Nutritional information per serving

Calories	298	Cal. from Fat (%)	23.6	Sodium (mg)	232
Fat (g)	7.8	Saturated Fat (g)	4	Cholesterol (mg)	21

FRESH TOMATO AND CHEESE PIZZA ♥

Nothing impresses kids like a homemade pizza, especially when they can help assemble it. Let them spread the tomato slices, cooked onion, and garlic over the top and see how eager they are to eat their healthy masterpiece.

2 thin slices of red onion, cut
in half
2 garlic cloves, thinly sliced
1 (10-ounce) can refrigerated
pizza crust dough
1 (15-ounce) carton nonfat
ricotta cheese

1 cup shredded part-skim
mozzarella cheese
¼ cup grated Parmesan
cheese, divided
1 tablespoon dried basil
4 Roma (plum) tomatoes,
thinly sliced

Preheat the broiler. Place the onion and garlic on a baking sheet coated with nonstick cooking spray. Broil 6 inches from the heat 8 to

10 minutes, or until charred; set aside. Reduce the temperature of the oven to 500°F. Roll the dough into a 12-inch circle and press into a pizza pan coated with nonstick cooking spray. Combine the ricotta cheese, mozzarella cheese, Parmesan cheese, and basil, stirring well. Spread the cheese over the dough, leaving a ½-inch border. Arrange the tomato slices over the cheese. Top with the onion and garlic. Bake on the bottom rack of the oven for 10 to 12 minutes, or until the crust is browned. Transfer the pizza to a cutting board.

Makes 8 slices

Nutritional information per slice

Calories	184	Cal. from Fat (%)	21.5	Sodium (mg)	351
Fat (g)	4.4	Saturated Fat (g)	2.1	Cholesterol (mg)	10

BROCCOLI PIZZA

You can make this pizza easily with a prepared crust.

1 (10-ounce) can refrigerated
  pizza crust
1 teaspoon minced garlic
2 tablespoons chopped onion
2 tablespoons balsamic or
  red wine vinegar
½ teaspoon dried basil
½ teaspoon dried thyme
½ teaspoon dried oregano
¼ teaspoon crushed red
  pepper flakes

1 cup shredded part-skim
  mozzarella cheese
1 (10-ounce) package frozen
  chopped broccoli, thawed
  and well drained
2 Roma (plum) tomatoes,
  sliced
¼ cup grated Romano
  cheese

Preheat the oven to 425°F. In a 12-inch-round pizza pan coated with nonstick cooking spray, unroll the dough and press in the pan to cover. Bake for 5 to 8 minutes, or until light golden brown. In a food processor, combine the garlic, onion, vinegar, basil, thyme, oregano, and red pepper flakes; process until smooth and spread over the partially baked crust. Then sprinkle with the mozzarella cheese. Spread the broccoli and tomatoes evenly over the cheese. Sprinkle with the Romano cheese. Bake for 15 minutes, or until the edges of the crust are deep golden brown. Serve immediately.

Makes 8 slices

Nutritional information per slice

Calories	152	Cal. from Fat (%)	25.5	Sodium (mg)	302
Fat (g)	4.3	Saturated Fat (g)	2.1	Cholesterol (mg)	11

BROCCOLI AND RICE STRATA

The brown rice gives an earthy flavor to the medley of vegetables. This dish can also be made ahead up to the point of baking and then refrigerated.

1 onion, coarsely chopped	½ teaspoon dried dillweed
1 green bell pepper, seeded and coarsely chopped	1 teaspoon dried thyme
	1 teaspoon dried oregano
½ pound fresh mushrooms, sliced	4 cups cooked brown rice
	1 (8-ounce) package part-skim mozzarella cheese, shredded
1 large bunch broccoli, florets only	
1 teaspoon minced garlic	1 cup nonfat sour cream

Preheat the oven to 350°F. In a large pan coated with nonstick cooking spray, sauté the onion, green pepper, mushrooms, and broccoli over medium heat until tender, about 7 minutes. Add the garlic, dillweed, thyme, and oregano. In a 3-quart oblong baking dish, spread the rice on the bottom and cover with the vegetable mixture. Sprinkle with the cheese and cover all with the sour cream. Sprinkle with the paprika. Bake for 20 minutes, or until bubbly.

Makes 6 main-course servings

Nutritional information per serving

Calories	335	Cal. from Fat (%) 20.7	Sodium (mg)	238
Fat (g)	7.7	Saturated Fat (g) 4.1	Cholesterol (mg)	26

ITALIAN RICE WITH SPRING VEGETABLES ♥

This is a good alternative to pasta primavera. If you can find orzo, a rice-shaped pasta, in your grocery store, use it instead of rice.

1 medium zucchini, chopped	1 cup rice
4 asparagus spears, chopped	½ cup white wine
⅓ cup sliced fresh mushrooms	3 cups canned fat-free chicken broth
½ cup chopped broccoli florets	1 medium tomato, chopped
	¼ cup grated Parmesan cheese
1 medium onion, chopped	

Steam or cook the zucchini, asparagus, mushrooms, and broccoli in a small amount of boiling water until crisp-tender, about 5 minutes. Drain and set aside. Coat a large skillet with nonstick cooking spray and add the onion, sautéing over medium-high heat until golden brown, about 7 minutes. Add the rice to the pan and stir 2 minutes. Add the wine and chicken broth to the pan and bring to a boil. Reduce the heat, cover, and cook until the liquid is absorbed, about 20 minutes. Add the tomato and cooked vegetables to the rice, stirring well. Toss in the cheese and serve immediately.

Makes 4 to 6 servings

Nutritional information per serving

Calories	191	Cal. from Fat (%)	6.6	Sodium (mg)	311
Fat (g)	1.4	Saturated Fat (g)	0.7	Cholesterol (mg)	3

GARDEN BAKED POTATOES

This attractive potato dish will be a favorite as a side dish or even as a quick lunch.

4 baking potatoes, scrubbed
½ cup finely chopped onion
2 tablespoons buttermilk or skim milk
½ cup nonfat cottage cheese
2 cups broccoli florets, roughly chopped

2 cups sliced yellow squash
½ cup water
⅓ cup chopped green onion (scallion) stems (green parts)
¼ cup shredded part-skim mozzarella cheese

Preheat the oven to 400°F. Pierce the potatoes with a fork and bake for 1 hour, or until soft. Set aside until cool enough to handle. Lower the oven temperature to 350°F. Cut the potatoes in half lengthwise and scoop out the flesh into a bowl, being careful not to rip the potato shells. Set aside.

In a small pan coated with nonstick cooking spray, sauté the onion until tender, about 5 minutes. In a mixing bowl, combine the sautéed onion, potato pulp, buttermilk, and cottage cheese, mixing well. Stuff each potato shell with the mixture. In a microwaveproof dish, microwave the broccoli florets and squash in a small amount of water for about 7 minutes, or until the vegetables are tender; drain. Top the potatoes evenly with the cooked vegetables, green onion stems, and mozzarella cheese. Place the potatoes on a baking sheet and bake for 15 minutes, or until the cheese is melted.

Makes 8 servings

Nutritional information per serving

Calories	156	Cal. from Fat (%)	8.1	Sodium (mg)	96
Fat (g)	1.4	Saturated Fat (g)	0.8	Cholesterol (mg)	5

QUICK VEGETARIAN CHILI

If you can work a can opener and accept compliments graciously, you can prepare this hearty dish and look impressive. Serve with shredded Monterey Jack cheese, if desired.

1 (10-ounce) can chopped tomatoes and green chilies
1 (28-ounce) can no-salt-added whole tomatoes with their juice, crushed
1 (15-ounce) can pinto beans, drained and rinsed
1 (15-ounce) can red kidney beans, drained and rinsed
1 (19-ounce) can garbanzo beans, drained and rinsed
1 (4½-ounce) can chopped green chilies, drained

1 green bell pepper, seeded and chopped
½ teaspoon minced garlic
1 onion, chopped
2 medium zucchini, halved lengthwise and thinly sliced
2 tablespoons chili powder
½ teaspoon ground cumin
½ teaspoon sugar
1 teaspoon dried oregano

In a large pot, combine the tomatoes and green chilies, crushed tomatoes, pinto beans, kidney beans, garbanzo beans, green chilies, green pepper, garlic, onion, zucchini, chili powder, cumin, sugar, and oregano. Heat to boiling. Reduce the heat and simmer, covered, for 40 minutes, stirring occasionally.

Makes 8 one-cup servings

Nutritional information per serving

Calories	207	Cal. from Fat (%)	9.5	Sodium (mg)	872
Fat (g)	2.2	Saturated Fat (g)	0.2	Cholesterol (mg)	0

LAYERED MEXICAN VEGETARIAN DISH ♥

This dish is great served with salsa and a dollop of nonfat sour cream. You may also top it with shredded reduced-fat Monterey Jack cheese for the last 10 minutes of baking.

1 cup chopped onion
1 (15½-ounce) can kidney
   beans, rinsed and drained
1 (16-ounce) can no-salt-
   added whole tomatoes,
   chopped, with their juice
1 (10-ounce) package frozen
   corn

2 cups chopped green bell
   pepper
2 tablespoons chili powder
1 teaspoon ground cumin
1 tablespoon Worcestershire
   sauce
8 flour tortillas

Preheat the oven to 400°F. In a bowl, combine the onion, kidney beans, tomatoes, corn, pepper, chili powder, cumin, and Worcestershire sauce. Place 2 tortillas in the bottom of a 2-quart casserole. Top with about ¼ of the vegetable mixture. Repeat the layers, alternating with the tortillas and vegetables, ending with the vegetables on top. Bake for 45 minutes.

Makes 6 to 8 servings

Nutritional information per serving

Calories	245	Cal. from Fat (%)	10.3	Sodium (mg)	720
Fat (g)	2.8	Saturated Fat (g)	0.6	Cholesterol (mg)	0

GARDEN ENCHILADAS ♥

These enchiladas take a bit of time and require more than one pan, but the happy faces around the dinner table will make it all worthwhile.

1 cup chopped onion
1 cup peeled shredded
  carrots
2 cups sliced fresh
  mushrooms
1 (10-ounce) package frozen
  chopped spinach, thawed
  and squeezed dry
1 (10-ounce) can diced
  tomatoes and green chilies

3 cups cooked brown rice
2 tablespoons chili powder
½ teaspoon ground cumin
2 (14-ounce) cans enchilada
  sauce
20 to 24 flour tortillas
½ cup shredded reduced-fat
  Cheddar cheese
½ cup shredded reduced-fat
  Monterey Jack cheese

Preheat the oven to 350°F. In a large skillet coated with nonstick cooking spray, sauté the onion, carrots, and mushrooms over medium heat until tender, about 5 minutes. Stir in the spinach and tomatoes and chilies, cooking for 5 minutes. Stir in the rice, chili powder, and cumin. Remove from the heat.

In a small skillet, pour in 1 can of enchilada sauce over medium heat a little at a time and heat briefly. Dip the tortillas in the heated sauce to soften, dipping only one side of the tortilla; lay on a plate, dry side up. Fill each tortilla with filling after it is dipped. Roll up, sauce side down, and lay in a large pan coated with nonstick cooking spray. Repeat until all the enchiladas are filled. Pour the other can of enchilada sauce over the stuffed enchiladas and sprinkle with both the cheeses. Cover with foil and bake for 30 minutes.

Makes 10 to 12 servings

Nutritional information per serving

Calories	415	Cal. from Fat (%)	12.6	Sodium (mg)	1,641
Fat (g)	5.8	Saturated Fat (g)	1.7	Cholesterol (mg)	3

ENCHILADA BAKE ♥

You can get this all ready to bake, then seal it up with aluminum foil and pop it in the freezer so it will be all ready to bake when you want a satisfying dinner in a hurry.

½ cup yellow or red bell pepper, seeded and chopped
1 green bell pepper, seeded and chopped
1 onion, chopped
1 garlic clove, minced
½ cup sliced fresh mushrooms
1 (15-ounce) can pinto beans, drained and rinsed

1½ cups chopped tomatoes
1 tablespoon chili powder
½ teaspoon ground cumin
¾ cup part-skim ricotta cheese
¼ cup plain nonfat yogurt
6 corn tortillas (flour can be used)
½ cup shredded reduced-fat Monterey Jack cheese

Preheat the oven to 350° F. In a saucepan coated with nonstick cooking spray, sauté the peppers, onion, garlic, and mushrooms over medium heat until tender, about 5 minutes. Add the beans, tomatoes, chili powder, and cumin. Simmer gently for about 30 minutes.

In a bowl, mix the ricotta and yogurt together and set aside. Soften the tortillas by putting them in a covered dish and microwaving for 15 to 30 seconds. On each tortilla, place 1½ teaspoons shredded cheese, 2 tablespoons of the yogurt mixture, and 2 tablespoons of the bean mixture. Roll each tortilla around the mixture and place the filled tortillas, seam side down, in a baking dish coated with nonstick cooking spray. Top the tortillas with the remaining bean mixture and cheese. Bake, uncovered, for 15 to 20 minutes, or until the cheese melts.

Makes 6 to 8 servings

Nutritional information per serving

Calories	167	Cal. from Fat (%)	23.2	Sodium (mg)	221
Fat (g)	4.3	Saturated Fat (g)	2.1	Cholesterol (mg)	12

VEGETARIAN ENTRÉES

CAKES,
COOKIES,
and
BROWNIES

APRICOT CAKE ♥

These ingredients can be kept in your pantry to whip up this outstanding cake in minutes. Everyone will think you're a gourmet!

⅓ cup canola oil
1 (16-ounce) can light apricot halves, drained and chopped
½ cup apricot nectar
1 (18¼-ounce) box light white cake mix

1 (3-ounce) box apricot gelatin
3 large eggs
1 teaspoon vanilla extract
1 teaspoon butter extract
Apricot Frosting (recipe follows)

Preheat the oven to 350°F. Coat three 9-inch cake pans with non-stick cooking spray and dust with flour. In a mixing bowl, combine the oil, apricots, and apricot nectar. In another bowl, combine the cake mix and gelatin. Add to the liquid mixture and beat well. Add the eggs and beat again. Mix in the extracts. Pour evenly into the cake pans and bake for 20 to 25 minutes, or until the center springs back when touched. Cool for 10 minutes in the pans, then remove to wire racks. Frost the cooled cakes with Apricot Frosting.

Apricot Frosting

6 tablespoons (¾ stick) light stick margarine, at room temperature
1 (16-ounce) box confectioners' sugar

¼ cup apricot nectar
1 teaspoon vanilla extract
½ teaspoon butter extract

In a mixing bowl, blend together the margarine, confectioners' sugar, nectar, and vanilla and butter extracts until smooth.

Makes 16 slices

Nutritional information per slice

Calories	349	Cal. from Fat (%)	27	Sodium (mg)	165
Fat (g)	10.5	Saturated Fat (g)	1.4	Cholesterol (mg)	40

LEMON BUNDT CAKE ♥

It's hard to believe this cake is "light." Serve up slices with a mug of tea in the afternoon. Don't overbake it so it will be moist.

½ cup (1 stick) light stick margarine, at room temperature
¾ cup plus ⅓ cup sugar
3 large egg whites, at room temperature
1 teaspoon vanilla extract
1 teaspoon lemon extract

2½ cups all-purpose flour
1 teaspoon baking soda
1 cup low-fat lemon yogurt, drained of any excess liquid
1 tablespoon grated lemon rind
⅓ cup lemon juice

Preheat the oven to 325°F. Coat a 10-inch bundt pan with nonstick cooking spray and dust with flour. In a mixing bowl, cream together the margarine and ¾ cup of the sugar. Add the egg whites and beat 4 minutes with a mixer on medium speed. Add the vanilla and lemon extracts. In another bowl, combine the flour and baking soda. In another small dish, combine the yogurt and lemon rind. Add the dry ingredients alternately with the yogurt, beginning and ending with the flour.

Pour into the bundt pan and bake for 40 to 50 minutes, until a toothpick inserted in the middle comes out clean. In a small saucepan or in the microwave, heat the remaining ⅓ cup sugar and the lemon juice until the sugar is melted; set aside. Let the cake sit in the pan 10 minutes, then turn out onto a serving plate and pour the hot glaze over.

Makes 16 slices

Nutritional information per slice

Calories	168	Cal. from Fat (%)	17	Sodium (mg)	174
Fat (g)	3.2	Saturated Fat (g)	0.6	Cholesterol (mg)	1

LEMON POPPY SEED CAKE ♥

You always see poppy seed cakes at the bakery and think they must be difficult to make. Not so! If possible, use fresh lemon juice. With this recipe, you can enjoy a wonderful combination with little effort. This one will disappear quickly.

1 (18½-ounce) box light
   yellow cake mix
¼ cup canola oil
¼ cup water
1⅓ cups plain nonfat yogurt
1 large egg
3 large egg whites

1 teaspoon almond extract
⅓ cup lemon juice
1 tablespoon poppy seeds

LEMON GLAZE
1 cup confectioners' sugar
3 tablespoons lemon juice

Preheat the oven to 350°F. Coat a 10-inch bundt pan with nonstick cooking spray and dust with flour. In a large mixing bowl, combine the cake mix, oil, water, yogurt, egg, egg whites, almond extract, and lemon juice. Beat with a mixer at medium speed for 6 minutes. Stir in the poppy seeds. Pour the batter into the bundt pan and bake for 40 minutes, or until a wooden pick inserted in the center of the cake comes out clean. Cool in the pan on a wire rack 10 minutes. Meanwhile, make the Lemon Glaze: Combine the confectioners' sugar and lemon juice, stirring until smooth. Remove the cake from the pan onto a serving plate and drizzle with the Lemon Glaze.

Makes 16 to 20 slices

Nutritional information per slice

Calories	170	Cal. from Fat (%) 28.6	Sodium (mg)	91
Fat (g)	5.4	Saturated Fat (g) 0.6	Cholesterol (mg)	11

PINEAPPLE SHEET CAKE

This cake gets excellent reviews at birthday parties, for after-school snacks, or just about any time.

2 large eggs, beaten
1⅓ cups sugar
2 cups all-purpose flour
1 teaspoon vanilla extract
2 teaspoons baking soda

1 (15¼-ounce) can crushed
   pineapple, in juice
Creamy Frosting (recipe
   follows)

Preheat the oven to 350°F. Coat a 17 × 11 × 1-inch jelly-roll pan with nonstick cooking spray. In a bowl, combine the eggs, sugar, flour, vanilla, baking soda, and pineapple with its juice and mix well. Pour into the jelly-roll pan and bake for 15 to 20 minutes, until the top springs back when touched. Frost while hot with the Creamy Frosting.

Creamy Frosting

3 tablespoons light stick
   margarine, softened
4 ounces light cream cheese,
   softened

2 cups confectioners' sugar
1 teaspoon vanilla extract
1 teaspoon butter extract

In a mixing bowl, beat the margarine and cream cheese. Blend in the confectioners' sugar and vanilla and butter extracts, mixing until smooth.

Makes 32 slices

Nutritional information per slice

Calories	116	Cal. from Fat (%)	12.4	Sodium (mg)	120
Fat (g)	1.6	Saturated Fat (g)	0.6	Cholesterol (mg)	15

I think of this recipe during the holiday season, but it's so good that it's worth freezing the cranberries when they're in season to have the cake year-round.

½ cup (1 stick) light stick margarine, at room temperature
1 cup sugar
1 large egg
1 tablespoon grated orange rind
2¼ cups all-purpose flour
1 teaspoon baking soda
½ cup orange juice

½ cup skim milk
1½ cups chopped fresh cranberries
⅔ cup chopped dates

ORANGE GLAZE
½ cup confectioners' sugar
1½ tablespoons orange juice

Preheat the oven to 350°F. Coat a 10-inch bundt pan with nonstick cooking spray and dust with flour. In a mixing bowl, cream the margarine and sugar until light and fluffy. Add the egg and orange rind, beating well. Combine the flour and baking soda and add to the creamed mixture alternately with the orange juice and milk. Stir in the cranberries and dates. Pour into the bundt pan and bake for 40 minutes.

Meanwhile, make the glaze. In a small saucepan, combine the confectioners' sugar and orange juice and cook over low heat until smooth. Invert the cake onto a serving platter and pour the orange glaze over while the cake is still hot.

Makes 16 slices

Nutritional information per slice

Calories	151	Cal. from Fat (%)	16.2	Sodium (mg)	131
Fat (g)	2.7	Saturated Fat (g)	0.5	Cholesterol (mg)	11

COCONUT CAKE ♥

By using coconut extract in the cake, you have all the flavor of coconut without the fat. If desired, you can sprinkle a little flaked coconut on the top.

1 (18¼-ounce) box light
   yellow cake mix
1 (4-serving) box vanilla
   instant pudding and pie
   filling mix
1⅓ cups water
1 large egg

3 large egg whites
¼ cup canola oil
1 teaspoon coconut extract
1 teaspoon almond extract
Cream Cheese Icing (recipe
   follows)

Preheat the oven to 350°F. Coat three 9-inch cake pans with non-stick cooking spay and dust with flour. Blend the cake mix, vanilla pudding mix, water, egg, egg whites, oil, and coconut and almond extracts in a mixing bowl. Beat at medium speed for 4 minutes. Pour even amounts into the cake pans and bake for 15 to 18 minutes. Cool in the pans at least 15 minutes, then turn out on racks to cool completely. Frost with Cream Cheese Icing.

Cream Cheese Icing

2 tablespoons light stick
   margarine, at room
   temperature
1 (8-ounce) package light
   cream cheese, softened

4 cups confectioners' sugar
1 teaspoon vanilla extract

Combine the margarine and cream cheese in a mixing bowl. Gradually add the confectioners' sugar, mixing until smooth. Add the vanilla. Frost between the layers and on the top and sides of the cake.

Makes 16 slices

Nutritional information per slice

| Calories | 345 | Cal. from Fat (%) 24.5 | Sodium (mg) | 272 |
| Fat (g) | 9.4 | Saturated Fat (g) 2.5 | Cholesterol (mg) | 20 |

COFFEE ANGEL FOOD CAKE ♥

Few things are simpler than this light coffee cake.

1 (14½-ounce) box angel
food cake mix
1 teaspoon vanilla extract
1 teaspoon almond extract

1 tablespoon instant coffee
dissolved in 1 tablespoon
water
Coffee Icing (recipe follows)

Prepare the angel food cake according to the directions on the box. Blend the vanilla and almond extracts and the coffee into the batter, then bake according to the directions on the box and when cool ice with Coffee Icing.

Coffee Icing

6 tablespoons light stick
margarine, at room
temperature
2 tablespoons instant coffee
dissolved in 1 tablespoon
water

1 (16-ounce) box
confectioners' sugar
3 to 4 tablespoons skim milk

In a mixing bowl, cream the margarine with the dissolved coffee and confectioners' sugar, adding milk as needed until the icing reaches spreading consistency. Ice the top, sides, and center of the cake.

Makes 16 slices

Nutritional information per slice

Calories	230	Cal. from Fat (%)	9.1	Sodium (mg)	246
Fat (g)	2.3	Saturated Fat (g)	0.4	Cholesterol (mg)	0

CAKES, COOKIES, AND BROWNIES

BLUEBERRY COBBLER CAKE ♥

You can substitute peaches for the blueberries for a delicious peach dessert. The topping forms a cake on top of the filling. As the cobbler cake cools, the filling thickens. Serve this one with a big spoon.

⅓ cup light brown sugar
1 tablespoon cornstarch
1½ tablespoons water
1 tablespoon lemon juice
3 cups fresh or frozen
   blueberries
1 cup all-purpose flour

½ cup sugar
1½ teaspoons baking
   powder
½ cup skim milk
¼ cup (½ stick) light stick
   margarine, softened

Preheat the oven to 375°F. Coat an oblong 1½-quart baking dish with nonstick cooking spray. In a saucepan, mix the brown sugar and cornstarch together, then stir in the water and cook over medium heat until thick, stirring constantly. Remove from the heat. Add the lemon juice and blueberries. Turn into the baking dish. Combine the flour, sugar, and baking powder in a bowl. Blend in the milk and margarine. Spread the topping over the blueberry mixture and bake 30 minutes. Cool slightly before serving.

Makes 8 slices

Nutritional information per slice

Calories	295	Cal. from Fat (%)	14	Sodium (mg)	178
Fat (g)	3.2	Saturated Fat (g)	0.5	Cholesterol (mg)	0

WAIT CAKE ♥

The most difficult part of this cake is waiting to cut it, which gives it its name. Don't feel bad if you get impatient—I've cheated before and it's still good!

1 (18¼-ounce) box light
   yellow cake mix
1 teaspoon baking powder
2 cups light sour cream

1½ cups sugar
1 teaspoon almond extract
1½ cups frozen light
   whipped topping, thawed

Preheat the oven to 350°F. Coat two 9-inch-round cake pans with nonstick cooking spray and dust with flour. Prepare the cake mix according to package directions, adding the baking powder to the batter. Pour the batter into the cake pans and bake for 25 to 30 minutes. Cool the layers on wire racks.

Meanwhile, in a bowl, combine the sour cream, sugar, and

almond extract, blending well to make the filling. Chill in the refrigerator while the cake is baking. When the cake has cooled, split each layer in half with a serrated knife. Spread the filling between the layers, reserving 1 cup for frosting. Combine the reserved 1 cup filling with the whipped topping, mixing until smooth. Spread the frosting on the sides and top of the cake. Seal the cake in an airtight container or cover tightly with plastic wrap and refrigerate for 36 to 48 hours before serving.

Makes 16 to 20 slices

Nutritional information per slice

Calories	217	Cal. from Fat (%)	22.8	Sodium (mg)	220
Fat (g)	5.5	Saturated Fat (g)	3.5	Cholesterol (mg)	40

STRAWBERRY ANGEL FOOD CAKE ♥

This is great during strawberry season. It's so light and so quick!

1 (16-ounce) angel food cake
1 (8-ounce) package light
   cream cheese, softened
½ cup sugar

¼ cup evaporated skimmed
   milk
2 pints strawberries, hulled
   and sliced

Slice the angel food cake horizontally into 3 equal layers with a serrated knife. Prepare the filling by creaming together the cream cheese, sugar, and evaporated skim milk. Top the bottom cake layer with the filling and strawberries. Repeat the layers.

Makes 10 to 12 slices

Nutritional information per slice

Calories	191	Cal. from Fat (%)	16.5	Sodium (mg)	379
Fat (g)	3.5	Saturated Fat (g)	2.2	Cholesterol (mg)	9

ITALIAN CREAM CAKE ♥

I am thrilled to offer this lighter version of my favorite cake. Now I can enjoy my birthdays again. It is definitely worth the effort. This cake was featured on the cover of the November/December 1995 issue of Cooking Light Magazine *as the "Best Cake Ever!"*

½ cup (1 stick) light stick margarine, at room temperature
¼ cup canola oil
2 cups sugar
2 large eggs, separated
2 cups all-purpose flour
1 teaspoon baking soda

1 cup buttermilk
1 teaspoon vanilla extract
1 teaspoon butter extract
1 teaspoon coconut extract
½ cup chopped pecans
4 large egg whites
Cream Cheese Icing (recipe follows)

Preheat the oven to 350°F. Coat three 9-inch pans with nonstick cooking spray and dust with flour. Cream the margarine and oil in a mixing bowl. Gradually add the sugar and beat until light and fluffy. Add the 2 egg yolks, one at a time, beating well after each addition. Mix the flour and baking soda together. Add the flour to the sugar mixture, alternating with the buttermilk and ending with the flour. Beat after each addition. Add the vanilla, butter, and coconut extracts and the pecans. Beat all 6 egg whites until stiff peaks form. Fold the beaten egg whites into the batter mixture.

Pour the batter evenly into the cake pans. Bake for 20 to 25 minutes, until the tops spring back when touched. Cool the cakes in the pans for 10 minutes, then turn them out onto racks to cool thoroughly. Frost the layers and sides with Cream Cheese Icing.

Cream Cheese Icing

1 (8-ounce) package light cream cheese, softened
3 tablespoons light stick margarine, softened

1 (16-ounce) box confectioners' sugar
1 teaspoon vanilla extract

In a mixing bowl, beat the cream cheese and margarine until smooth. Add the confectioners' sugar and beat until light. Blend in the vanilla.

Makes 16 to 20 slices

Nutritional information per slice

Calories	326	Cal. from Fat (%)	28.7	Sodium (mg)	229
Fat (g)	10.4	Saturated Fat (g)	1.1	Cholesterol (mg)	27

CARROT CAKE ♥

If carrot cake is one of your favorites, this is your lucky day because now you can have your cake and eat it too.

2 cups all-purpose flour
2 teaspoons baking soda
2 teaspoons ground
   cinnamon
1 cup light brown sugar
1 large egg
2 large egg whites
⅔ cup buttermilk

1 (8-ounce) can crushed
   pineapple in juice
2 cups grated peeled carrots
3 tablespoons canola oil
2 teaspoons vanilla extract
Orange–Cream Cheese Icing
   (recipe follows)

Preheat the oven to 350°F. Coat a 13 × 9 × 2-inch pan with nonstick cooking spray and dust with flour. In a bowl, combine the flour, baking soda, and cinnamon; set aside. In a large mixing bowl, combine the brown sugar, egg, egg whites, buttermilk, pineapple and juice, carrots, oil, and vanilla, beating at medium speed with a mixer until well blended. Pour the batter into the pan and bake for 30 to 35 minutes, or until a wooden pick inserted in the center comes out clean. Cool the cake in the pan completely. Spread the Orange–Cream Cheese Icing over the top of the cake. Cut into squares.

Orange–Cream Cheese Icing

6 ounces light cream cheese,
   softened
1 tablespoon light stick
   margarine, softened

1½ cups confectioners' sugar
1 teaspoon grated orange
   rind
½ teaspoon vanilla extract

In a mixing bowl, combine the cream cheese and margarine. Gradually add the confectioners' sugar, mixing until smooth. Add the orange rind and vanilla.

Makes 18 to 24 squares

Nutritional information per square

Calories	153	Cal. from Fat (%) 20.6		Sodium (mg)	141
Fat (g)	3.5	Saturated Fat (g)	1.1	Cholesterol (mg)	9

OATMEAL CHOCOLATE CAKE ♥

The oatmeal gives this snacking cake a nice, unusual consistency. It's great served with frozen vanilla yogurt on the side.

1½ cups boiling water	2 large egg whites
1 cup old-fashioned oatmeal	1½ cups all-purpose flour
1 cup light brown sugar	1 teaspoon baking soda
½ cup sugar	1 tablespoon cocoa
½ cup (1 stick) light stick margarine	½ cup semisweet chocolate chips
1 large egg	

Preheat the oven to 350°F. Coat a 13 × 9 × 2-inch baking pan with nonstick cooking spray and dust with flour. Pour the boiling water over the oatmeal in a bowl and let stand for 10 minutes. Add the brown sugar, sugar, and margarine. Stir until the margarine melts. Add the egg and egg whites; mix well. In another bowl, sift together the flour, baking soda, and cocoa. Add the dry ingredients to the sugar mixture, mixing well. Stir in the chocolate chips. Pour into the baking pan and bake for about 40 minutes. Let cool in the pan.

Makes 36 squares

Nutritional information per slice

Calories	87	Cal. from Fat (%) 23.8	Sodium (mg)	77
Fat (g)	2.3	Saturated Fat (g) 0.7	Cholesterol (mg)	6

APPLESAUCE–CHOCOLATE CHIP CAKE ♥

This is not a real sweet cake, more like a snack cake. The applesauce keeps it moist but it's not just a substitute for more oil; it also adds to the flavor.

¼ cup (½ stick) light stick margarine, at room temperature	2 large egg whites
	2 cups all-purpose flour
¼ cup canola oil	1½ teaspoons baking soda
1½ cups sugar	1 (16-ounce) jar applesauce
1 teaspoon cinnamon	1 teaspoon vanilla extract
3 tablespoons cocoa	½ cup semisweet chocolate chips
1 large egg	

Preheat the oven to 350°F. Coat a 13 × 9 × 2-inch baking pan with nonstick cooking spray and dust with flour. In a mixing bowl, cream the margarine, oil, and sugar. Add the cinnamon and cocoa; mix well. Blend in the egg and egg whites. In another bowl, combine the flour and baking soda and add to the creamed mixture. Stir in the applesauce and vanilla. Beat until the ingredients are well mixed. Pour the batter into the baking pan and sprinkle with the chocolate chips. Bake for 30 minutes. Cool in the pan and cut into squares.

Makes 36 squares

Nutritional information per square

Calories	102	Cal. from Fat (%)	27.7	Sodium (mg)	74
Fat (g)	3.1	Saturated Fat (g)	0.7	Cholesterol (mg)	6

TRIPLE CHOCOLATE CAKE

This recipe was always a favorite standby of mine in my first "very fattening" cookbook. I adjusted it so now you can enjoy it without guilt.

Cocoa
1 (18½-ounce) box of light or
 regular devil's food cake
 mix
1 (4-serving) box instant
 chocolate pudding mix
1 cup nonfat sour cream
¼ cup canola oil
⅓ cup skim milk
1 large egg
3 large egg whites

⅓ cup almond liqueur (such
 as Amaretto)
1 teaspoon almond extract
⅓ cup semisweet chocolate
 chips

ALMOND GLAZE
1½ cups confectioners' sugar
¼ cup skim milk
1 teaspoon almond extract

Preheat the oven to 350°F. Coat a 10-inch fluted bundt pan with non-stick cooking spray and dust with cocoa. Place the cake mix, pudding mix, sour cream, oil, skim milk, egg, egg whites, liqueur, and almond extract in a large mixing bowl. Beat with a mixer for 2 minutes, or until the mixture is well blended. Stir in the chocolate chips. Pour into the bundt pan and bake for 40 to 50 minutes, until a toothpick inserted in the middle comes out clean. Meanwhile, make the Almond Glaze: Mix the confectioners' sugar, milk, and almond extract together in a small bowl. Let stand at room temperature until ready to use. Cool the cake on a rack for 10 minutes before inverting onto a serving plate. Drizzle the Almond Glaze over the warm cake.

Makes 16 slices

Nutritional information per slice

Calories	303	Cal. from Fat (%)	29.9	Sodium (mg)	392
Fat (g)	10.1	Saturated Fat (g)	2.1	Cholesterol (mg)	16

BANANA UPSIDE-DOWN CAKE

This luscious treat is best when eaten the same day and, of course, hot out of the oven. If you're a banana lover, this cake is for you!

⅔ cup light brown sugar
2 tablespoons light tub
  margarine
2 large ripe bananas, sliced
1½ cups all-purpose flour
1 teaspoon baking soda
½ teaspoon baking powder
1 cup mashed ripe bananas
  (approximately 2)

½ cup buttermilk
1 teaspoon vanilla extract
⅔ cup sugar
⅓ cup canola oil
1 large egg
2 large egg whites

Place a rack in the lowest position in the oven and preheat to 350°F. Coat a 9 × 9 × 2-inch-square pan with nonstick cooking spray. In a mixing bowl, cream the brown sugar and margarine until mixed. Spread the brown sugar mixture over the bottom of the pan. Arrange the banana slices atop the brown sugar mixture, covering it completely. Combine the flour, baking soda, and baking powder in a bowl. Mix the mashed bananas, buttermilk, and vanilla in another bowl. With a mixer, cream the sugar and oil until fluffy. Add the egg and egg whites, one at a time, beating well. Add the dry ingredients alternately with the banana-buttermilk mixture, mixing until just combined. Pour the batter over the bananas and bake for 30 minutes. Immediately turn the cake onto a plate and serve.

Makes 12 servings

Nutritional information per serving

Calories	257	Cal. from Fat (%)	27.6	Sodium (mg)	186
Fat (g)	7.9	Saturated Fat (g)	0.9	Cholesterol (mg)	18

PUMPKIN-BUTTERSCOTCH CAKE

You might not even realize there is pumpkin in this cake—it tastes more like a wonderful spice cake. Because there's no frosting, it makes a nice treat to tuck into lunch boxes or bring along on a picnic.

2½ cups all-purpose flour	2 large eggs
1 tablespoon baking powder	2 large egg whites
1 teaspoon baking soda	1½ cups light brown sugar
2 teaspoons ground cinnamon	⅓ cup canola oil
1 teaspoon ground nutmeg	⅔ cup butterscotch morsels
1 (16-ounce) can solid-pack pumpkin	

Preheat the oven to 350°F. Coat a 13 × 9 × 2-inch baking pan with nonstick cooking spray and dust with flour. In a medium bowl, combine the flour, baking powder, baking soda, cinnamon, and nutmeg. In a large mixing bowl, beat the pumpkin, eggs, egg whites, brown sugar, and oil with a mixer at medium speed for 3 minutes. Stir in the dry ingredients just until blended. Spread the batter in the baking pan and sprinkle with butterscotch morsels. Bake for 40 to 45 minutes, until a toothpick inserted in the middle comes out clean. Cool in the pan on a wire rack. Cut into squares.

Makes 24 squares

Nutritional information per square

Calories	166	Cal. from Fat (%)	27.4	Sodium (mg)	144
Fat (g)	5.0	Saturated Fat (g)	1.5	Cholesterol (mg)	18

CHOCOLATE CHIP COOKIES

Finally, here's a chocolate chip cookie that will satisfy you. If you want you can add chopped pecans, but remember it will increase your fat content. A cookbook isn't complete without a chocolate chip cookie recipe and you'll love this one.

½ cup (1 stick) light stick margarine, softened	2 cups all-purpose flour
⅓ cup sugar	1 teaspoon baking soda
¾ cup light brown sugar	1 teaspoon vanilla extract
1 large egg	½ cup semisweet chocolate chips

Preheat the oven to 375°F. In a mixing bowl, beat the margarine until creamy. Gradually add the sugar and brown sugar, beating well. Add the egg and beat well. Combine the flour and baking soda in another bowl. Add to the margarine mixture and beat just until blended. Add the vanilla. Stir in the chocolate chips. Drop the dough by level tablespoonfuls 2 inches apart onto cookie sheets coated with nonstick cooking spray. Bake for 5 to 6 minutes. Remove from the cookie sheets and let cool completely on a wire rack.

Makes 48 cookies

Nutritional information per cookie

Calories	56	Cal. from Fat (%)	26.1	Sodium (mg)	55
Fat (g)	1.6	Saturated Fat (g)	0.5	Cholesterol (mg)	4

OATMEAL ROCKIES ♥

My mother loves oatmeal cookies, so I always include a recipe for her. You can add ½ cup of toasted pecans for the deluxe version of these cookies. I put the cookies in zip-top bags in the freezer and pull them out when I have a sweet craving.

½ cup canola oil	½ teaspoon baking soda
1⅓ cups light brown sugar	2 cups old-fashioned
1 tablespoon vanilla extract	oatmeal
2 large egg whites	½ cup golden raisins
1½ cups all-purpose flour	
1 teaspoon ground cinnamon	

Preheat the oven to 350°F. Coat a baking sheet with nonstick cooking spray. In a large bowl, stir together the oil and brown sugar until combined. Add the vanilla extract and egg whites. In a small bowl, combine the flour, cinnamon, and baking soda. Stir the flour mixture into the sugar mixture. Add the oatmeal and raisins. Drop by spoonfuls onto the baking sheet and bake for 8 to 10 minutes.

Makes 42 to 48 cookies

Nutritional information per cookie

Calories	76	Cal. from Fat (%)	29.9	Sodium (mg)	19
Fat (g)	2.5	Saturated Fat (g)	0.2	Cholesterol (mg)	0

CHOCOLATE BROWNIES ♥

There's nothing better than old-fashioned brownies with chocolate frosting. Sprinkle toasted pecans on top for the ultra-deluxe version.

½ cup (1 stick) light stick margarine, at room temperature
1⅓ cups sugar
6 large egg whites
1 cup nonfat sour cream
⅓ cup skim milk

2 teaspoons vanilla extract
1⅓ cups all-purpose flour
1 teaspoon baking powder
½ teaspoon salt (optional)
⅔ cup cocoa
Chocolate Frosting (recipe follows)

Preheat the oven to 350°F. Coat a 13 × 9 × 2-inch baking pan with nonstick cooking spray and dust with flour. In a mixing bowl, beat the margarine until fluffy. Gradually add the sugar and beat well. Add the egg whites, sour cream, milk, and vanilla; beat well. Combine the flour, baking powder, salt, if using, and cocoa in another bowl. Add the flour mixture to the creamed mixture, mixing well. Pour the batter into the baking pan and bake for 25 minutes, or until a wooden pick inserted in the center comes out clean. Cool in the pan on a wire rack. Spread the Chocolate Frosting over the cooled brownies and cut into squares.

Chocolate Frosting

3 cups confectioners' sugar
¼ cup cocoa

1½ teaspoons vanilla extract
¼ cup skim milk, as needed

In a mixing bowl, blend the confectioners' sugar, cocoa, vanilla, and skim milk until the frosting is of spreading consistency.

Makes 48 brownies

Nutritional information per brownie

Calories	83	Cal. from Fat (%)	13	Sodium (mg)	89
Fat (g)	1.2	Saturated Fat (g)	0.3	Cholesterol (mg)	1

CHOCOLATE MINT BROWNIES

I am not sure if I love these brownies for the mint flavoring or for their pretty color. Either way, you will find yourself making them for party pick-up sweets, especially during the holidays

½ cup (1 stick) light stick margarine
⅔ cup cocoa
1½ cups sugar
1 large egg
2 large egg whites
1½ cups all-purpose flour

¼ cup nonfat plain yogurt
1 tablespoon vanilla extract
½ teaspoon peppermint extract
Mint Frosting (recipe follows)

Preheat the oven to 350°F. Coat a 15 × 10 × 1-inch baking sheet with nonstick cooking spray. In a small saucepan or in the microwave, melt the margarine with the cocoa over low heat. Transfer the melted chocolate mixture to a mixing bowl. Add the sugar, egg, and egg whites, beating well. Add the flour alternately with the yogurt to the chocolate mixture. Add the vanilla and peppermint extracts. Pour into the baking sheet and bake for 15 minutes, or until a toothpick inserted in the middle comes out clean. Do not overbake. Cool and spread with the Mint Frosting.

Mint Frosting

3 tablespoons light cream cheese, softened
1 tablespoon light stick margarine, softened
2 cups confectioners' sugar

½ teaspoon peppermint extract
Few drops of green food coloring

In a mixing bowl, blend the cream cheese and margarine until creamy. Gradually add the confectioners' sugar, mixing until smooth. Add the peppermint extract and green food coloring.

Makes 48 brownies

Nutritional information per brownie

Calories	53	Cal. from Fat (%)	21.1	Sodium (mg)	28
Fat (g)	1.2	Saturated Fat (g)	0.3	Cholesterol (mg)	4

COFFEE TOFFEE BROWNIES ♥

These are wonderful, with a rich caramel flavor. Coffee is a secret ingredient that just adds to the flavor.

½ cup (1 stick) light stick margarine
1 (16-ounce) box dark brown sugar
2 tablespoons instant coffee
1 tablespoon hot water
1 large egg

2 large egg whites
1 tablespoon vanilla extract
2 cups all-purpose flour
2 teaspoons baking soda
⅛ teaspoon salt
½ cup semisweet chocolate chips

Preheat the oven to 350°F. Coat an 11 × 8 × 2-inch baking pan with nonstick cooking spray and dust with flour. In a small saucepan, melt the margarine and brown sugar over low heat. Combine the instant coffee with the hot water to dissolve and combine with the brown sugar mixture in a mixing bowl. Stir and let cool.

Beat together the egg, egg whites, and vanilla; mix into the brown sugar mixture. Combine the flour, baking soda, and salt and stir into the brown sugar mixture. Stir in the chocolate chips. Pour the batter into the baking pan and bake for 30 minutes, until a toothpick inserted in the middle comes out clean. Do not overcook. Cool in the pan and cut into squares.

Makes 28 brownies

Nutritional information per brownie

Calories	128	Cal. from Fat (%)	19.6	Sodium (mg)	162
Fat (g)	2.8	Saturated Fat (g)	0.9	Cholesterol (mg)	8

ROCKY ROAD BROWNIES

Rocky Road Brownies in a low-fat cookbook? Yes, and they're just fabulous. You can keep the fact that they are light to yourself and just enjoy the praise.

1 (20½-ounce) package light fudge brownie mix
1 (5-ounce) can evaporated skimmed milk
1 (10-ounce) bag miniature marshmallows

½ cup coarsely chopped pecans
⅓ cup semisweet chocolate chips

Preheat the oven to 350°F. Coat a 13 × 9 × 2-inch baking pan with nonstick cooking spray. Prepare the brownie mix according to package directions, substituting the evaporated milk for the water. Pour into the baking pan and bake according to package directions. Do not overbake. Remove from the oven and top evenly with the marshmallows, pecans, and chocolate chips. Return to the oven for 3 to 5 minutes, or just until the topping is warmed and begins to melt together. Cool in the pan on a rack for 20 to 30 minutes before cutting into squares.

Makes 48 brownies

Nutritional information per brownie

| Calories | 85 | Cal. from Fat (%) | 18 | Sodium (mg) | 52 |
| Fat (g) | 1.7 | Saturated Fat (g) | 0.3 | Cholesterol (mg) | 0 |

PEANUT BUTTER BROWNIES

These swirled cakelike brownies are the answer to a peanut butter lover's dream.

½ cup (1 stick) light stick margarine, softened
1¼ cups light brown sugar
1 large egg
4 large egg whites
1 teaspoon vanilla extract

1½ cups all-purpose flour
½ teaspoon baking powder
2 tablespoons cocoa
¼ cup 25% less fat creamy peanut butter

Preheat the oven to 350°F. Coat a 13 × 9 × 2-inch baking pan with nonstick cooking spray and dust with flour. In a large mixing bowl, blend the margarine and brown sugar until creamy. Add the egg, egg whites, and vanilla, beating until thoroughly mixed. In a small bowl, combine the flour and baking powder. Add to the creamed mixture, mixing well. Divide the batter in half. Stir the cocoa into half of the batter and the peanut butter into the other half. Spoon dollops of each batter alternately into the baking pan and bake for 25 minutes, or until a toothpick inserted in the middle comes out clean.

Makes 48 brownies

Nutritional information per brownie

Calories	56	Cal. from Fat (%)	25.7	Sodium (mg)	44
Fat (g)	1.6	Saturated Fat (g)	0.3	Cholesterol (mg)	4

CHEWY CARAMEL BROWNIES

These indulgent brownies will be the talk of the town. These brownies harden as they cool and become easier to cut, so try to wait—I never can!

9 ounces caramels, unwrapped
1 (14-ounce) can low-fat sweetened condensed milk
1 (18¼-ounce) box light devil's food cake mix

½ cup (1 stick) light stick margarine, melted
½ cup semisweet chocolate chips

Preheat the oven to 350°F. Coat a 13 × 9 × 2-inch baking pan with nonstick cooking spray and dust with flour. In the top of a double boiler or in the microwave, melt the caramels with ⅓ cup of the milk. Keep warm and set aside. In a large mixing bowl, combine the cake mix, margarine, and remaining milk. Beat at high speed with a mixer until very well combined.

Spread half of the dough into the bottom of the baking pan. Bake for 6 minutes, then sprinkle the chocolate chips over the partially baked dough. Spread the caramel mixture over the chocolate chips. Crumble the remaining dough on top. Return to the oven and continue baking for 15 minutes, or until the sides pull away from the pan. Do not overcook. Cool in the pan on a rack and cut into squares.

Makes 48 brownies

Nutritional information per brownie

Calories	116	Cal. from Fat (%)	22.5	Sodium (mg)	127
Fat (g)	2.9	Saturated Fat (g)	1.4	Cholesterol (mg)	2

LEMON SQUARES ♥

This might be one of my favorite recipes in the book. Lemon lovers, beware, as you might find yourself working your way through the whole pan! Use fresh lemon juice if possible.

1¾ cups all-purpose flour, divided	1 tablespoon grated lemon rind
⅓ cup plus 3 tablespoons confectioners' sugar	1 teaspoon baking powder
⅓ cup light stick margarine, chilled and cut into small pieces	3 large egg whites
	1 large egg
	⅓ cup plus 1 tablespoon lemon juice
1⅓ cups sugar	½ teaspoon butter extract

Preheat the oven to 350°F. Coat a 13 × 9 × 2-inch baking pan with nonstick cooking spray. Combine 1½ cups of the flour and ⅓ cup of the confectioners' sugar in a bowl; cut in the margarine with a pastry blender or 2 knives until the mixture resembles coarse meal. Press the mixture firmly and evenly into the bottom of the baking pan. Bake for 20 minutes, or until lightly browned.

Combine the sugar, ¼ cup of the flour, the lemon rind, baking powder, egg whites, and egg in a medium bowl and blend with a whisk. Stir in ⅓ cup of the lemon juice and the butter extract. Pour the mixture over the prepared crust. Bake for 20 minutes, or until set. In a small dish, combine the remaining ¼ cup confectioners' sugar with the remaining 1 tablespoon lemon juice to make a glaze. Spread the glaze over the hot Lemon Squares. Cool completely in the pan.

Makes 48 squares

Nutritional information per square

Calories	52	Cal. from Fat (%)	13.5	Sodium (mg)	32
Fat (g)	0.8	Saturated Fat (g)	0.1	Cholesterol (mg)	4

ALMOND CHESS SQUARES

These make a great pick-up dessert. The Almond Chess Squares are very rich in taste, so serve them in small squares.

1 (18¼-ounce) box light
yellow cake mix
1 large egg
½ cup (1 stick) light
margarine, melted
1 tablespoon water
1½ teaspoons almond
extract, divided

1 (8-ounce) package fat-free
cream cheese, softened
1 (16-ounce) box
confectioners' sugar
3 large egg whites
1 teaspoon butter extract

Preheat the oven to 350°F. Coat a 13 × 9 × 2-inch baking pan with nonstick cooking spray. In a large mixing bowl, combine the cake mix, egg, margarine, water, and ½ teaspoon of the almond extract. Beat by hand until well blended. Pat the batter into the bottom of the baking pan. In a mixing bowl, beat the cream cheese, confectioners' sugar, and 3 egg whites until the mixture is smooth and creamy. Add the remaining teaspoon almond extract and the butter extract. Pour over the batter in the pan. Bake for 45 minutes, or until the top is golden brown. Cool in the pan on a rack and cut into squares.

Makes 48 squares

Nutritional information per square

Calories	96	Cal. from Fat (%)	15.9	Sodium (mg)	119
Fat (g)	1.7	Saturated Fat (g)	0.5	Cholesterol (mg)	5

DESSERTS

CHERRY CRISP ♥

Lots of times we forget about canned cherries, but you won't ever forget this delicious recipe.

1 (16-ounce) can tart cherries, drained	¼ teaspoon baking powder
½ cup sugar, divided	½ cup old-fashioned oatmeal
1½ tablespoons tapioca	3 tablespoons light stick margarine, softened
½ cup all-purpose flour	

Preheat the oven to 350°F. In a bowl, mix the cherries, ¼ cup sugar, and the tapioca; let stand for 15 minutes. In another bowl, combine the remaining ¼ cup sugar, flour, and baking powder; then stir in the oatmeal. Cut in the margarine until the mixture is fine and crumbly. Place the cherry mixture in a pie plate and sprinkle with the oatmeal mixture. Bake for 25 minutes, until browned.

Makes 4 to 6 servings

Nutritional information per serving

Calories	219	Cal. from Fat (%)	14.4	Sodium (mg)	96
Fat (g)	3.5	Saturated Fat (g)	0.6	Cholesterol (mg)	0

HOLIDAY APPLE CRISP ♥

For those who don't like their desserts too sweet, this will surely be a hit. You can serve it with frozen nonfat vanilla yogurt, if desired.

2 pounds tart cooking apples	⅔ cup all-purpose flour
1 (16-ounce) can jellied cranberry sauce	½ cup light brown sugar
1 teaspoon ground cinnamon	1 teaspoon vanilla extract
	5 tablespoons light stick margarine, chilled and cut
1 cup old-fashioned oatmeal	into pieces

Preheat the oven to 350°F. Peel and core the apples and slice thin. Arrange in a 9-inch-square baking dish coated with nonstick cooking spray. Spread the cranberry sauce evenly over the apples. Mix the cinnamon, oatmeal, flour, brown sugar, and vanilla together. Cut in the margarine until crumbly. Spread the mixture over the cranberry layer and bake approximately 40 minutes.

Makes 8 servings

Nutritional information per serving

Calories	299	Cal. from Fat (%)	14.3	Sodium (mg)	112
Fat (g)	4.7	Saturated Fat (g)	0.8	Cholesterol (mg)	0

BLUEBERRY CRUMBLE ♥

When blueberries are in season, run right for this recipe. Serve with frozen low-fat vanilla yogurt for a real treat.

4 cups blueberries
2 tablespoons all-purpose
  flour
⅔ cup sugar
1 teaspoon almond extract
½ teaspoon ground
  cinnamon

1 (1-pound 5-ounce) box
  low-fat wild blueberry
  muffin mix
6 tablespoons (¾ stick) light
  stick margarine, melted

Preheat the oven to 350°F. Coat an 8 × 8 × 2-inch baking pan with nonstick cooking spray. In a saucepan, combine the blueberries, flour, and sugar. Cook until the mixture comes to a boil, stirring gently. Cook for 1 or 2 minutes, until thickened. Remove from the heat and add the almond extract. Pour into the prepared 8 × 8 × 2-inch baking pan. In a bowl, combine the cinnamon and muffin mix. Stir in the margarine until the mixture is crumbly. Sprinkle the crumbs over the filling. Bake for 25 to 35 minutes, or until the top is golden brown.

Makes 8 servings

Nutritional information per serving

Calories	401	Cal. from Fat (%) 12.8		Sodium (mg)	506
Fat (g)	5.7	Saturated Fat (g)	0.8	Cholesterol (mg)	0

BLUEBERRY COBBLER ♥

I have a sweet neighbor who picks me fresh blueberries and gives them to me to freeze so I can have blueberry treats like this one yearlong with fresh blueberries!

4 cups thawed fresh or
  frozen unsweetened
  blueberries
½ cup sugar
2 tablespoons cornstarch
1 cup all-purpose flour
1½ teaspoons baking
  powder

½ teaspoon ground
  cinnamon
⅛ teaspoon salt
3 tablespoons light stick
  margarine, melted

Preheat the oven to 400°F. Coat a 9-inch pie plate with nonstick cooking spray. In a small saucepan, combine the blueberries, sugar, and cornstarch. Cook over medium heat, stirring occasionally for 5 minutes, or until the berries are very soft; remove the pan from the heat and set aside. In a medium bowl, combine the flour, baking powder, cinnamon, and salt, stirring to combine. Stir in the margarine and mix until a soft dough forms. Turn onto a lightly floured surface and roll out with a floured rolling pin to a 10- to 11-inch circle. Stir the berry mixture and pour it into the prepared pie plate. Cover with the crust and crimp to seal. Bake for 25 minutes.

Makes 8 servings

Nutritional information per serving

| Calories | 174 | Cal. from Fat (%) 13.5 | Sodium (mg) | 190 |
| Fat (g) | 2.6 | Saturated Fat (g) 0.4 | Cholesterol (mg) | 0 |

PUMPKIN-APRICOT CRUMBLE PIE ♥

When I came up with this apricot-pumpkin dessert, it was the first time I truly liked a pumpkin pie.

1 (6-ounce) package dried apricots, finely chopped
¾ cup light brown sugar
1 unbaked 9-inch pie shell
2 large eggs, lightly beaten
1 (16-ounce) can solid-pack pumpkin
⅓ cup sugar
¼ cup apricot preserves

1 teaspoon ground cinnamon
¼ teaspoon ground ginger
1¼ cups evaporated skimmed milk
1 tablespoon light stick margarine, melted
2 tablespoons all-purpose flour

Preheat the oven to 425°F. Mix the apricots and brown sugar in a small bowl. Place ¾ cup of the mixture in the bottom of the pie shell; reserve the remaining mixture for the topping. Combine the eggs, pumpkin, sugar, apricot preserves, cinnamon, ginger, and evaporated milk in a large bowl; mix well. Pour into the pie shell and bake for 15 minutes. Reduce the temperature to 350°F. and bake for another 30 minutes. Add the margarine and flour to the reserved crumb mixture, sprinkle over the pie, and bake for another 20 minutes. Cool on a wire rack.

Makes 8 servings

Nutritional information per serving

| Calories | 349 | Cal. from Fat (%) 19.5 | Sodium (mg) | 199 |
| Fat (g) | 7.6 | Saturated Fat (g) 2.3 | Cholesterol (mg) | 55 |

APPLE CRUMBLE PIE ♥

I always have to include an Apple Crumble Pie in each book because it is one of my favorites. I think this is the best recipe yet—see what you think!

CRUST
1 cup all-purpose flour
2 tablespoons cold water
2 tablespoons canola oil

1 teaspoon vanilla extract
1 teaspoon ground
cinnamon
1 tablespoon water

1 tablespoon all-purpose
flour
¼ cup sugar
4 cups peeled, sliced tart
apples
Topping (recipe follows)
½ cup confectioners' sugar
2 tablespoons lemon juice

Preheat the oven to 350°F. In a small bowl, mix the flour, cold water, and oil together and press into a 9-inch pie plate. Combine the vanilla, cinnamon, 1 tablespoon water, flour, sugar, and apples. Fill the crust with the filling. Sprinkle the filling with the Topping. Bake for 1 hour, or until the apples are done and the pie is bubbly. Drizzle with a glaze made from mixing the confectioners' sugar and lemon juice together in a measuring cup.

Topping

½ teaspoon ground
cinnamon
½ cup crushed nonfat
pretzels
¼ cup light brown sugar

1 cup all-purpose flour
5 tablespoons light stick
margarine, chilled and
cut into pieces

Combine the cinnamon, pretzels, brown sugar, and flour in a small bowl. Cut in the margarine until the mixture is crumbly.

Makes 8 slices

Nutritional information per slice

Calories	314	Cal. from Fat (%)	21.8	Sodium (mg)	179
Fat (g)	7.6	Saturated Fat (g)	0.9	Cholesterol (mg)	0

BANANA CREAM PIE ♥

If you like banana pudding, this might become your favorite dessert. To make vanilla wafer crumbs, just crush the vanilla wafers in a food processor or between two sheets of wax paper with a rolling pin.

1 cup reduced-fat vanilla
wafer crumbs
2 tablespoons (¼ stick) light
stick margarine, melted
¼ cup plus ⅓ cup sugar
2 tablespoons cornstarch

1½ cups skim milk
1 large egg, beaten
1 tablespoon vanilla extract
3 bananas, sliced
3 large egg whites

Preheat the oven to 375°F. In a pie plate, mix the vanilla wafer crumbs and margarine. Press it into the bottom and up the sides of the pie plate and bake for 5 to 7 minutes; set aside. Raise the oven temperature to 400°F. In a saucepan, combine ¼ cup of the sugar and the cornstarch. Gradually add the skim milk, stirring until blended. Cook over medium heat, stirring constantly until the mixture thickens and comes to a boil. Boil 1 minute longer, stirring constantly. In a small bowl, gradually stir ⅓ of the hot mixture into the beaten egg. Return this to the remaining hot mixture, stirring constantly. Cook for another 2 minutes, stirring constantly. Remove from the heat and add the vanilla.

Spread the sliced bananas on the baked piecrust and then cover with the custard. With a mixer, beat the egg whites until soft peaks form. Gradually add the remaining ⅓ cup sugar, beating until stiff peaks form. Spread the meringue over the filled pie and bake for 4 to 5 minutes, until the meringue begins to turn golden. Watch closely.

Makes 8 servings

Nutritional information per serving

Calories	200	Cal. from Fat (%) 18.2	Sodium (mg)	123
Fat (g)	4	Saturated Fat (g) 1	Cholesterol (mg)	34

LEMON MERINGUE PIE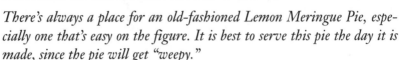

There's always a place for an old-fashioned Lemon Meringue Pie, especially one that's easy on the figure. It is best to serve this pie the day it is made, since the pie will get "weepy."

PIECRUST
1 cup all-purpose flour
1 tablespoon sugar
⅛ teaspoon baking powder
3 tablespoons light stick
   margarine

2 tablespoons water
½ teaspoon vanilla extract
Lemon Filling (recipe
   follows)
Meringue (recipe follows)

Preheat the oven to 375°F. In a bowl, combine the flour, sugar, and baking powder. Cut in the margarine until coarse crumbs form. Stir in the water and vanilla with a fork. Gather the dough into a small flattened round ball and roll out on a floured surface to fit a 9-inch pie plate. If the dough is too stiff, you can add more water. Transfer into the pie plate and pierce with a fork. Bake for 10 to 15 minutes, or until lightly browned. Lower the oven temperature to 350°F. Cool the piecrust slightly. Fill with the Lemon Filling. Spread the Meringue over the pie filling, spreading it all the way to the crust. Bake the pie for 10 to 12 minutes, or until lightly brown. Refrigerate until well chilled and ready to serve.

Lemon Filling

¼ cup cornstarch
1 cup sugar
⅓ cup cold water
1 cup hot water
½ cup lemon juice

1 teaspoon grated lemon
   rind
2 large egg yolks, slightly
   beaten

In a saucepan, combine the cornstarch and sugar. Blend in the cold water. Add the hot water. Cook over medium-high heat, stirring constantly, until the mixture is thick and clear, about 10 minutes. Remove from the heat and add the lemon juice and lemon rind. Return to the stove and continue cooking for 2 minutes. Blend about ½ cup of the hot mixture into the egg yolks. Return to the saucepan and continue cooking for 2 more minutes, stirring constantly.

Meringue

3 large egg whites
¼ teaspoon cream of tartar

¼ cup sugar
½ teaspoon vanilla extract

In a mixing bowl, beat the egg whites with the cream of tartar at high speed until soft peaks form. Gradually add the sugar, beating well after each addition. Add the vanilla. Continue beating until the meringue stands in soft peaks.

Makes 8 servings

Nutritional information per serving

Calories	244	Cal. from Fat (%)	13.6	Sodium (mg)	88
Fat (g)	3.7	Saturated Fat (g)	0.8	Cholesterol (mg)	54

CHOCOLATE ESPRESSO PIE

This recipe will replace your old favorite mocha pie. The marshmallows give the pie a creamy consistency. Instant espresso powder can be found in the grocery store with the coffees.

1 cup chocolate wafer
  crumbs
3 tablespoons light stick
  margarine, melted
2 tablespoons water
25 marshmallows
¾ cup skim milk
2 tablespoons cocoa

1 tablespoon instant espresso
  powder
2 tablespoons coffee liqueur
1 teaspoon vanilla extract
1 package instant whipped
  topping mix, prepared
  according to directions
  using skim milk

Preheat the oven to 375°F. Combine the chocolate wafer crumbs, melted margarine, and water in a 9-inch pie plate, mixing with a fork. Press down on the bottom and up the sides. Bake for 5 minutes; cool. Meanwhile, combine the marshmallows, milk, cocoa, and espresso powder in a heavy saucepan over medium-low heat, cooking until melted. Add the coffee liqueur and vanilla. Cool completely. Fold half of the prepared whipped topping into the pie mixture and pour into the baked shell. Spread the chocolate pie with the remaining whipped topping. Refrigerate until set.

Makes 8 servings

Nutritional information per serving

Calories	210	Cal. from Fat (%)	27	Sodium (mg)	173
Fat (g)	6.3	Saturated Fat (g)	2.7	Cholesterol (mg)	1

WHITE CHOCOLATE–ALMOND BROWNIE PIE ♥

When the praise started rolling in, I was too embarrassed to admit that I just opened boxes so I smiled and said, "Thanks!" (You can do the same.) Top with toasted sliced almonds, if desired.

1 (1-pound 4½-ounce) box low-fat fudge brownie mix	1 (1.8-ounce) package white chocolate mousse dessert mix
2 teaspoons almond extract, divided	

Preheat the oven to 350°F. Coat a 9 × 9 × 2-inch-square baking pan with nonstick cooking spray. Prepare the brownie mix according to package directions and stir in 1 teaspoon almond extract. Pour the batter into the prepared baking pan and bake for 20 to 25 minutes. Do not overbake. Cool the cake. Prepare the dessert topping mix according to directions, using skim milk. Blend in the remaining teaspoon of almond extract. Spread the cake with the topping.

Makes 12 to 16 servings

Nutritional information per serving

Calories	170	Cal. from Fat (%)	19.6	Sodium (mg)	140
Fat (g)	3.7	Saturated Fat (g)	1.3	Cholesterol (mg)	0

CHERRIES JUBILEE ♥

Even the name of this dessert sounds festive! It is truly a grand finale.

½ cup orange juice	1 (16-ounce) can pitted red tart cherries in water
¼ cup sugar	
1 tablespoon grated orange rind	⅓ cup almond liqueur
	Low-fat vanilla frozen
1 tablespoon cornstarch	yogurt

In a large shallow skillet, combine the orange juice, sugar, orange rind, and cornstarch. Drain the cherries, reserving ⅓ cup cherry liquid, and add the liquid to the skillet; set the cherries aside. Heat the mixture over medium heat and bring to a boil, stirring constantly. Reduce the heat and stir in the cherries. Heat the liqueur in a small dish in the microwave and add to the corner of the skillet. Then ignite carefully with a long match. Stir gently until the flame dies out. Serve immediately over frozen vanilla yogurt.

Makes 6 servings

| Calories | 126 | Cal. from Fat (%) | 1.3 | Sodium (mg) | 7 |
| Fat (g) | 0.2 | Saturated Fat (g) | 0 | Cholesterol (mg) | 0 |

COFFEE CHEESECAKE

This recipe makes an old-fashioned-type cheesecake, one that you will make over and over. The coffee can be left out for a traditional cheesecake, which can then be served plain or with a fruit topping.

Cheesecakes can be made ahead of time and stored in the freezer. When you are ready to serve the cheesecake, remove from the freezer and defrost at room temperature for several hours or place in the refrigerator overnight.

¾ cup graham cracker
  crumbs
1 tablespoon cocoa
¾ cup plus 2 tablespoons
  sugar
2 tablespoons (¼ stick) light
  stick margarine, melted
1 (8-ounce) package light
  cream cheese, softened
1 (8-ounce) package fat-free
  cream cheese, softened

⅓ cup all-purpose flour
1 tablespoon cornstarch
1 large egg
2 tablespoons instant coffee
  dissolved in 1 teaspoon
  vanilla extract
⅓ cup nonfat sour cream
½ cup skim milk
4 large egg whites

Preheat the oven to 325°F. Combine the graham cracker crumbs, cocoa, 2 tablespoons of sugar, and the melted margarine. Press into the bottom of a 9-inch springform pan. In a mixing bowl, combine the cream cheeses, flour, cornstarch, ½ cup of the sugar, the egg, and the coffee dissolved in vanilla, beating until well combined. Add the sour cream and milk, mixing well. In a separate bowl, beat the egg whites until stiff, gradually adding the remaining ¼ cup sugar. Fold into the cream cheese mixture and pour over the crust in the springform pan. Bake for 1 hour. Leave in the oven with the door slightly open for another hour. Refrigerate for at least 2 hours.

Makes 12 servings

Nutritional information per serving

| Calories | 187 | Cal. from Fat (%) | 24.1 | Sodium (mg) | 270 |
| Fat (g) | 5 | Saturated Fat (g) | 2.6 | Cholesterol (mg) | 30 |

BANANA-COFFEE FLAMBÉ

This is a fabulous, impressive ending to a meal. You won't have to travel to New Orleans for Bananas Foster anymore. By heating the liqueur first, you will have no trouble igniting the sauce. Be very careful when flambéeng a dish.

3 tablespoons light stick margarine	4 firm bananas, peeled, halved, and split lengthwise
⅓ cup light brown sugar	
4 tablespoons brewed strong coffee	4 tablespoons coffee liqueur
	Nonfat vanilla frozen yogurt

In a large, wide skillet, heat the margarine, brown sugar, and coffee until melted and bubbly. Add the banana slices, cooking for 5 minutes, turning as needed. Meanwhile, heat the coffee liqueur in a microwaveproof dish for 30 seconds. Pour in one corner of the skillet, remove from the heat, and ignite with a long match to flame. Stir carefully until the flame dies out. Serve immediately over nonfat vanilla frozen yogurt.

Makes 6 servings

Nutritional information per serving

Calories	181	Cal. from Fat (%)	16.5	Sodium (mg)	79
Fat (g)	3.3	Saturated Fat (g)	0.6	Cholesterol (mg)	0

CRANBERRY CHEESECAKE

This is a holiday treat with the combination of cranberries and cheesecake. Cheesecakes freeze well, so if freezing, spread with the Cranberry Topping just before serving.

½ cup graham cracker crumbs	½ cup sugar
	½ teaspoon almond extract
1 tablespoon light stick margarine, melted	3 large egg whites
	Cranberry Topping (recipe follows)
1 (8-ounce) package light cream cheese, softened	
1 (8-ounce) container part-skim ricotta cheese	

Preheat the oven to 350°F. Coat a 9-inch pie plate with nonstick cooking spray. In a small bowl, combine the graham cracker crumbs and margarine. Pat the mixture into the bottom of the pie plate. In a mixing bowl, combine the cream cheese and ricotta until well blended. Add the sugar and almond extract, mixing well.

In another mixing bowl, beat the egg whites until soft peaks form. Fold the egg whites gradually into the cheese mixture until well combined. Pour half of the batter into the pie shell. Spread with ³/₄ cup of the Cranberry Topping and cover with the remaining cheesecake batter. Bake for 40 to 45 minutes, until set. Remove from the oven to cool on a rack. When cool, spread with the remaining Cranberry Topping. Refrigerate until chilled, about 2 hours. The cheesecake will keep, covered, in the refrigerator for up to a week.

Cranberry Topping

1 (16-ounce) can whole berry cranberry sauce
¹/₄ cup sugar

1 tablespoon cornstarch
¹/₄ cup water

In a medium saucepan, cook the cranberry sauce and sugar over medium-low heat until the sugar is dissolved and the mixture is bubbly. In a small bowl, combine the cornstarch and water; add to the saucepan. Cook over medium heat, stirring constantly, until the mixture thickens. Refrigerate until lukewarm, about 15 to 20 minutes, stirring in the refrigerator from time to time. Remove ³/₄ cup cranberry topping for the inside of the cheesecake. Refrigerate the remaining topping until well chilled.

Makes 8 to 10 servings

Nutritional information per serving

Calories	239	Cal. from Fat (%)	24.1	Sodium (mg)	203
Fat (g)	6.4	Saturated Fat (g)	3.8	Cholesterol (mg)	18

BREAD PUDDING WITH RUM SAUCE ♥

For people who've never experienced a bread pudding, this is an incredible low-fat introduction to a Southern delight.

1 (16-ounce) loaf French bread	1 (12-ounce) can evaporated skimmed milk
1 (16-ounce) can light sliced peaches, drained	½ teaspoon ground cinnamon
½ cup golden raisins	¼ teaspoon ground nutmeg
2 large eggs	1 teaspoon butter extract
2 large egg whites	1 teaspoon coconut extract
¾ cup sugar	1 tablespoon vanilla extract
2 cups skim milk	Rum Sauce (recipe follows)

Preheat the oven to 350°F. Break the bread into 3-inch pieces and place in a 3-quart baking dish. Add the sliced peaches and raisins to the bread, mixing gently. In a bowl, combine the eggs and egg whites with the sugar, mixing well. Add the skim milk, evaporated milk, cinnamon, nutmeg, and butter, coconut, and vanilla extracts, blending well. Pour the egg mixture evenly over the bread and press the bread with a fork so it will soak up the liquid. Bake for approximately 30 to 40 minutes, or until set. Serve hot with the Rum Sauce.

Rum Sauce

2 tablespoons (¼ stick) light stick margarine	⅓ cup sugar
2 tablespoons all-purpose flour	1⅓ cups skim milk
	1 tablespoon rum extract

In a small saucepan, melt the margarine and add the flour and sugar, mixing well. Gradually add the milk, stirring constantly. Cook until the mixture comes to a boil and boil for 1 minute. Remove from the heat and stir in the rum extract.

Makes 10 servings

Nutritional information per serving

Calories	356	Cal. from Fat (%)	9.7	Sodium (mg)	418
Fat (g)	3.8	Saturated Fat (g)	1	Cholesterol (mg)	45

FRUIT TRIFLE ♥

When summer fruit is in season, this dessert is the one to make. Everyone always seems to fight for the last piece. Just buy your angel food cake premade in the grocery store and then you'll be pleasantly surprised by how little time is involved in putting the dessert together. Feel free to use the fruits of your choice!

½ cup sugar	1 pound strawberries,
⅓ cup cornstarch	stemmed and sliced
3 cups skim milk	2 bananas, peeled and sliced
2 large egg yolks, slightly	1 pint blueberries
beaten	2 kiwis, peeled and sliced
1 teaspoon vanilla extract	1 (12-ounce) container light
1 (16-ounce) angel food cake,	frozen whipped topping,
cut into ½-inch slices	thawed
½ cup sherry	

In a 2-quart saucepan, stir together the sugar and cornstarch. Gradually add the milk, stirring until smooth. Stir in the beaten egg yolks. Cook over medium heat, stirring constantly, until the mixture comes to a boil. Boil for 2 minutes and remove from the heat. Stir in the vanilla. Transfer to a bowl, cover with wax paper, and refrigerate until chilled, about 30 minutes.

Arrange half of the angel food cake slices in a single layer in a trifle dish or a deep glass bowl. Sprinkle with ¼ cup of the sherry. Layer with half of the fruit, half of the custard, and half of the whipped topping. Repeat layering with the remaining ingredients, beginning with the angel food cake and sherry again and ending with the whipped topping. Refrigerate until ready to serve.

Makes 16 servings

Nutritional information per serving

Calories	232	Cal. from Fat (%)	25.6	Sodium (mg)	257
Fat (g)	6.6	Saturated Fat (g)	5.6	Cholesterol (mg)	28

PISTACHIO LAYERED DESSERT

The green filling makes this dessert something to think about around Christmas or even St. Patrick's Day. Chocolate wafers are found in most stores, but you can always use the tops and bottoms of chocolate sandwich cookies.

1½ cups chocolate wafer
  crumbs
3 tablespoons light stick
  margarine, melted
1 (8-ounce) package fat-free
  cream cheese, softened
1 cup confectioners' sugar

1 (8-ounce) carton light
  frozen whipped topping,
  thawed and divided
2 (4-serving) packages
  pistachio instant pudding
  mix
3 cups skim milk

Combine the crumbs with the margarine in a small bowl and pat it into a 2-quart oblong baking dish or a 13 × 9 × 2-inch pan. Refrigerate until firm. In a mixing bowl, combine the cream cheese and confectioners' sugar, blending until smooth. Blend in half of the whipped topping (about 1 cup) thoroughly. Spread the mixture with a knife over the crumbs. (Be careful, as this will pull up the crumbs.) Refrigerate until firm.

Meanwhile, in a mixing bowl, mix the pistachio pudding mix and skim milk, beating until thick. Spread over the cream cheese mixture and return to the refrigerator until firm. Carefully spread the remaining whipped topping on top. Refrigerate 1 hour before serving.

Makes 18 servings

Nutritional information per serving

| Calories | 157 | Cal. from Fat (%) 24.6 | Sodium (mg) | 325 |
| Fat (g) | 4.3 | Saturated Fat (g) 2.4 | Cholesterol (mg) | 2 |

TIRAMISÙ ♥

The name Tiramisù means "pick me up," so get ready! This recipe was on the cover of Cooking Light Magazine's *March 1995 issue. If you've never had Tiramisù, this is the perfect time to try making it. I know it requires using a few bowls, but it is worth the effort. You can find instant espresso coffee at the grocery store to make espresso without any special appliances.*

½ cup espresso coffee
¼ cup plus 1 tablespoon
   sugar
3 tablespoons coffee liqueur
1 (8-ounce) package light
   cream cheese, softened
¾ cup confectioners' sugar

1½ cups light frozen
   whipped topping, thawed
   and divided
3 large egg whites
20 ladyfingers, split
Cocoa, for sprinkling

In a small bowl, combine the espresso coffee, 1 tablespoon sugar, and the coffee liqueur; set aside. In a mixing bowl, combine the cream cheese with the confectioners' sugar, beating until well blended. Fold in 1 cup frozen whipped topping. In another mixing bowl, beat the egg whites until soft peaks form, add the remaining ¼ cup sugar, and continue beating until stiff peaks form. Fold into the cream cheese mixture.

In a 9 × 9 × 2-inch dish, place a layer of the split ladyfingers across the bottom of the dish. Drizzle with half of the espresso mixture, half of the cream cheese mixture, and repeat the layers, beginning with split ladyfingers and ending with the cream cheese mixture. Spread with the remaining ½ cup whipped topping in a thin layer on top of the dessert and sprinkle with cocoa. Refrigerate until well chilled.

Makes 16 servings

Nutritional information per serving

Calories	147	Cal. from Fat (%)	30.6	Sodium (mg)	102
Fat (g)	5	Saturated Fat (g)	3.5	Cholesterol (mg)	57

CARAMEL DELIGHT CRUNCH

This quick and easy recipe can be made ahead and frozen. Everyone will think there are nuts in the crust but it is actually just pretzels. A clever way to use up those crushed bits in the bottom of the bag.

1½ cups all-purpose flour
1 cup old-fashioned oatmeal
½ cup light brown sugar
½ cup crushed fat-free pretzels
1 teaspoon vanilla extract

½ cup (1 stick) light stick margarine, melted
⅔ cup caramel topping (bought in grocery store)
½ gallon nonfat vanilla frozen yogurt

Preheat the oven to 350°F. In a medium bowl, combine the flour, oatmeal, brown sugar, and pretzels; stir in the vanilla and melted margarine. Spread a thin layer of the mixture on a cookie sheet and bake until brown, about 20 minutes. Cool, then crumble, reserving ¼ cup of the crumbs for topping. In a 13 × 9 × 2-inch pan, layer ¾ of the crumbled mixture on the bottom, pour the caramel topping over the crumbs, and spread the vanilla yogurt over both. Sprinkle the remaining cup of crumbs on top and freeze until ready to serve. Cut into squares to serve.

Makes 16 servings

Nutritional information per serving

Calories	270	Cal. from Fat (%)	11	Sodium (mg)	220
Fat (g)	3.3	Saturated Fat (g)	0.6	Cholesterol (mg)	0

CHOCOLATE SAUCE

Thought you'd have to give up chocolate sundaes? No way! This chocolate sauce is irresistible served hot or even right out of the refrigerator. Store in the refrigerator and use as needed—if it lasts that long.

½ cup sugar
⅓ cup cocoa
⅓ cup light corn syrup

⅓ cup water
1 teaspoon vanilla extract

Combine the sugar, cocoa, corn syrup, and water in a saucepan. Bring to a boil over medium heat, stirring frequently. Boil 1 minute. Remove from the heat and add the vanilla. Cool.

Serve over frozen nonfat yogurt.

Makes 8 servings

| Calories | 96 | Cal. from Fat (%) | 4.6 | Sodium (mg) | 18 |
| Fat (g) | 0.5 | Saturated Fat (g) | 0.3 | Cholesterol (mg) | 0 |

CARAMEL SAUCE ♥

Serve over frozen vanilla yogurt, angel food cake, or pound cake. For the ultimate indulgence, pair this with Chocolate Sauce (opposite).

½ cup water
⅓ cup light brown sugar
1 teaspoon vanilla extract

2 teaspoons cornstarch
1 (5-ounce) can evaporated
  skimmed milk

In a heavy, small saucepan, heat the water and brown sugar over low heat until the sugar dissolves. Increase the heat and bring to a boil without stirring until the sugar mixture turns deep golden brown, about 2 minutes. Reduce the heat and stir in the vanilla. Combine the cornstarch and evaporated milk in a small bowl to make a thin paste and stir into the sauce. Cook until the sauce is slightly thickened.

Makes 8 servings

Nutritional information per 2-tablespoon serving

| Calories | 54 | Cal. from Fat (%) | 1 | Sodium (mg) | 27 |
| Fat (g) | 0 | Saturated Fat (g) | 0 | Cholesterol (mg) | 1 |

Almond Chess Squares . . . . 1 fruit, 0.5 bread/starch
Angel Hair and Sun-Dried Tomatoes . . . . 4 bread/starch, 1.5 vegetable
Apple Crumble Pie . . . . 2 fruit, 1.5 bread/starch, 1.5 fat
Apple Muffins . . . . 0.5 fruit, 1.5 bread/starch
Applesauce–Chocolate Chip Cake . . . . . . 1 fruit, 0.5 bread/starch
Apricot Bread . . . . 1 fruit, 1 bread/starch
Apricot Cake . . . . 3 fruit, 1 bread/starch, 2 fat
Apricot Delight . . . . 3 fruit
Artichoke Dip . . . . 0.66 vegetable
Asparagus and Brie Pizza . . . . 0.5 bread/starch, 0.5 fat, 1 vegetable
Baby Lima Beans . . . . 2 bread/starch, 1.5 vegetable, 1 lean meat
Baked Beans . . . . 1.5 bread/starch, 1 vegetable, 0.25 lean meat
Baked Corn in Sour Cream . . . . 1.5 bread/starch, 0.5 vegetable, 0.5 lean meat
Baked French Toast . . . . 3 bread/starch, 0.5 fat
Baked Macaroni and Cheese Primavera . . 1 bread/starch, 1 fat, 2 vegetable, 0.5 skim milk
Baked Mexican Spinach Dip . . . . 2 vegetable, 1 lean meat
Banana-Coffee Flambé . . . . 2.5 fruit, 0.5 fat
Banana Cream Pie . . . . 1 fruit, 1.5 bread/starch, 0.5 fat
Banana Upside-Down Cake . . . . 1.5 fruit, 1.5 bread/starch, 1 fat
Barley Casserole . . . . 1 bread/starch, 1 vegetable
Barbecue Shrimp . . . . 3 lean meat
Bean and Corn Salad . . . . 1.5 bread/starch, 1 fat, 0.5 vegetable
Beef and Rice . . . . 1 bread/starch, 2 vegetables, 2 lean meat
Beef Stroganoff . . . . 4 lean meat, 0.5 skim milk
Beefy Vegetable Soup . . . . 1.5 bread/starch, 1 vegetable, 1.5 lean meat
Beer Bread Muffins . . . . 2 bread/starch
Black Bean Soup . . . . 2 bread/starch, 1 vegetable, 0.5 lean meat
Black-Eyed Pea Dip . . . . 0.5 bread/starch, 0.5 fat, 2 vegetable
Blueberry Cobbler . . . . 2 fruit, 0.5 bread/starch
Blueberry Cobbler Cake . . . . 1 fruit, 1.5 bread/starch, 0.5 fat
Blueberry Crumble . . . . 4.5 fruit, 1 bread/starch, 1 fat
Bran Muffins . . . . 0.5 fruit, 1 bread/starch, 1 fat
Breakfast Casserole . . . . 0.5 bread/starch, 0.33 fat, 1 vegetable, 1 lean meat
Bread Pudding with Rum Sauce . . . . 2 fruit, 2 bread/starch, 0.5 fat, 0.5 skim milk
Broccoli and Rice Strata . . . . 2.5 bread/starch, 2 vegetable, 1 medium fat meat
Broccoli Casserole . . . . 2.5 vegetable, 1 lean meat
Broccoli Pizza . . . . 1 bread/starch, 1 fat, 1 vegetable
Broccoli Vermicelli Salad . . . . 2 bread/starch, 1 fat, 1 vegetable
Broccoli with Dijon Sauce . . . . 1.5 vegetable
Broiled Marinated Shrimp . . . . 2 lean meat
Broiled Tomatoes . . . . 1 vegetable
Butterscotch Banana Bread . . . . 0.5 fruit, 1 bread/starch, 1 fat
Caesar Salad . . . . 2 vegetable
Caponata . . . . 1 vegetable
Caramel Delight Crunch . . . . 1.5 fruit, 2 bread/starch, 0.5 fat
Caramel Sauce . . . . 0.33 fruit, 0.33 skim milk
Carrot Cake . . . . 1 fruit, 1 bread/starch, 0.33 fat
Cauliflower with Creamy
     Mustard Sauce . . . . 0.33 bread/starch, 2 vegetable
Cheese-Stuffed Shells . . . . 2 bread/starch, 2 vegetable, 1 lean meat
Cheesy Corn Muffins . . . . 1 bread/starch, 0.5 fat
Cheesy Spicy Squash . . . . 1.5 vegetable, 0.5 medium fat meat
Cherries Jubilee . . . . 2 fruit
Cherry Crisp . . . . 3 bread/starch

Cherry Gelatin Mold .... 2.25 fruit
Chewy Caramel Brownies .... 1 fruit, 0.5 bread/starch, 0.5 fat
Chicken and Dumplings .... 1 bread/starch, 0.5 vegetable, 3 lean meat
Chicken and Peppers .... 3 vegetable, 3.5 lean meat
Chicken and Sausage Gumbo .... 4.5 lean meat, 2 bread/starch, 0.5 vegetable
Chicken Breasts with Lemon
    and Capers .... 0.5 bread/starch, 3 lean meat
Chicken Chili con Queso .... 1 bread/starch, 1 vegetable, 2 lean meat
Chicken Fajitas .... 2.5 bread/starch, 1 vegetable, 4 lean meat
Chicken in Cream Sauce .... 1 vegetable, 3 lean meat
Chicken Mediterranean Pasta .... 4 bread/starch, 0.5 fat, 2 vegetable, 2 lean meat
Chicken Pot Pie .... 0.5 bread/starch, 2.5 vegetable, 3 lean meat,
    0.5 skim milk
Chicken Scaloppine .... 1 vegetable, 5 lean meat
Chicken Scampi .... 4 lean meat
Chicken Soup .... 0.5 vegetable, 3.5 lean meat
Chicken Vermicelli .... 1.5 bread/starch, 1.5 vegetable, 4 lean meat
Chili .... 1 bread/starch, 2 vegetable, 4 lean meat
Chocolate Brownies .... 1 bread/starch
Chocolate Chip Cookies .... 1 fruit
Chocolate Espresso Pie .... 1.5 fruit, 1 bread/starch, 1 fat
Chocolate Mint Brownies .... 0.33 fruit, 0.5 bread/starch
Chocolate Sauce .... 1.5 fruit
Cinnamon Bread .... 0.5 fruit, 1.25 bread/starch
Coconut Cake .... 3 fruit, 1 bread/starch, 2 fat
Coffee Angel Food Cake .... 2 fruit, 1 bread/starch, 0.5 fat
Coffee Cheesecake .... 0.33 fruit, 1.5 bread/starch, 1 fat
Coffee Toffee Brownies .... 1 fruit, 0.5 bread/starch, 0.5 fat
Cold Peach Soup .... 1 fruit, 1 skim milk
Corn and Zucchini Salsa .... 1 bread/starch, 1.5 vegetable
Corn Soup .... 1 bread/starch, 0.5 skim milk
Cornish Hens with Wild Rice Stuffing ... 0.5 fruit, 2.5 bread/starch, 1 fat, 5 lean meat
Crab and Spinach Casserole .... 3 vegetable, 4 lean meat
Cranberry Cheesecake .... 1.5 fruit, 1 bread/starch, 1 fat, 0.5 lean meat
Cranberry-Pumpkin Bread .... 1 fruit, 1.25 bread/starch, 1 fat
Cranberry-Glazed Baby Carrots .... 1 vegetable, 0.5 fruit
Crawfish-Eggplant Bake .... 3 vegetable, 1 lean meat
Cream of Spinach Soup .... 2 vegetable, 0.5 fat
Creamy Corn Casserole .... 1 bread/starch, 0.5 lean meat
Creamy Potato Soup .... 1 bread/starch, 1 fat, 1 vegetable
Curried Chicken Salad .... 1 vegetable, 3 lean meat, 0.5 skim milk
Dilly Stuffed Potatoes .... 1.5 bread/starch
Dip for Fresh Fruit .... 0.2 skim milk
Eggplant and Pepper Bake .... 0.5 fat, 2.5 vegetable
Eggplant and Zucchini Lasagne .... 1 bread/starch, 1.5 vegetable, 1 lean meat,
    0.5 skim milk
Eggplant Parmesan .... 1 bread/starch, 4 vegetable, 2 lean meat
Enchilada Bake .... 1.5 bread/starch, 1 vegetable, 0.5 lean meat
Excellent Eggplant Pasta .... 3 bread/starch, 1 fat, 0.33 lean meat
Extra-Special Herbed Garlic Bread ...... 1 bread/starch, 0.5 fat
Fettuccine Florentine .... 2.5 bread/starch, 1 vegetable, 0.5 lean meat
Fettuccine with Shrimp, Tomatoes,
    and Artichoke Hearts .... 3 bread/starch, 3 vegetable, 1.5 lean meat
Fiesta Potato Casserole .... 1.5 bread/starch, 0.33 skim milk

Fresh Tomato and Cheese Pizza . . . . 1 bread/starch, 1 vegetable, 1.5 lean meat
Fruit Bread . . . . 1 fruit, 1 bread/starch, 0.33 fat
Fruit Trifle . . . . 2.5 fruit, 1 fat, 0.5 skim milk
Fruity Tossed Green Salad with
  Strawberry Dressing . . . . 2 vegetable, 0.5 fat
Garden Baked Potatoes . . . . 2 bread/starch
Garden Enchiladas . . . . 4 bread/starch, 2 fat, 3.5 vegetable
Garden Pasta . . . . 2.5 bread/starch, 1 fat, 0.33 lean meat
Garlic Mashed Potatoes . . . . 2 bread/starch
Garlic Pasta . . . . 2.5 bread/starch, 2 fat
Glazed Chicken Strips . . . . 1 fruit, 0.5 vegetable, 3 lean meat
Good Morning Grits . . . . 1 bread/starch, 1 vegetable, 1 lean meat
Gooey Rolls . . . . 1.5 fruit, 1 bread/starch, 1 fat
Greek Shrimp and Pasta . . . . 3 bread/starch, 1.5 vegetable, 2 lean meat
Greek Tortellini Salad . . . . 1.5 bread/starch, 1 fat, 2.5 vegetable
Green Bean Casserole . . . . 0.5 bread/starch, 1.5 vegetable, 1 lean meat
Grilled Chicken Teriyaki . . . . 0.5 fruit, 4 lean meat
Hamburger Dip . . . . 0.33 lean meat
Holiday Apple Crisp . . . . 3 fruit, 1 bread/starch, 1 fat
Honey-Glazed Turkey Breast . . . . 0.25 fruit, 3 lean meat
Hot Creamy Veggie Dip . . . . 0.33 vegetable
Hot Fruit Casserole . . . . 2.5 fruit, 0.75 bread/starch, 0.5 fat
Hot Spinach Dip . . . . 2 vegetable
Indoor Barbecued Chicken . . . . 4 lean meat
Italian Cream Cake . . . . 1.5 bread/starch, 2 fruit, 2 fat
Italian Linguine Casserole . . . . 2 bread/starch, 1 fat, 1.5 vegetable, 1 lean meat
Italian Pasta Salad . . . . 1 bread/starch, 1.5 vegetable
Italian Rice with Spring Vegetables . . . . . 1.5 bread/starch, 2 vegetable, 0.5 fat
Italian Soup . . . . 1 bread/starch, 1.5 vegetable, 0.5 lean meat
Italian Spinach Pie . . . . 2.5 vegetable, 1 lean meat
Italian Squares . . . . 1 vegetable
Italian-Style Pot Roast . . . . 3 vegetable, 6 lean meat
Jalapeño Corn Bread . . . . 3 bread/starch, 1 fat
Layered Eggplant and Pasta Casserole . . . 2 bread/starch, 1 vegetable, 1 lean meat
Layered Mexican Vegetarian Dish . . . . . . 3 bread/starch
Layered Veggies . . . . 0.5 bread/starch, 0.5 fat, 1.5 vegetable
Lemon Bread . . . . 2 bread/starch
Lemon Bundt Cake . . . . 0.5 fruit, 1.5 bread/starch, 0.5 fat
Lemon-Feta Chicken . . . . 3.5 lean meat
Lemon Meringue Pie . . . . 2.5 fruit, 1 bread/starch, 0.5 fat
Lemon Poppy Seed Cake . . . . 1 fruit, 1.5 bread/starch
Lemon Squares . . . . 0.2 fruit, 0.5 bread/starch
Macaroni and Cheese . . . . 1 bread/starch, 1 fat, 1 lean meat, 1 skim milk
Macaroni Salad . . . . 1 bread/starch, 1 vegetable
Marinated Broccoli and Artichokes . . . . . 2.5 vegetable
Meat Sauce . . . . 1.5 vegetable, 3 lean meat
Meatballs with Tomato Sauce . . . . 3 bread/starch, 4 vegetable, 4 lean meat
Mediterranean Capellini . . . . 3 bread/starch, 1 fat, 1 vegetable
Mexican Lasagne . . . . 1.5 bread/starch, 1 vegetable, 3.5 lean meat
Mexican Tamale Dip . . . . 1 vegetable
Morning Muffins . . . . 1 fruit, 1.5 bread/starch,
New Potato Salad . . . . 1.5 bread/starch
Oatmeal Chocolate Cake . . . . 1 bread/starch
Oatmeal Rockies . . . . 1 bread/starch

RECIPE EXCHANGES

Smothered Pork Chops	0.5 bread/starch, 3 lean meat
Smothered Round Steak	1 vegetable, 3.5 lean meat
Southwestern Chicken Lasagne	1 bread/starch, 2 vegetable, 2 lean meat
Southwestern Grits	1 bread/starch, 0.5 vegetable, 0.5 medium fat meat
Southwestern Pasta Salad	5 bread/starch, 0.5 vegetable, 0.5 fat
Southwestern Quiche	1 bread/starch, 1 vegetable, 1 medium fat meat
Southwestern Rice Salad	3 bread/starch, 2 vegetable
Southwestern Round Steak	2 vegetable, 3.5 lean meat
Special Fish	1 vegetable, 5 lean meat
Special Spinach Casserole	0.5 fat, 2.5 vegetable
Speedy Bean Soup	2.5 bread/starch, 1 vegetable
Spicy Meat Loaf	1 vegetable, 3 lean meat
Spicy Southwestern Pasta	4 bread/starch, 0.5 vegetable, 0.5 lean meat
Spinach and Cheese Tortilla Pizza	0.5 bread/starch, 0.5 vegetable
Spinach Balls with Jezebel Sauce	0.5 fruit, 1 vegetable
Spinach Bread	1 bread/starch, 1 vegetable
Spinach Salad	1 fruit, 1.5 vegetable, 0.33 lean meat
Spinach Stroganoff	3.5 vegetable, 1 fat
Split Pea Soup	1.5 bread/starch, 1.5 vegetable, 0.5 lean meat
Squash and Zucchini Medley	1 vegetable
Stewed Okra	2 vegetable
Strawberry Angel Food Cake	2 fruit, 0.5 fat, 0.5 skim milk
Stuffed Catch of the Day	0.5 bread/starch, 1 vegetable, 5 lean meat
Stuffed Mushrooms	1 vegetable
Stuffed Peppers	1 bread, 1 vegetable, 2 lean meat
Superb Salmon Steaks	0.5 fruit, 6 lean meat
Sweet-and-Sour Shrimp and Peppers	1.5 vegetable, 1 lean meat
Sweet Potato Casserole with Praline Topping	1 fruit, 1 bread/starch, 0.5 fat
Tamales	0.5 bread/starch, 0.5 lean meat
Tequila Chicken	0.5 vegetable, 4 lean meat
Tex-Mex Dip	0.75 bread/starch
Tipsy Mushrooms	0.5 fat, 1 vegetable
Tiramisù	0.5 fruit, 1 bread/starch, 1 fat
Tortilla Shrimp Bites	0.25 bread/starch, 0.25 lean meat
Tortilla Soup	1 bread/starch, 0.5 vegetable, 1 lean meat
Triple Chocolate Cake	1.5 fruit, 1.5 bread/starch, 2 fat
Tropical Romaine Salad	1 fruit, 1 fat, 1 vegetable
Tuna and White Bean Salad	0.5 bread/starch, 1 vegetable, 2 lean meat
Tuna Pasta Casserole	2 bread/starch, 1 vegetable, 1.5 lean meat
Tuna Steaks with Horseradish Sauce	6 lean meat, 1 fat
Veal Marengo	1 vegetable, 2 lean meat
Vegetable Lasagne	1.5 bread/starch, 1 lean meat
Vegetable Rice	2 bread/starch, 0.5 fat, 1.5 vegetable
Wait Cake	1.5 fruit, 1 bread/starch, 1 fat
Waldorf Carrot Salad	1 fruit
White Chocolate–Almond Brownie Pie ..	1 fruit, 1 bread/starch, 0.5 fat
Wild Rice and Feta Salad	1 vegetable, 1 bread/starch, 1 fat
Wild Rice Soup	2.5 bread/starch, 0.5 vegetable, 1 lean meat

INDEX

CONVERSION CHART
Equivalent Imperial and Metric Measurements

American cooks use standard containers, the 8-ounce cup and a tablespoon that takes exactly 16 level fillings to fill that cup level. Measuring by cup makes it very difficult to give weight equivalents, as a cup of densely packed butter will weigh considerably more than a cup of flour. The easiest way therefore to deal with cup measurements in recipes is to take the amount by volume rather than by weight. Thus the equation reads: *1 cup = 240 ml = 8 fl. oz.* *½ cup = 120 ml = 4 fl. oz.*

It is possible to buy a set of American cup measures in major stores around the world.

In the States, butter is often measured in sticks. One stick is the equivalent of 8 tablespoons. One tablespoon of butter is therefore the equivalent to ½ ounce/15 grams.

SOLID MEASURES

U.S. and Imperial Measures		Metric Measures	
ounces	pounds	grams	kilos
1		28	
2		56	
3½		100	
4	¼	112	
5		140	
6		168	
8	½	225	
9		250	¼
12	¾	340	
16	1	450	
18		500	½
20	1¼	560	
24	1½	675	
27		750	¾
28	1¾	780	
32	2	900	
36	2¼	1000	1
40	2½	1100	
48	3	1350	
54		1500	1½
64	4	1800	
72	4½	2000	2
80	5	2250	2¼
90		2500	2½
100	6	2800	2¾

LIQUID MEASURES

Fluid ounces	U.S.	Imperial	Milliliters
	1 teaspoon	1 teaspoon	5
¼	2 teaspoons	1 dessertspoon	10
½	1 tablespoon	1 tablespoon	14
1	2 tablespoons	2 tablespoons	28
2	¼ cup	4 tablespoons	56
4	½ cup		110
5		¼ pint or 1 gill	140
6	¾ cup		170
8	1 cup		225
9			250
10	1¼ cups	½ pint	280
12	1½ cups		340
15		¾ pint	420
16	2 cups		450
18	2¼ cups		500
20	2½ cups	1 pint	560
24	3 cups		675
25		1¼ pints	700
27	3½ cups		750
30	3¾ cups	1½ pints	840
32	4 cups or 1 quart		900
35		1¾ pints	980
36	4½ cups		1000
40	5 cups	2 pints or 1 quart	1120
48	6 cups		1350
50		2½ pints	1400
60	7½ cups	3 pints	1680
64	8 cups or 2 quarts		1800
72	9 cups		2000

OVEN TEMPERATURE EQUIVALENTS

Fahrenheit	Celsius	Gas Mark	Description
225	110	¼	Cool
250	130	½	
275	140	1	Very Slow
300	150	2	
325	170	3	Slow
350	180	4	Moderate
375	190	5	
400	200	6	Moderately Hot
425	220	7	Fairly Hot
450	230	8	Hot
475	240	9	Very Hot
500	250	10	Extremely Hot

EQUIVALENTS FOR INGREDIENTS

all-purpose flour–plain flour
arugula–rocket
confectioners' sugar–icing sugar
cornstarch–cornflour
eggplant–aubergine

granulated sugar–castor sugar
half and half–12% fat milk
lima beans–broad beans
scallion–spring onion
shortening–white fat

unbleached flour–strong, white flour
vanilla bean–vanilla pod
zest–rind
zucchini–courgettes or marrow